Trees & Shrubs

by Derek Fell

Photography by Derek Fell • Illustrations by Joan Frain

HPBooks
a division of
PRICE STERN SLOAN
Los Angeles

CONTENTS

About the Author

Derek Fell is a prolific garden writer and plant photographer, as well as a winner of many awards from the Garden Writers Association of America. He is the author of three other gardening books for HPBooks: *Vegetables, How to Select, Grow & Enjoy; Annuals, How to Select, Grow & Enjoy;* and *How to Photograph Flowers, Plants & Landscapes.*

A consultant to The White House during the Ford Administration, Mr. Fell also served for several years as director of the National Garden Bureau, and has more than 20 years of experience in gardening. He lives with his wife and five children on a 2-acre farm in Bucks County, Pennsylvania, where he is constantly testing new plants and new growing techniques. Mr. Fell took all the photos in this book.

Acknowledgments

We would like to thank the following individuals for their contributions to this book:

Dr. Ann Rhoads, Morris Arboretum, Philadelphia, PA
H. Thomas Hallowell Jr., Deerfield Garden, Philadelphia, PA
Ruth Levitan, Stamford, CT
William Nelson, Pacific Tree Farms, Chula Vista, CA

Cover photo: Azaleas and white dogwood bloom against a background of white pines at Deerfield Garden near Philadelphia, Pennsylvania. Photo by Derek Fell.

Published by HPBooks
A division of Price Stern Sloan, Inc.
360 North La Cienega Blvd.
Los Angeles, CA 90048
ISBN: 0-89586-372-3
Library of Congress Catalog Card Number: 85-81858
©1986 HPBooks, Inc., Printed in U.S.A.
9 8 7 6 5

1
The Splendor of Trees & Shrubs

Although trees and shrubs perform different functions in the landscape, their planting and care have much in common, so there is good reason to combine them into a single book. Both belong to a distinct group within the plant kingdom, known collectively as *woody plants,* because they have the ability to form a tough, durable cell structure called *wood.* Wood forms the sturdy framework that permits trees and shrubs to grow larger and live longer than other plants. In fact, there is no botanical difference between a tree and a shrub. These are simply common terms that make a distinction on the basis of appearance, or *growth habit.*

The accepted definition of a *tree* is a woody plant that tends to form a single main trunk and is capable of growing 15 feet or higher. *Shrubs* are generally defined as woody plants under 15 feet high that form multiple stems and a thicket of twiggy branches.

However, these definitions have no scientific recognition because there are too many anomalies to make any hard and fast rules. For example, in its juvenile stage, *Euonymus alatus*—known as burning bush for its red fall coloring—grows shrubby with a cluster of main stems and a thicket of branchlets. But with the passing of time, it

produces a thick main trunk and spreading canopy to become a handsome 15- to 20-foot tree.

Conversely, many trees can be kept shrublike by pruning to control size and encourage multiple stems. There are also dwarf forms of many standard-size tree species.

From a design standpoint, trees and shrubs perform different functions. Shrubs are usually used as low, decorative highlights. They are often used as *understory* plants to landscape areas beneath tall trees in woodland and garden settings. Trees, on the other hand, tend to be planted for skyline effects, tall windbreaks, making wooded lots and creating shade. They are the most dominant plants in the landscape. Trees and shrubs become perfect companions when the trees provide a backdrop and the shrubs are used at eye level in the foreground for ornamental accents. H. Thomas Hallowell Jr., the owner of the large estate garden of Deerfield, near Philadelphia, typified the attitude of most home gardeners when he said of his garden, "For me, trees and shrubs exist for one purpose—to make a pretty picture."

For the most part, shrubs are expected to be more ornamental and functional than trees. Their ornamental impact comes mostly from flowers, fruits and leaves—the more colorful their appearance, the more highly rated they tend to be among home gardeners. At the other extreme, when shrubs are needed for practical reasons, such as for hedges and screens, we want them to be as unobtrusive as possible so that other plantings and design elements can be accentu-

ated. An example is a tall hedge of yew or privet that provides a solid green backdrop for a colorful flower bed.

Shrubs are not expected to be as long-lived as trees, so the loss of a shrub is little cause for tears because they are usually replaced easily at modest cost. Trees, however, are valued more for their stature, shape and form. If a tree provides good color, we tend to look on it as a bonus. Furthermore, the loss of a large, mature tree can be distressing, for it can take many years to replace.

Without question, some of the world's most impressive tree plantings have been established by the British. At Chatsworth, a large estate garden in England, the value of old trees was so acutely appreciated that wide avenues were planted to look their best 300 years into the future!

ABOUT THIS BOOK

Trees and shrubs represent a vast group of plants from many climates. It is impossible to cover every aspect of their uses and needs in a single book. Some tree books are *nature* books, primarily intended for identification of individual wayside or forest trees. This is a *garden* book, and its intent is to satisfy three essential gardening needs:

● *Ideas*—suggestions for using various kinds of trees and shrubs in the landscape.

● *Planting and care*—practical information on how to grow and care for trees and shrubs.

● *Recommendations*—an encyclopedic listing of garden-worthy trees and shrubs, giving specific descriptions and growing information.

Left: Suburban backyard garden owes its spectacular beauty to a profusion of flowering trees and shrubs underplanted with perennials and woodland wildflowers. Dogwoods and azaleas are the dominant woody plants. Use of evergreen conifers is limited to mature Canadian hemlock and juniper at upper left.

Towering tulip poplar offers cool shade, shadow pattern and a magnificent silhouette against the sky.

Because their life span is normally much longer than that of man, they carry their associations from generation to generation. But mostly it is a matter of beauty—the ability of trees to significantly improve the quality of our surroundings, whether it is the blizzard of snow-white blossoms produced by an ornamental crabapple in spring or the pencil-straight trunk and lofty lime-green leaf canopy of a tulip poplar in summer.

Mr. Henry F. duPont, owner of the famous woodland garden of Winterthur near Wilmington, Delaware, once lectured his staff on what to do in the event of a fire. Although his house contained a priceless collection of antiques, his instructions were ". . . to hose down the trees. I can always rebuild the house but I can't replace the trees."

The famous American landscape architect Thomas D. Church put it well when he wrote "Never underestimate the value of a handsome tree. Protect it. Build your house and garden compositions around it, for it offers you shade, shadow, pattern against the sky, protection over your house, a ceiling over your terrace."

Newspaper magnate Randolph Hearst valued the beauty of native California live oaks so highly at his famous Hearst Castle estate near San Simeon, California, that he thought nothing of relocating 100-year-old oaks to make room for construction or just to place them in a better view. Today, there is hardly a mature oak on the grounds that has not been moved at least once, involving dozens of men, mules and heavy equipment to dig and transport the enormous root balls, some weighing more than 200 tons.

Today, a serious collector of ornamental trees may pay thousands of dollars for a fine-looking specimen of Japanese maple, for example, then pay thousands more to have it moved. A fine weeping form of Nootka false cypress was recently purchased for a private estate from a Pennsylvania nursery for $50,000, exclusive of moving costs. The root ball alone weighed over 20 tons and the tree had to be transported to New York State.

SHRUBS

Shrubs bridge the size gap between perennials and trees in the home landscape. Horticulturally, the term *peren-*

This book is also intended as a feast of images—colorful photographs that show a world of stunning beauty we may sometimes take too much for granted.

TREES

"Men seldom plant trees till they are old and wise and find by experience the prudence and necessity for it."
—John Evelyn, English philosopher, 1664.

The Chinese have a saying: "For a life of complete fulfillment, a person must do three things—write a book, have a child and *plant a tree.*" Few of us have the time or the talent to write a book, and not everyone can be blessed with a child, but anybody can plant a tree.

North America is richly endowed with trees. At last count there were over 1,180 different native and naturalized species. Hawthorns *(Crataegus)* represent the largest genus, with 168 spe-

cies identified, excluding hybrids and cultivated varieties. Oaks *(Quercus)* also constitute a large genus, with over 60 species. The Southeast has the largest concentration of different kinds of trees, with Florida possessing the largest number of any state. The state with the fewest different native trees is South Dakota. It is mostly treeless prairie, with the exception of cottonwoods and willows growing along stream banks.

In all the plant kingdom, nothing seems to evoke greater awe and admiration than trees. The thought of a 300-year-old oak falling victim to a developer's chainsaw will rally whole neighborhoods into saving the tree. Even at home, the loss of a stately maple or other prominent tree from natural causes can produce intense feelings of personal loss.

What *is* it in a tree that evokes such feelings? Partly it seems to be that trees are natural landmarks and memorials.

nial refers to *herbaceous* plants whose topgrowth usually dies back to the ground in winter and regrows the following spring. Though perennials are usually grouped with annuals, biennials and flowering bulbs, some of them do form living woody parts at their base, and because of this tendency they are known as *sub-shrubs*. Examples of sub-shrubs are lavender, tree peonies, rosemary, kitchen sage and candytuft. For this reason, they are often included in books on shrubs, but because they are more frequently confined to perennial borders, they are better treated as perennials, in my experience, and therefore not featured in this book.

Perhaps no genus of shrub has ever excited people more than *Rhododendron*—which includes the large group of plants known as azaleas—though the genus *Camellia* comes close. At the height of his mania for collecting rhododendrons, the famous international banker Lord Lionel de Rothschild readily financed expeditions to remote areas of India and China in search of new plants. He once sent his chauffeur on a 900-mile journey to the North of Scotland for pollen from a superior plant to help in his hybridizing program, even though good-looking plants of the same species grew on his doorstep.

Emperors in ancient China valued certain camellia plants so highly, they forbade the collecting of seeds or taking of cuttings, and organized special elaborate viewing parties for privileged people when plants were in full flower.

The introduction of tender Indica azaleas from Belgium into South Carolina in the 1840s began a tradition for planting azaleas in the South that has made Magnolia Garden—and other famous Southern gardens—a mecca for tourists every April, when thousands of these plants bloom spectacularly around the margins of lakes shaded by ancient bald cypress trees, loblolly pines and cabbage palms. Thick, sinuous wisteria vines coil up into the lofty branches, dipping fragrant blue blossoms to the mirror-smooth surface of the water. White 'Cherokee' roses and yellow 'Lady Banks' roses arch their canes into the leafy canopy, mingling their shining blossoms with garlands of Spanish moss and jasmine. The color from so many flowering shrubs, reaching into the

trees, is so spellbinding that published travel guides have rated Magnolia Garden's spring extravaganza as a scenic wonder comparable to Niagara Falls and the Grand Canyon!

Another important milestone for shrub planting in North America was the introduction of the hardy, evergreen Kurume hybrid azaleas from Japan. These low, spreading, extremely free-flowering azaleas were first shown at the Panama Pacific Exposition in San Francisco in 1915. They created such a sensation that Northern gardeners began a planting frenzy with these azaleas that has been gaining momentum ever since.

The most common use for shrubs today is around house foundations, where they provide decoration and soften large expanses of wood or masonry. When used in this manner, such shrubs are referred to by landscapers as *foundation plants*. Slow-growing evergreens are particularly popular as foundation plants because they require relatively little care

and can be trimmed into tidy, geometric shapes, such as globes, pyramids and columns. However, a more pleasing effect is often achieved by interplanting a few flowering shrubs, such as azaleas, rhododendrons, hydrangeas and viburnums, and allowing them to grow to their natural size and shape.

Shrubs are also favorite choices for defining garden areas, creating barriers and ensuring privacy by screening. Low shrubs make good large-scale ground covers and can also be used as corridors to direct pedestrian traffic. Vining shrubs are used to cover walls and structures. Shrubs to satisfy these needs do not have to be flowering or ornamental varieties with exotic fruit displays or variegated foliage. Most often it is sufficient that they provide dense, leafy growth that is restful to the eye.

Still relatively scarce in North American gardens—but gaining in popularity—is the *mixed-shrub border*, which is meant to be admired from the

Beautiful sunken garden at Winterthur Garden, Delaware, is surrounded by native and naturalized deciduous trees that leaf out in spring to completely screen garden from house. White dogwoods and pink azaleas stand out among the greenery.

Terraced garden features predominantly evergreen conifers. Weeping hemlock cascades down wall at right. Dwarf blue spruce decorates border. Topiary hemlock squirrel and potted topiary ivies decorate gravel terrace midway down the vista. Towering pines underplanted with white azaleas provide dramatic background and skyline effect to highlight romantic *Temple of Love.*

It is worth a great deal to be able to stand back from your house and see it visually framed by the branches of a beautiful tree. Large trees add character to the landscape. Fortunate indeed is the owner of a new home that has an existing large tree in close proximity to the house. Just one large tree can help give any subsequent landscaping and garden design the semblance of maturity, softening the severity of architectural lines and expanses of new masonry.

Homeowners plant trees and shrubs for beauty and comfort—spring bloom and fragrance, a green leafy canopy that provides cool shade in summer, color from leaves or berries in fall and interesting branch or bark patterns in winter.

Shade trees give protection from the sun. They make summer heat more tolerable and filter the dazzling reflection from masonry and concrete. Shrubs and trees around house foundations, and vines on walls, can accentuate vertical or horizontal architectural details.

The shadow pattern cast by the leaves and branches of large trees can be an important design feature in the landscape. Across lawns, paving, decks and terraces, trees provide a constantly changing silhouette as the sun moves across the sky. These shadow patterns help decorate vast expanses of sterile man-made landscapes, making them look more natural.

Similarly, beside a pool, lake or stream, water movement reflected up onto the boughs of overhanging trees can be a pleasant embellishment. This is quite distinct from the exquisite water reflections that trees themselves cast on the water's surface.

Trees and shrubs also form vistas, frame views and define special areas. Trees and shrubs are invaluable as screens to provide privacy, hide undesirable sights, provide a setting for garden structures and offer wind protection. A solid hedge creates a backdrop for flower borders. Hedges of evergreen shrubs or trees provide a year-round green wall.

Trees and tall shrubs—especially evergreens—make far more effective windbreaks than a solid wall. Wind can hit a wall, jump over it and continue on with equal or even greater velocity, but trees and shrubs will dissipate the full force of the wind into gentle breezes.

house. Like perennial borders, mixed-shrub borders are much more common in Europe. In North America, mixed-shrub borders generally rely heavily on dwarf conifers, largely because of their easy maintenance, compared to a border of various flowering shrubs. Borders confined to a mass display of a particular kind of shrub, such as red-flowering azaleas, white-flowering hydrangeas or yellow forsythias, are also easier to maintain than borders of mixed flowering shrubs.

But times are changing. American gardeners are rapidly becoming more adventurous and more creative with their home surroundings. "Painting" the home landscape with shrubs is an endeavor more and more people are finding immensely satisfying.

TREES AND SHRUBS IN THE LANDSCAPE

Beautiful trees and shrubs can be a good investment in many ways. For example, plantings of mature shrubs and trees considerably increase the cash value of a house. Recognition of this fact has led to the enormous popularity of fast-growing shade trees, such as hybrid varieties of poplar that have growth rates of up to 8 feet a year.

Water reflections double the beauty of trees and shrubs. Here at Magnolia Gardens, South Carolina, towering bald cypress and a lone palmetto are mirrored in glass-smooth surface of Big Cypress Lake.

Trees and shrubs also control soil erosion. Plantings of low, closely spaced shrubs are one of the best ways to control soil erosion on slopes.

Large trees form a beautiful backdrop or cyclorama to enhance the skyline—and surely every child has known the pleasure trees provide for hours of exhilarating play—a rope swing across a swimming hole, a climbing tree, a tree house, a tire swing, a tightrope bridge across a stream or a hollow tree to hide in.

For more on landscape uses of trees and shrubs, see pages 23-35.

Shadow patterns on lawn are an important element of good landscape design that includes trees.

Flowering dogwood provides canopy of flowers and cooling shade over patio.

FOUR SEASONS OF COLOR FROM TREES

Spring: Delicate, double, pink blossoms of a weeping Higan cherry complement a naturalized planting of yellow daffodils.

Summer: Slash of bright crimson from a serpentine bed of scarlet sage contrasts brilliantly with dark, soothing greens of midsummer in Victorian-style garden.

Fall: Carpet of fallen leaves from Kwanzan cherries covers slope, beautifying garden as effectively as any mass planting of flowers.

Winter: Naked, dormant branches of deciduous maples and ashes etch the sky. The arching, graceful branches are highlighted by fresh fall of snow.

ANATOMY OF TREES AND SHRUBS

Trees and shrubs are unique among all forms of plants in that they produce *woody* parts—usually a trunk, roots and branches. Other parts such as flowers, leaves, fruit and seeds are similar to those found on other plants, including annuals and perennials. This woody structure gives trees and shrubs *strength, endurance* and *stature*—thus, trees and most shrubs have the ability to grow much larger than other plants and to live for many years. The tallest trees in the world are the giant redwoods *(Sequoia sempervirens)*. In a grove of these "tall trees" growing in Humboldt County, California, some specimens are over 360 feet high. The oldest known living tree is a bristle-cone pine *(Pinus aristata var. longaeva),* growing at 10,000 feet in the White Mountains of the Sierra Nevada range in California. Nicknamed "Methuselah," it is reputedly 4,600 years old. The most massive tree depends on how you measure stature. The famous "General Sherman" sequoia *(Sequoiadendron giganteum)* in Sequoia National Park, California, has the broadest girth (79.8 feet) but measured by total spread, the record is claimed by a banyan tree *(Ficus bengalensis)* in the Calcutta Botanical Garden, India. Its total leaf canopy covers 4 acres, supported by more than 1,000 brace roots.

Even shrubs are not excluded from the record books. The oldest living object on earth is listed in the *Guinness Book of World Records* as a creosote bush *(Larrea tridentata)* located in the southwestern Sonora Desert. Nicknamed "King Clone," the plant's woody, spreading root system is estimated to be 11,700 years old, dead in the middle but still supporting active growth around the perimeter in an ever-widening circle. This record is now being challenged by an ancient box-huckleberry plant *(Gaylussacia brachycera)* in Pennsylvania. Extending for 1-1/4 miles, it is estimated by botanists to be over 13,000 years old.

HOW TREES AND SHRUBS GROW

The 4,600-year-old "Methuselah" bristle-cone pine, the 3,000-year-old "General Sherman" big tree and the 11,700-year-old "King Clone" creosote bush all started life the same way. A tiny

Sunlight shining on leaves is the primary source of energy for trees. Roots absorb mineral nutrients and water from the soil.

seed dropped to the ground in fall, remained dormant over winter and germinated in spring when the soil warmed and moisture was provided.

When a seed germinates, it immediately sprouts *roots* to penetrate the soil in search of anchorage and nutrients, and *leaves* to help it manufacture additional nutrients from the atmosphere. The seedling does this by a process known as *photosynthesis*. In this process, millions of tiny pores *(stomata)* on the leaf surfaces absorb carbon dioxide. The carbon dioxide combines with water to provide sugar. A green substance in the leaf, called *chlorophyll,* and sunlight are necessary for photosynthesis to occur. In the process, the leaves release oxygen into the air.

The most favorable conditions for photosynthesis are mild temperatures and diffused light. On hot, bright, cloudless, sunny days, photosynthesis slows down. An ample supply of water is also essential to photosynthesis. This is because water is a raw material for the manufacture of sugar, and because plants on the verge of wilting close their stomata. Stomatal closure reduces water loss but also restricts carbon dioxide intake.

When a seed first germinates, the growing point of the seedling is situated between the first pair of seed leaves,

called *cotyledons*. This growing point becomes a lead shoot or *leader,* which, along with similar growth points at the tips of all branches, continues to grow as long as the tree or shrub lives.

Besides the root tips and branch tips, another vital growing part is established during the first year, called the *cambium layer*. Only one cell thick, this layer is located between the wood and the bark, and is the origin of the *wood* that makes the tree or shrub grow in stature. In spring when the cambium layer becomes active, it splits off rows of wood cells to the inside and rows of bark cells to the outside. The bark is continually eroding and remains relatively thin, but the inner wood accumulates in ever-widening circles or *rings*. Each ring represents 1 year's growth, and individual rings can be distinguished because the wood formed in spring is composed of larger-diameter cells and therefore is more porous than wood formed in summer. You can tell the age of a tree by counting the rings. You can also tell periods of drought or abundant rainfall by the thickness of the rings, because less wood is formed during a dry year.

Some trees and shrubs have the ability to survive long periods of drought, but inadequate moisture is still the most common cause of stress. Like other plants, trees and shrubs continuously transpire moisture from the surface of their leaves, so water must be available to the root system in a more-or-less steady supply.

Many trees are fast growing during their juvenile stage. Black walnuts and dawn redwoods can grow 6 feet a year in their early years. Some hybrid poplars reliably grow 8 feet a year when young. As a tree gets older, height growth slows down and the tree tends to spread outward.

The growth rate of certain woody vines is even more astounding. The native trumpet creeper (*Campsis radicans*) will easily grow 15 feet in 1 year.

After a suitable period of time, trees and shrubs will flower and set seeds. Many shrubs and some trees—such as *Amelanchier*—will flower the next season after germinating. Others, like tulip trees and walnuts, may take 10 years or more to flower. The flowers can take on many forms. They can be produced singly like tulip trees, or in clusters like the catkins of a beech. The flowers then produce fruits, which can take on the form of a *nut, capsule, berry, cone* or other form.

Trees and shrubs are often referred to as either *flowering* or *foliage* trees and shrubs. Foliage trees and shrubs are grown primarily for their leaves—they also produce flowers but these are usually so small or inconspicuous that they have little or no ornamental value.

The life span of a tree or shrub varies from species to species. Some are naturally short-lived. Forty years for poplars is old. Oaks are capable of living to more than 1,000 years, redwoods to more than 3,000 years.

PARTS OF A TREE

The most important physical features of a tree are shown on the facing page. The parts described below are also found on shrubs, which are also woody plants.

The *trunk* is the tree's main support. Some trees form a single trunk and others are multi-stemmed, either by nature or as a result of *suckering* when the main trunk is damaged. The outer skin of a tree trunk is called *bark*. This serves for protection. Beneath the bark are layers of wood that serve different purposes. The *inner bark* is part of the circulatory system, permitting the downward flow of sap. The *cambium* is only one cell thick and the source of all new wood. The *sapwood* is responsible for sap flow up the tree. Sap carries water and nutrients in soluble form to branches and leaves. The *heartwood* is dead sapwood that contributes to the tree's strength and rigidity. The tree's vital functions are carried on by the narrow layers just beneath the bark. If a band of cambium layer is destroyed completely around the trunk, the sap flow is cut off and the tree will die. This is called *girdling*.

The *outline* or *growth habit* of a tree or shrub is the shape created by its canopy of leaves and branches. Broadly speaking, the outline can be rounded and spreading or upright and spirelike. Some trees are highly variable in their outlines. In nature, the outline fits a tree for survival—a spreading rounded shape is efficient for photosynthesis, while an upright, spirelike shape helps a tree resist wind damage. The drawings on pages 21 and 22 show typical outlines of trees and shrubs.

Leaves produce food by means of photosynthesis, and transpire moisture and oxygen. Leaf shape is important to the tree's survival. Broad leaves are efficient at photosynthesis, presenting a large area for capturing sunlight. The fine needles of a conifer present a small surface area to the elements and allow a tree to conserve moisture to endure winters in an evergreen state.

A leaf cross-section shows it is composed of cells containing *chlorophyll*, a green substance that allows the leaf to convert sunlight, water and carbon dioxide into food. Pores in the leaf called *stomata* allow the leaf to absorb carbon dioxide and release both oxygen and water. Leaves can also absorb plant nutrients in soluble form. Applying liquid fertilizers or plant food directly on leaves is known as *foliar feeding*.

Branches support leaves, flowers and fruit. They also form *buds*, which are the growing points for undeveloped leaves, flowers or new branches. The principal growing branch is called a *leader* and the side branches are called *laterals*. The tip of a branch contains a *terminal bud* and the side buds are called *lateral buds*.

Flowers can be showy and ornamental, as on flowering cherries and crabapples, or small and inconspicuous. Many trees and shrubs have *perfect* flowers that contain both male and female parts. Others have separate male and female flowers. If male and female flowers are borne on the same plant, the tree or shrub is called *monoecious*. On *dioecious* trees and shrubs, male and female flowers are borne on separate plants. In this case, only the female plant can produce fruit and seeds, but must have a male plant nearby to pollinate it. Tulip trees and flowering crabapples are examples of trees with perfect flowers. Monoecious trees include oaks and beech; dioecious trees include holly and ash.

Fruits follow flowering and can take many forms—including nuts and berries. On conifers, the seeds are produced in a *cone*. Most trees produce fruits that contain seeds adapted for dispersal by animals, but some trees, such as maples, produce naked, winged seeds for dispersal by wind.

Roots anchor the tree and allow it to absorb water and nutrients. Water and nutrients in soluble form are absorbed by minute *root hairs*, located just behind the actively growing tips of the *feeder roots*. This is important to remember when feeding a tree, because the feeder roots are generally concentrated near the soil surface in an area which may extend from the trunk out to a distance equal to the height of the tree. Most trees and shrubs have fibrous roots close to the soil surface; some also have long taproots that can dig deep in search of moisture.

PARTS OF A TREE

This composite drawing shows the most important physical features of a typical tree. These parts are also found on shrubs, which are also woody plants.

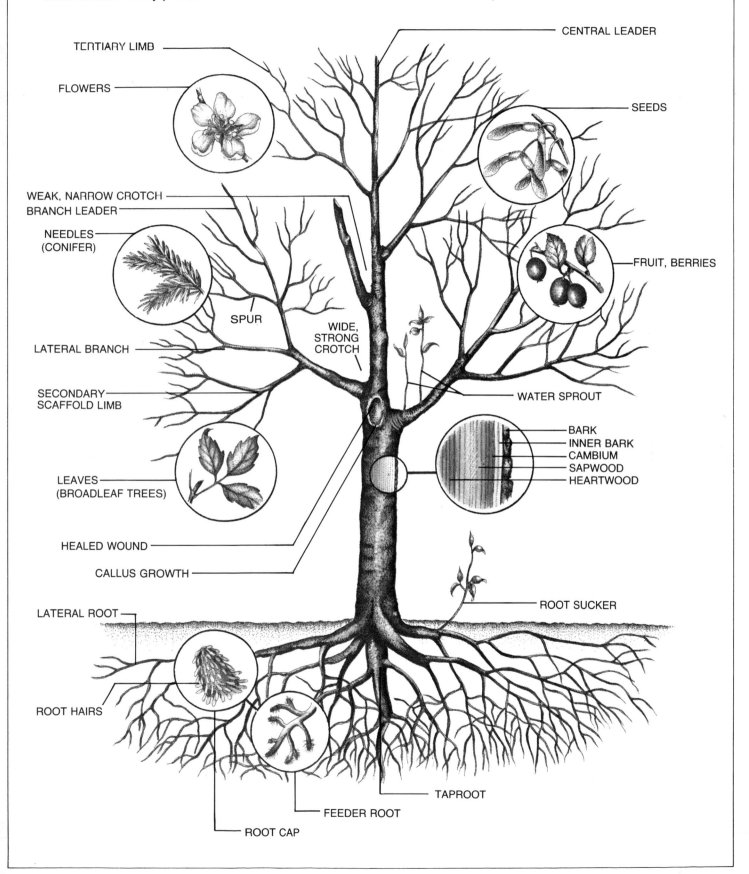

TERTIARY LIMB

FLOWERS

CENTRAL LEADER

SEEDS

WEAK, NARROW CROTCH

BRANCH LEADER

NEEDLES (CONIFER)

FRUIT, BERRIES

SPUR

WIDE, STRONG CROTCH

LATERAL BRANCH

SECONDARY SCAFFOLD LIMB

WATER SPROUT

BARK
INNER BARK
CAMBIUM
SAPWOOD
HEARTWOOD

LEAVES (BROADLEAF TREES)

HEALED WOUND

CALLUS GROWTH

ROOT SUCKER

LATERAL ROOT

ROOT HAIRS

TAPROOT

FEEDER ROOT

ROOT CAP

Many trees and shrubs produce fruits, nuts or berries that enclose seeds for dispersal by animals. Brilliant red berries of *Virburnum* are shown here.

Red maple *(Acer rubrum)* is one of several trees that produce winged seeds for dispersal by wind.

Needleleaf evergreens have developed slender, needlelike leaf surface to resist cold weather. Shown here is Norway spruce *(Picea abies)*.

DECIDUOUS VS. EVERGREEN

Basically, all trees and shrubs can be classified as *deciduous* or *evergreen*. Deciduous trees and shrubs drop all their leaves in fall, go dormant in winter and leaf out again in spring with renewed growth and vigor. Before a deciduous plant goes dormant, it removes much of the nutrient value from the leaves before shedding them. In its dormant state, most trees or shrubs can withstand severe cold.

Evergreens, on the other hand, do not drop their leaves all at one time but hold them year round, losing and renewing them continuously. The leaves of evergreens have adapted to surviving cold winters. Many tropical and subtropical plants remain evergreen, but they do not survive temperatures much below freezing (28F/-4C).

Evergreens are further divided into *needleleaf evergreens* and *broadleaf evergreens*. Most needleleaf evergreens are *conifers* (cone-bearing plants) that have developed a slender, needlelike leaf surface to help them resist the effects of cold winter winds. The leaves of certain broadleaf evergreens, such as rhododendrons and hollies, have developed special cell structures to help these plants endure winter cold. A few needleleaf conifers are deciduous, including larch, dawn redwood and bald cypress.

You may hear a plant described as being *semi-evergreen*. This means that in colder climates it may lose its leaves in winter, but in mild climates or frost-free areas it will stay green all year.

WHY LEAVES CHANGE COLOR IN FALL

Fall colors are displayed in collection of leaves, mostly those of maples.

During the time of the green leaves, *Ho-e-ma-ha, the Winter Man,* lives far in the North, according to the Cheyenne legend. As the days grow shorter, *Ho-e-ma-ha* begins his journey south. Wherever his moccasins touch, the grass withers and turns brown, the running streams are ice-locked and stilled, and where he breathes, the leaves turn yellow and red. Nowadays, the myths and legends of old have succumbed to the more-prosaic scientific explanations for the changing of leaf colors in fall.

Leaves of most trees and shrubs are relatively short lived. Most deciduous trees and shrubs lose their foliage all at one time to go dormant at the onset of winter, then regrow new leaves the following spring. This process helps deciduous plants conserve energy during the cold months. Evergreens, such as pine trees, shed and regrow their needlelike leaves sporadically throughout the year. They have adapted themselves to conserve moisture with a small leaf profile, allowing them to survive the winter permanently green.

Before a deciduous tree sheds its leaves, it withdraws sugars and minerals from the leaves for the tree to store. That's why certain trees like maples can be freely "tapped" during early spring to release their sugary sap. In the fall, the arrival of short days and cool nights causes a layer of cells at the base of the leaf to harden and seal off the sugar flow, so it builds up in the leaf tissue. At the same time, the green chlorophyll is disappearing and allowing other pigments in the leaf to show more distinctly. Yellow coloring comes mainly from *carotin* and *xanthophyll,* the same pigments that make egg yolks yellow and carrots orange. Intense red coloring, and occasionally purple, comes from *tannin* and *anthocyanin.* Trapped in the leaf, these pigments combine to create the kaleidoscope of colors often seen in individual leaves, with red, yellow and bronze the predominating colors.

On most deciduous trees, the leaves finally fall when cells break down at the point where the leaf is attached to the twig. On other trees, such as those of beech and pin oak, the leaves will die, but remain connected to the twigs, staying on the tree all winter until new leaves literally push them off in spring.

The intensity of coloring can vary from year to year, depending on several factors. A warm, cloudy autumn and late frost will tend to produce poor colors, and excessive winds can strip the leaves from the trees before they have turned on their most brilliant display. Cool nights and warm, sunny days produce the best show of fall color.

Also, certain trees are distinctly better at changing colors than others. Most deciduous trees native to North America exhibit good autumn colors, and so do some in eastern Asia. There is apparently a valid reason for this.

About 1 million years ago, the world's climate began to change dramatically as the first of four Ice Ages crept across much of the earth from the polar ice caps. With the advancing cold and ice, entire families of trees were wiped out because they could not adapt to the changing climate, or retreat (by seed dispersal) across level land

Hickories and maples provide fall color among oaks, pines and firs. Sumac provides brilliant red foliage at left.

masses from the slowly advancing ice. In North America and parts of Asia, such as China, retreat was possible, and many original tree species made a comeback when each of the Ice Ages ended. But across vast areas of Europe and South Africa, many original species became extinct, because retreat was blocked by some natural barrier such as a mountain range or a sea.

It seems the original species that survived the Ice Ages developed the ability to produce dramatic color changes in autumn, while tree species which evolved anew after the last Ice Age lack this ability.

The Ice Ages also produced some interesting mutations among trees. Persimmon, for example, was a tropical tree that survived the Ice Ages in China and North America by mutations that developed hardy characteristics. The leaves turn purple in autumn, and in the North American species, the flavor of the late-ripening fruit is actually enhanced after frost.

In other tropical trees, a stable climate and warm temperatures throughout the year allow photosynthesis to go on uninhibited, so there is no winter leaf drop and no color change. When a leaf reaches maturity, it withers and drops.

2
Trees & Shrubs in the Landscape

Of all plants, trees and shrubs are the most prominent in a landscape. They are the most permanent, the least demanding of care, and they establish a sense of place and design better than all other plants.

Well-planned landscapes use a combination of *needleleaf evergreens, broadleaf evergreens* and *deciduous trees and shrubs* in varying proportions. Needleleaf evergreens establish a greater sense of permanence than other plants, not only because of their stature, but also because of their cold tolerance. Landscape architects often refer to evergreens as the *bones* of a garden. Planted as skyline and lawn accents, windbreaks, screens and hedges, or borders and edging, evergreens can delineate garden space or create permanent *outdoor rooms* and provide dominant highlights. Apart from a brighter leaf color in spring, their appearance changes little from one season to the next.

Because evergreens make especially good background plants, they are usually the first plants to be fitted into a landscape plan.

Deciduous trees and shrubs, on the other hand, are constantly changing with the seasons. Certain deciduous trees can even provide four seasons of dramatic

---

Left: Azaleas make excellent understory plants for woodlands and groves. They prefer light shade and acid soil.

color changes—such as lovely flowers in spring, lush greenery in summer, brilliant leaf coloring in fall and an artistic branch silhouette through winter.

Trees are the most influential design elements in a garden. For instance, palms instantly suggest a tropical climate. A small garden hedged in by tall evergreens becomes a secret garden—a refuge from the pressures of civilization.

DESIGNING WITH TREES AND SHRUBS

The placement of trees and shrubs in a garden is based on a relatively few basic design principles. In some cases, a tree or shrub is planted so its branches partially conceal a structural feature—such as a wall or fence—or drape over it as an embellishment. In other cases, trees and shrubs serve as a background to bring into relief special foreground features—such as a boulder, sculpture or a planting highlight.

The best gardens avoid symmetrical placement of trees and shrubs, except where an avenue, hedge or grove is desired. In informal plantings, trees and shrubs should never be planted in straight lines, but *staggered*. Trees and shrubs intended to form hedges, avenues or sentinels should be planted at precise distances, in lines.

When trees and shrubs are grouped together in numbers, it is best to use different species that will contrast pleasingly with each other, unless the

intent is to create a natural woodland or grove of predominantly one type of tree—such as oaks, pines or tulip poplars.

Contrasts of form and line are especially important—for example, an open, irregular-branching tree such as a rugged pine or a drooping willow in contrast to the dense, smooth contours of mounded azaleas shaped by shearing. Contrasts in leaf size and color are also desirable.

Taller trees should be employed in the background. Unless a windbreak or curtain effect is desired, deciduous trees are best employed as background plants because of their wintry, bare silhouetted aspect that can be admired from a distance. An exception is made with flowering deciduous trees such as cherries and crabapples because of their profuse blossoming, which is best admired close up.

Clipped or sheared broadleaf evergreen shrubs, such as azaleas, hollies and boxwood, can be used as foreground features to contrast with background trees that present a rugged appearance. These mounded shrubs can form cushions, like clumps of moss, to soften a landscape. Mound-shaped shrubs can also be planted on a slope, towering one above the other, to give the appearance of gently rolling hills.

Often, a single specimen of an especially beautiful or interesting tree or shrub is featured as an accent or focal point in the garden. It is usually positioned so it does not compete with other plants for visual attention.

Authentic Japanese gardens rely heavily on evergreen trees and shrubs—the complete opposite of a traditional English garden, where deciduous trees often predominate.

A favorite practice in Oriental gardens is to highlight a *lone tree*—such as a pine, willow or plum—on a promontory or earth mound. The tree itself can be surgically shaped to simulate weathered trees found in the wild. Limbs are removed between prominent scaffold branches and remaining limbs bent and shaped with wires and splints until they assume wild, rather than cultivated, forms. In other instances, special weeping forms—such as hemlocks and cedars—are placed to represent cascades, fountains and torrents.

THE ORIENTAL INFLUENCE

In Oriental gardens it is a general rule that four-fifths of the vegetation should be *evergreens*, with a heavy emphasis on conifers, rhododendrons, camellias and bamboo. A few deciduous flowering trees—notably cherries, crabapples and wisteria—and a few deciduous shade trees—notably oaks, maples, ginkgo and willows—are used principally for their fall coloring or texture. However, the somewhat somber Oriental style is not to everyone's taste. In the English style of landscaping, this emphasis is often completely reversed to achieve a totally different, but no less pleasing, result—one that is more airy and informal. Whatever ethnic style is preferred, this comparison does serve to show that in garden design a boldness and clarity of purpose is needed from the very outset to determine the choice of plants.

Trees, Stone and Water—It is the Japanese who believe that only three elements are essential to create a beautiful garden. They are *stone, water* and *trees*.

Stone is a symbol of endurance, power and permanence. It brings to the garden an aura of rugged grandeur. Ancient Japanese landscapers would scour the mountains for rocks and boulders with interesting colors, shapes and textures. Some the size of grand pianos would be dug from the forest floor because just a nub of exposed stone revealed to the finder that something visually exciting lay hidden there. Others would be raised from river beds or hauled out of rock falls—moved by armies of men and mules, the rocks themselves carefully wrapped in quilts to protect their flawless texture or some delicate plant growing on them, such as a fern or a clump of moss. In the mind's eye, stones can conjure up visions of craggy peaks and windswept rocky islands, of dry water courses and pebble beaches.

Water is the *music* of nature—splashing, gurgling, trickling. Water is also a mirror, reflecting the moon, vistas and highlights—doubling the visual impact of its surroundings. Water is cool and fluid—a reminder that all life on earth originated there. In a still pool it can be dark as night or flashing with the silver and golden images of fish. Cascading over rocks or arching out from a bamboo spout, water can twinkle with a thousand flashing lights. The shapes of rocks and trees are contorted in its reflection. Still water is level. There is a mystery to water—unknown creatures can lurk in its depths.

Trees are the life of a garden. Their presence is soothing to the senses. They provide more color, more gradations of texture and more structure to a garden than rocks or water combined. Color comes not only from blossoms, but also from leaves, berries, bark and branches. Trees introduce texture from the size, shape and arrangement of leaves, from the density and configuration of twigs and from the patterns of bark. Structure is evident in the lines of a tree—a pencil-straight trunk or a multitude of stems. The horizontal spread or the weeping effect of its branches are other visual delights associated with structure. The earth, with its stones and water, is a canvas. The trees are brush strokes.

Apart from blossoms of a few kinds of trees and shrubs—notably cherry, camellias and azaleas—flowers are noticeably absent from Japanese gardens. A discreet clump of water lilies to embellish a pool of water, and an occasional clump of iris, admired more for its swordlike leaves, are virtually the only flowering perennial plants found in traditional Japanese gardens. If a delphinium or a marigold raised its head, it would be pounced upon and eradicated as a weed. When I was conducting a private tour of the Katsura Imperial Garden, in Kyoto, my guide announced that I had come at the perfect time—summer—because then the garden could be admired for its enduring beauty without the distraction of spring flowers or fall foliage.

The Japanese philosophy of garden design is an extreme example of tree worship, but most other garden styles also hold woody plants in high regard. The Italians and the French with their emphasis on grandeur and formality of design and the English with their liking for natural landscapes, have developed special uses for trees as part of a garden's overall design.

THE EUROPEAN INFLUENCE

One of the most important design concepts used in the European style of landscaping is the *vista,* whereby trees help to establish a beautiful view. The French and Italians do it with avenues of trees in parallel lines. The most famous French avenues, called *allees,* are on level ground, but the outstanding Italian examples are more often seen on hillsides where steps may descend a slope to give the illusion of greater distance. Usually, a large sculpture or an ornate structure such as a fountain is sited at the end as a focal point.

English-style vistas are more natural, often cutting through natural woodland and with a view of a free-form lake in the distance. To emulate these European concepts of landscaping it is not necessary to own large, parklike estates. The principles can be applied to the smallest home garden, using smaller trees and compact shrubs to delineate a narrow or short vista.

This is the antithesis of traditional Oriental styles, where winding paths and zig-zag bridges are used to create *stroll gardens,* with twists and turns at every opportunity to make maximum use of confined areas and provide surprises around every corner.

In modern times, neither style need be exclusive of the other. In fact, there are many fine American gardens that borrow tree and shrub planting ideas from both European and Oriental cultures.

Publisher's Note: Derek Fell is the author of a beautiful new hardcover book that illustrates in color the dynamics of using trees to make vistas. Called "Deerfield—An American Garden—Through Four Seasons," the 96-page book is available by mail from Capability Books, Box 114, Deer Park, WI 54007. Cost is $35.00, plus $1.50 shipping.

Beautiful harmony between evergreens and deciduous trees at Dumbarton Oaks Garden in Washington, D.C. Spire-shaped cedars frame a vista where fall coloring of billowing native deciduous trees provides a focal point.

Beautiful rock garden uses mostly evergreen conifers to enhance brighter colors of alpine plants and perennials, such as the pink *Astilbe* in foreground.

Little leaf linden *(Tilia cordata)* has an attractive rounded, pyramidal habit.

'Pendula' is a lovely weeping form of deodar cedar *(Cedrus deodara albrea)*.

GROWTH HABIT

The term *growth habit* refers to the height, spread, growth rate and outline of a tree or shrub. Because these characteristics are highly variable among different kinds of trees and shrubs, it is important to consider them when making design decisions in a landscape. Growth habit is not only variable from species to species, but also within a single species where mutations have been used by horticulturists in developing new varieties.

When you see the towering, spirelike growth habit of a standard Canadian hemlock and compare it to the low, billowing, weeping features of the mutant variety 'Sargent's' weeping hemlock, it's hard to believe they are the same species. Whereas the standard Canadian hemlock is limited to mundane uses in the garden, such as for a windbreak or hedge, the weeping form is invaluable as a sophisticated lawn highlight or accent plant.

The drawing on the facing page shows some of the basic growth habits of trees and shrubs, which are described here.

Columnar trees are mostly evergreens with a dense foliage cover. Width is more-or-less equal from the base of the tree to its crown. The top is usually blunt or rounded. American arborvitae, Irish yew, podocarpus and Italian cypress are the best examples of columnar trees. They are used for vertical highlights—to delineate an avenue or create tall screens and windbreaks—and singly as exclamation points in the landscape. Columnar trees are also good in pairs at entryways and as sentinels at the corners of a building.

Fastigate trees are mostly deciduous. They have branches that point upward, sometimes in a spiral form, and usually a tapered top. Lombardy poplar trees are a good example. The fastigate English oak is effective as a foundation plant against a tall building, as a landscape highlight similar to columnar trees, and especially as a skyline tree.

Pyramidal trees are mostly evergreen, though some deciduous trees form a distinct pyramid shape—notably the pin oak. Pyramidal trees have wide, spreading lower branches that often sweep the ground, but the top tapers to a definite point. This is a classical shape immensely popular as a lawn highlight and for decorating with lights at Christmas. Evergreen forms such as deodar cedar, Norway spruce and Colorado blue spruce also make sturdy windbreaks.

Spirelike trees are mostly evergreens with wide-spreading lower branches that quickly slant up to a long, slender point. A particularly beautiful spirelike tree is the mature Norfolk Island pine, looking like a gigantic feather pointing skyward. They are magnificent skyline trees, and it is a pity they can be grown outdoors only in mild-winter locations close to the ocean. For colder regions, Douglas fir and the deciduous dawn redwood make beautiful spires, and are valued for lining long driveways and as lawn highlights.

Conical trees are shaped like spinning tops or squat pyramids. They are generally slow-growing evergreens that are dwarf mutations of standard trees, particularly hemlock, yew and spruce. Dwarf forms are popular for rock gardens.

Weeping or pendant trees bring a softness to the landscape. Weeping willow and weeping cherry are the best examples. Branches first grow upright, then arch and descend downward. Weeping trees are especially effective when planted at the edge of ponds so the water surface reflects their weeping outline and the hanging branches can touch the surface as though flowing into the water like a waterfall. They also make wonderful skyline trees. Some weeping varieties are grafted onto the trunk of a closely related plant to provide a pedestal on which to display the weeping form.

Cascading trees are more umbrella-

BASIC TREE SHAPES

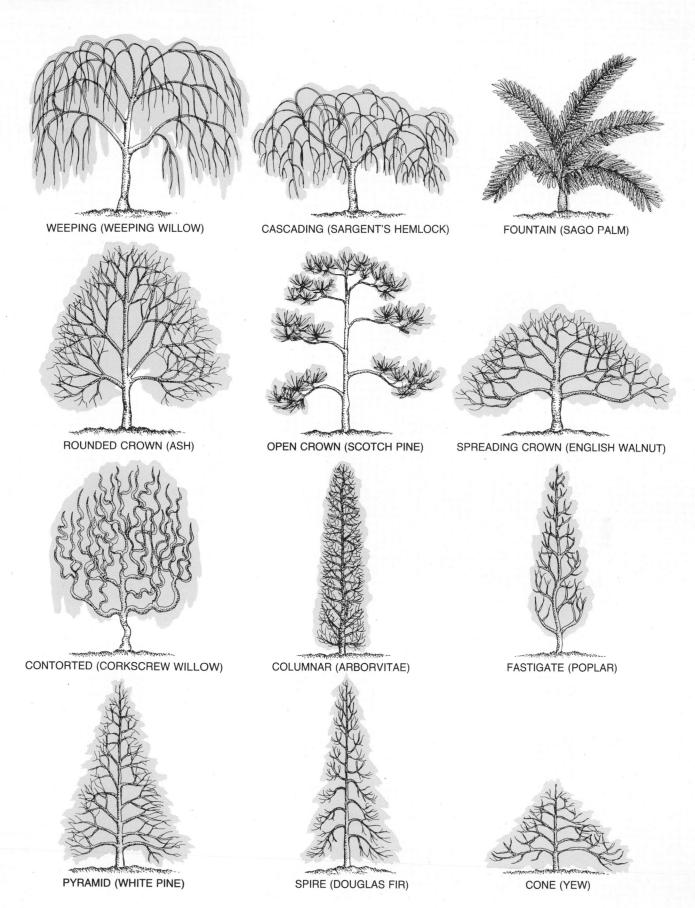

WEEPING (WEEPING WILLOW)

CASCADING (SARGENT'S HEMLOCK)

FOUNTAIN (SAGO PALM)

ROUNDED CROWN (ASH)

OPEN CROWN (SCOTCH PINE)

SPREADING CROWN (ENGLISH WALNUT)

CONTORTED (CORKSCREW WILLOW)

COLUMNAR (ARBORVITAE)

FASTIGATE (POPLAR)

PYRAMID (WHITE PINE)

SPIRE (DOUGLAS FIR)

CONE (YEW)

BASIC SHRUB SHAPES

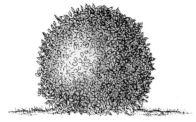

GLOBULAR (BOXWOOD)

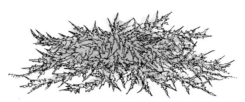

PROSTRATE (HORIZONTAL JUNIPER)

MULTI-STEMMED (FORSYTHIA)

VINING (WISTERIA)

like than weeping trees, though the terms are often used interchangeably. Cascading forms of catalpa, hemlock—particularly the Sargent's weeping hemlock—and mulberry are good examples, as are weeping crabapple and weeping cherry. All make excellent lawn highlights. *Pleaching* is a favorite pruning technique with cascading trees. The main trunk is *topped,* with few main scaffold branches left as stubs, to produce clusters of cascading whips.

Fountain-shaped trees and shrubs create an exploding fountain effect from outward-arching canes or fronds. Forsythia, fetterbush *(Leucothoe)* and Lady Banks roses have long, whiplike branches that do this. They are especially admired for their wintry outline where snow and ice can coat their limbs to sparkle in the sunlight. Plant them as informal hedges or highlights in odd corners. Used singly, they are best planted against a background of evergreens so the fountain effect can be emphasized. In frost-free areas, juvenile

Sago palms and tree ferns create a more tropical fountain effect.

Rounded-crown trees with straight, single trunks are perhaps everyone's image of the classic tree. Many deciduous trees grow this way, including beeches, ash, maples and many oaks. All are perfect as skyline trees, lawn highlights, shade trees, street trees and woodlots.

Open-crown trees have an irregular outline and sparse scaffold branches. Usually, this occurs on older trees. For example, Scotch pine, which begins its life pyramid-shaped, will shed branches as it ages. The gaps between the main side branches become greater and the tree opens up, often presenting a rugged, weathered silhouette to the landscape.

Spreading-crown trees are best for shade. Silk trees, Southern live oak and English walnut are excellent examples. Long, sinuous lower branches radiate out like the spokes of a wheel or arch elegantly. The crown presents a low profile to resist wind and avoid the possibility of the tree falling on the house in the

event of a storm. They are perfect trees from which to hang a swing.

Contorted trees have twigs and branches that twist and curl like the coils of a snake. The corkscrew willow and contorted form of hazel are the best-known examples. The contorted hazel is especially admired in foundation plantings where its tortuous, bare branches can be admired against a wall or screen during winter. The corkscrew willow grows tall and can make a dramatic skyline tree.

Multi-stemmed trees do not form a single main trunk. They sprout a cluster of main stems like shrubs. Usually, this cluster of stems can be thinned out by pruning to leave one main stem for the plant to be grown as a single-stemmed tree. Lilacs are good examples of multi-stemmed woody plants where the terms *tree* and *shrub* become interchangeable. In their juvenile years, lilacs are considered shrubs, but with age they are often referred to as trees.

In their natural state, multi-stemmed trees are good for creating a hedge, or in mixed-shrub borders and foundation plantings. For an especially artistic effect, the thicket of stems can be thinned out, stripped of lower side branches, and the dense overhead canopy shaped to form an umbrella or mushroom. This sculptural pruning is especially popular with camellias and European olives, so distant landscape features can be seen through boldly defined lines formed by the multiple trunks.

Another special effect possible with multi-stemmed trees and large shrubs is to form a *tunnel.* Planted on either side of a rustic path, large multi-stemmed shrubs, such as rhododendrons and camellias, can be encouraged to arch their upper branches to meet and form a leafy canopy. When flowers appear in summer, the spent petals drop like confetti to carpet the path.

Globular shrubs are round in shape and popular for foundation plantings. They are often referred to as *meat balls* when used in formal gardens. When rounded shrubs like boxwood and azaleas are heavily sheared to present a smooth outline, they have a soothing effect, like mounds of moss on a stream bank. Globular forms are extremely popular in Oriental gardens and rock gardens, arranged in informal groups of different heights to resemble a landscape of rolling hills.

Prostrate shrubs make effective ground covers for both decoration and erosion control. Many have branches that sweep across the ground, rooting along their length and suffocating all weed growth. Horizontal juniper species are the most frequently used prostrate shrubs for ground covers.

Vining shrubs come in many different forms. Some, like wisteria, will climb by twining—these will strangle a young tree if they get hold of it. Others, like trumpet vine, use clinging roots. Care should be taken to match the vine to its intended support. For example, honeysuckle is better used to cover an arbor than to decorate a tree. Virginia creeper is preferred for climbing up stone because of its clinging ability. Cherokee roses and jasmine are safer for garlanding trees. Many kinds of woody vines can be planted to serve as ground covers, such as English ivy.

TREES AND SHRUBS FOR DIFFERENT PURPOSES

Trees and shrubs are planted in the home landscape for both esthetic and practical reasons. Here are some of the uses for trees and shrubs:

Shade—Cooling shade is probably the most desirable reason for planting trees. A deck or patio may benefit from the shade of a spreading tree. When planting for shade, consider whether you need dense shade or light shade. Trees such as acacias, mimosa and honeylocust have delicate leaves that allow sufficient light to penetrate so that grass will grow right up to the trunk. Under the deeper shade of cedars, oaks and maples, grass may have to give way to a more shade-tolerant ground cover such as ivy, vinca or pachysandra.

When planting for shade, also consider whether or not the tree is messy, and if this trait is acceptable for the location you've chosen. For example, female ginkgos will drop unpleasant-smelling fruits, and the prickly nut cases of Chinese chestnuts can be a nuisance near heavily-used outdoor areas. Walnuts and fruiting varieties of mulberry are similarly messy. These trees would be poor choices around decks, patios, concrete driveways and swimming pools.

Ornamental Flowers—Few hardy trees

European olive is an excellent example of a multi-stemmed tree.

English boxwood *(Buxus sempervirens)* is pruned to globular form. Because of its small leaves and slow growth rate, boxwood is excellent for formal hedges and topiary subjects.

In the author's garden, raised deck allows striking pink blossoms of flowering crabapple (*Malus* species) to be admired close up.

and shrubs are *perpetual flowering*. This term refers to trees and shrubs that bloom over a long period of time during spring and summer. Those that are perpetual flowering—such as glossy abelia—tend to produce small blossoms. The exotic tropical hibiscus (*Hibiscus rosea-sinensis*) and bougainvillea are glorious exceptions for frost-free areas. Usually, woody plants have a brief period of bloom at a particular time of year. Amelanchiers and witchhazels are among the earliest to flower in spring, while camellias and franklinias are usually the last to flower in fall.

The prima donnas among hardy flowering trees and shrubs—magnolias, azaleas, rhododendrons, cherries, crabapples and dogwoods—squeeze their spectacular flowering displays into a brief 6-week period in spring. So it takes careful planning to achieve a continuous flowering display beyond spring, either by planting late-blooming varieties or summer-blooming trees and shrubs. Crape myrtle, silk tree, golden rain tree and pagoda tree are examples of summer-flowering trees. Good summer-flowering shrubs include oleander, hydrangeas, smoke tree and bottlebrush buckeye. Some flowering trees, such as hawthorns and crabapples, provide color twice—with flowers in spring and fruit in fall. A number of flowering trees and shrubs have the additional appeal of fragrance, such as lilac, jasmine, gardenia and many deciduous azaleas.

Ornamental Leaves—Though flowers can be fleeting, *perpetual color* is possible by choosing trees and shrubs with colorful leaves. 'Crimson King' maple and 'Thundercloud' plum, for example, are two of many trees with permanent bronze foliage. Colorado blue spruce has bluish needles. The selection among shrubs is even more extensive—golden barberry with golden yellow leaves, and 'Red Tips' photinia with shiny red leaves are two examples. Gray and silver are also common leaf colors besides the many gradations of green.

When fall coloring is considered, the color variation is even more extensive. Bright yellow, scarlet-red and deep maroon are common leaf colors among many native deciduous trees during fall.

Leaves also have ornamental value according to their shape. The fernlike leaves of staghorn sumac and the lacy leaves of Japanese cutleaf maples are especially attractive, aside from their beautiful fall coloring.

Ornamental Bark—The trunks of many trees are decorative because of colorful or textured bark. The paperbark maple is a prized lawn specimen because of its handsome, light-brown peeling bark. Similarly, the canoe birch is admired for its smooth, paper-white bark and contrasting black color bands. Deeply fissured bark can be an attractive feature—such as the basket-weave pattern of a black locust. Among shrubs with decorative bark, the red-twig dogwood is especially popular for coloring winter landscapes.

Trunks of trees can be straight as pencils—as in tulip or poplar trees—or twisted and gnarled. In some situations, English hawthorns are valued for their gnarled trunk and scaly bark. Observed against a stone wall or a wintry sunset, they can be appealing in their grotesqueness.

Because shrubs tend to be bushy, those with interesting trunks usually need lower branch pruning to reveal the trunk pattern, or, in the case of deciduous shrubs, are best admired in winter after the leaves have fallen. The evergreen English yews have beautiful red trunks revealed by lower branch pruning. Yellow-twig dogwood is strikingly beautiful after leaf fall.

Ornamental Roots—Though roots are normally hidden from view, those of many trees can be highly decorative, especially among trees with a natural tendency to form roots above ground. Beech trees in particular have decorative surface roots, extending a great distance from the trunk. Roots growing along a slope can be worn by footsteps to create natural stairways. Also, soil erosion from wind and rain can expose surface roots.

Ornamental Fruit—Many trees and shrubs produce decorative fruit after the flowers fade. Many have the added advantage of attracting songbirds. Those that produce red, orange and yellow fleshy fruits are especially appealing, though blue, black and even white fruits

American beech spreads a decorative network of roots over soil surface. To heighten ornamental effect, tiny blue Siberian squill have been planted among roots.

Handsome silver, orange and black bark patterns are strong decorative feature of Austrian pine *(Pinus nigra)*.

are not uncommon. Fruits that persist on the tree after the leaves have fallen are valuable for winter color, such as those of hawthorns, winterberry and berberis. *Caution:* Some ornamental berries are poisonous and should be avoided where children might be tempted to pick and eat them. Bittersweet and yew are potentially the most dangerous.

Some fruit-producing trees can be messy and undesirable for high-traffic areas. As mentioned, the female ginkgo produces malodorous, plumlike fruits. Black walnuts drop hard, oily nuts that are best kept clear of driveways. The most desirable trees with ornamental fruits are those that hold their fruit on the tree a long time and eventually are eaten by birds. Hawthorns and sarvistrees are good examples.

Shrubs As Ground Covers—Shrubby, ground-hugging plants have distinct advantages over grass. They never need mowing, can crowd out weeds more effectively than grass and require less care. Dense plantings of low shrubs make effective ground covers on slopes to prevent soil erosion. Horizontal junipers work well on dry, sunny slopes where grass would burn up, while low-growing forms of azaleas can work well in shade.

Additional shrubs to use as ground covers include berberis, cotoneaster,

Multicolored Japanese maples are backlighted by sun in early spring. As colorful as any flowers, these leaves all turn brilliant orange in fall.

Evergreen windbreak of blue spruce and white spruce is more effective at cushioning force of winds than a wall or fence.

winter creeper, euonymus, heathers, English ivy, dwarf hollies and honeysuckle.

Hedges—Some trees and many shrubs make good formal hedges. Plants like boxwood, holly and hemlock have dense, evergreen growth that can be severely pruned to create clean, straight lines and an impenetrable thicket of branches. Small-leaved shrubs make better formal hedges than large-leaved shrubs. Billowing plants such as spirea and forsythia lend a more informal effect and produce beautiful flowers in the bargain. Hedges can mark a property line, form corridors or create screens. They can form straight lines and gentle curves. Columnar evergreens such as American arborvitae make excellent tall hedges. Dwarf boxwood and dwarf berberis can be used to create *parterres,* as described on page 31.

Windbreaks—Trees and large shrubs make far more effective windbreaks than solid fences or walls. Whereas a strong wind can hit a solid wall and jump over it with equal or greater force, the branches

of trees and shrubs cushion the force of the wind, dissipating it. Tall, dense needleleaf evergreens such as spruce and pines are favored trees for windbreaks. Among broadleaf evergreens, holly makes a good windbreak. In coastal gardens where protection from salt spray is also important, salt-tolerant plants are vital—such as Japanese black pine, Atlas cedar, Monterey cypress and Russian olive.

Foundation Plantings—Tidy, mixed-shrub borders against the house, with an occasional tree used as a highlight, are highly useful design features—they can enhance the desirable architectural features of a house and hide undesirable features. However, a common mistake among new homeowners is to cram beds around the house foundation with a "horticultural zoo" of shrubs and trees, leaving the perimeter of the property bare and forlorn.

Beware of cluttered, overgrown foundation plantings. They can give a house a reclusive, suffocated appearance. The wrong plant in a foundation

planting can quickly become untidy and overgrown, cutting light from windows. Desirable architectural features can become hidden and underground wiring and drains interfered with. Frequent pruning will be required to keep shrubs and trees from growing against the house itself. It's better to confine large, fast-growing shrubs and billowing trees to island beds on the lawn and to borders edging the property.

Foundation borders should contain a balance of needleleaf evergreens and broadleaf evergreens, plus an occasional deciduous tree or shrub for maximum interest. Because architectural lines generally run horizontal and vertical, a blend of upright and spreading plants is desired to soften the vast expanses of wall. Upright yews, pittosporum and arborvitae are good for planting at corners and entryways. Dwarf mounded plants, such as Japanese holly and azaleas, are good to locate under windowsills.

Shade tolerance should be considered along north-facing walls, heat and sun tolerance along south- or west-facing walls. Also, excessive soil alkalinity due to lime leaching from a masonry foundation or walls can sometimes be a problem.

When selecting and placing foundation plantings, plan for their ultimate mature size and allow enough space for them to reach their mature height and spread without interfering with the house structure or nearby walkways. Slow-growing plants are best, particularly those that withstand severe annual pruning. Above all, avoid any trees and shrubs that have a tendency to *sucker,* such as Lombardy poplar, tree of heaven and sumacs.

Rough Woodland—Lord Lionel de Rothschild, head of the famous banking family—and an eminent rhododendron breeder—once lectured a group of horticulturists, and said: "Every garden, no matter how small, should have its two acres of rough woodland." He himself lived on a vast estate called Exbury, in the South of England, and thought of gardens in terms of hundreds of acres, rather than hundreds of square feet, like most of us do. However, the advice does serve to illustrate the point that rough woodland—an uncared-for wilderness of mostly native trees—can be a conscious and desirable element of garden design, just as a meadow of wildflowers can be.

A source of firewood and wildlife shelter, rough woodland has a natural, informal, carefree beauty that can be a pleasant contrast from the formality of parkland and garden rooms, especially when threaded with winding paths. Rough woodland need not be an untended jungle of weedy trees choked with vines. Glades, glens and clearings can be made to expose the best native species or to introduce some desirable foreign kinds. Pines and deciduous trees with large leaves are particularly desirable for rough woodland because they carpet the ground with a thick layer of mulch and leaf mold that can effectively smother excessive weed growth and keep the woodland floor clean.

Though 2 acres is certainly the most desirable size for a woodlot and wildlife refuge, even 1/2 acre of rough woodland can provide a haven for birds and small wildlife, and offer a moderate amount of firewood.

Groves—Even if you don't have room for 1/2 acre of rough woodland, the effect can be achieved on a much smaller scale by planting a grove of trees. For example, a small grove of just a dozen trees, randomly planted, need not occupy more than a few hundred square feet at the edge of a lawn to provide a cool, peaceful retreat. A bench circling a trunk, or a hammock strung between two stout trees, can provide a peaceful spot for reading or contemplation. Pines, oaks, maples and tulip poplars are good trees for planting in groves because the cover from their fallen leaves will deter weeds. After the trees have grown to a desirable height, the lower branches should be pruned off to make it easy to walk among the trees.

Orchards—Orchards are groves of trees that produce fruit or nuts and are best planted with equal spacing between them to allow maximum air circulation and access by bees for maximum yields. Even spacing also facilitates harvesting, pruning, spraying and other special care that food-producing trees demand. Trees for home orchards are best planted in staggered rows, forming a diamond pattern. Apples, cherries and English walnuts make particularly fine ornamental orchards. Apples and cherries are highly

Woodland garden of deciduous trees underplanted with evergreens creates pleasant contrast of colors in fall around a clearing with picnic table.

ornamental in spring when covered with white blossoms, and English walnuts have a dense, spreading crown that forms a cool, green leaf canopy.

Even a small fruit orchard (100 x 100 feet) can accommodate a good assortment of favorite fruits, such as apples, pears, peaches apricots and plums. However, many nut trees grow large before they begin bearing, such as walnuts, pecans, hickory and butternuts, so planting more than two kinds might be impractical.

For extra ornamental effect, fruit trees can be underplanted with shade-tolerant shrubs such as azaleas. If you do this, make sure shrubs don't interfere with tree care and harvesting.

Where space is limited, dwarf fruit trees can be chosen to make an orchard. For extra decorative appeal, the dwarf trees can be criss-crossed with miniature hedges of dwarf boxwood, dwarf barberry or similar edging plants. For more on fruit and nut trees, refer to the book *Fruit, Berries & Nuts for the Midwest and East* by Theodore James Jr., or

Western Fruit, Berries & Nuts by Lance Walheim and Robert L. Stebbens. Both books are published by HPBooks.

Skyline Trees—Trees visible against the sky, on a hill, at the edge of a property or distant landscape are known as *skyline trees*. These trees help define the skyline of a particular area. Few natural landscape features add character to a location better than skyline trees. Tall, gnarled conifers with open branches, weeping willows with arching boughs and Southern live oaks festooned with wisps of Spanish moss can present a magnificent silhouette to admire against sunrises and sunsets or against monotone winter skies and seascapes.

Perhaps the most familiar effect from skyline trees is the *lone tree*—a single specimen perched on a cliff edge or crowning a hilltop. It is a symbol of survival, defying the elements. Perhaps the most famous example is a single gnarled Monterey cypress clinging to a rocky promontory overlooking the Pacific Ocean near Carmel, California. Named the "Lone Cypress," it has often been referred to as "the most photographed tree in the world."

A line of trees on the skyline can be equally picturesque. In the New York Finger Lakes region, Lombardy poplars cresting the slopes of vineyards help create an aura suggestive of the Italian or French countryside. A riverbank billowing with weeping willows conjures up visions of the English countryside. A mild-climate resort with an avenue of tall palms is transformed into an image of tropical splendor. A line of Japanese black pines lends an Oriental look and spirelike Italian cypresses a Mediterranean appearance.

Street Trees—In much the same way that skyline trees can lend a distinctive feel or look to an area, so can street trees. An avenue of Southern live oaks draped in Spanish moss identifies many Southern towns, while an avenue of sugar maples is the trademark of many New England communities. Fort Myers, on the Gulf Coast of Florida, has an avenue of royal palms 3 miles long.

It must be realized, however, that a street in a quiet country town and one in a busy, bustling, industrialized metropolis are completely different environments. Also, coastal and inland locations differ in the amount of salt-tolerance needed. Salt tolerance should also be considered in areas where salt is used to control ice on streets during winter. Where pollution is a problem, the choice becomes limited to trees noted for surviving noxious fumes, soot and grime. The London plane tree and Bradford pear are examples of pollution-tolerant trees.

In addition to the above considerations, street trees planted in planting strips between the street and sidewalk should have non-invasive root systems that won't tear up paving or interfere with underground utilities. The tree must be the right shape and size for the space to which it will be fitted—it should not interfere with overhead wires, parking, traffic (both vehicular and pedestrian) or street lighting, nor block street signs.

Topiary—Pronounced *TOE-pee-air-ee,* the word describes what many experts believe to be the most challenging of all horticultural endeavors. It is the art of training plants into special shapes. The shapes can be highly realistic—

TOPIARY

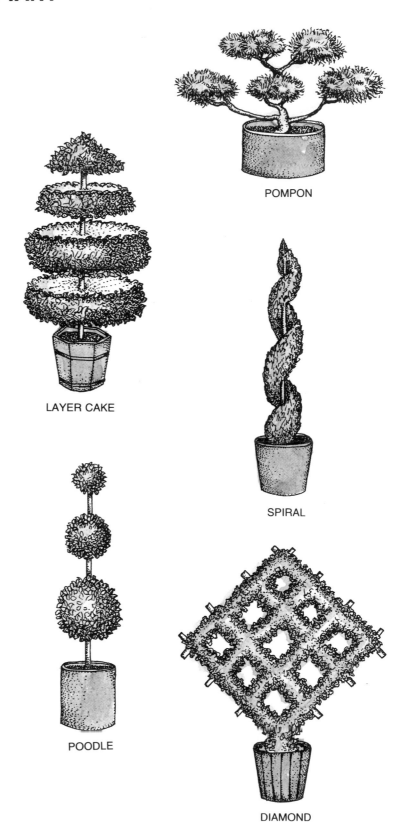

POMPON

LAYER CAKE

SPIRAL

POODLE

DIAMOND

Shown here are several standard topiary forms. Topiary can be trained to geometric shapes such as those shown here, or can represent natural or whimsical figures such as the fox chase pictured on the facing page.

Horse and rider chase a pack of hounds across a lawn at Ladew Topiary Garden in Monkton, Maryland. Plants used are Hick's Japanese yew.

Eastern white pine *(Pinus strobus)* is favorite subject for bonsai training.

recognizable as animals, humans and other whimsical animated objects—or they can be abstract as spirals, pyramids and other geometric shapes. The work is especially challenging because the outlines must be clean and well-defined to look good, requiring special skill in pruning and constant attention. Outdoor topiaries are demanding of space, plants need good care to maintain dense growth, and the work of shaping is labor intensive.

Few plants make good topiaries. The main need is for slow, dense, evergreen growth. Japanese yew, Canadian hemlock and English boxwood are the preferred choices for Northern gardens. Pittosporum and creeping fig are the popular choices for Southern gardens.

There are three ways to create topiary. The old-fashioned way is to shape plants into free-standing units. A bushy shrub is shaped with shears, similar to a sculptor chopping away at a block of stone. The more modern method is to grow plants over preshaped metal frames that serve as pruning guides as the foliage grows to cover them. The third method is more often used for *table-top topiaries*. A shape made of styrofoam or tightly packed sphagnum moss is kept moist for roots of vines to cover the surface—especially vines of English ivy and creeping fig. Roots from the creeper penetrate the mold and the surface is

hidden by a thin, dense covering of leaves. These table-top topiaries are the easiest to grow. They can be planted quickly and the shape covered within a matter of months, whereas topiaries planted as free-standing units, or through frames, can take years to reach a decent size.

The best examples of outdoor topiary work in America can be seen at Ladew Gardens in Monkton, Maryland; Green Animals in Portsmouth, Rhode Island; and Disneyworld in Florida. The photo above depicts an especially elaborate design at the Ladew Gardens of a horse and rider jumping a fence in pursuit of five hounds and a fox, all clipped out of Japanese yew grown around metal frames. During a trip to England, the garden's founder Harvey S. Ladew saw the topiary foxhunting scene along the top of a hedge. Though he copied the design, he made the figures more animated—and improved on the original—by planting them across his front lawn.

Bonsai—Pronounced *Bone-SIGH*, this is the Oriental art of dwarfing and shaping trees in shallow pots known as *bonsai dishes*. Contrary to popular belief, bonsai was not invented by the Japanese. Nature produced the first bonsai trees. Miniature trees and trees with gnarled trunks with sparse foliage are found in many mountainous areas of the world

where rocky conditions restrict normal growth by confining root systems, while wind, rain, ice and salt spray bend trunks and branches into dramatic and beautiful shapes.

The Chinese are credited with being the first to recognize the special beauty of their dwarf tree forms, and centuries ago began collecting specimens from the wild, digging them up and transferring them to pots. The Japanese are credited with being the first to discover that the same dwarfing and twisted effects can be created artificially by special training techniques, involving judicious pruning of trees and roots, use of wire to direct branches and restricting the roots to a small container.

One way to create a bonsai tree is to start it from seed and deliberately stunt its growth in a shallow, confined container. Another, more widespread practice is to prune young trees down to miniature size and sculpt them into interesting forms.

The least successful method is to actually dig a tree up from the wild—it can take 5 to 15 years to *condition* a wild bonsai before it will grow in a container and the survival rate is low.

Evergreen trees such as spruce, juniper, pine and cedar are the easiest to start with. Shrubs such as azaleas and camellias are also popular bonsai subjects.

Espaliered firethorn *(Pyracantha coccinea)* trained against bare wall to soften expanse of garish brick.

This intricate horticultural maze planted from English boxwood is a half-size replica of the one at Hampton Court, England. It proves the superb quality of boxwood as a hedge.

Espalier—Pronounced *es-PAL-yay* or *es-PAL-yer,* this is the art of training trees and shrubs to a single plane, either against flat, vertical surfaces like walls, or along wires or wooden frames. Those grown horizontally along wires or wooden railings are called *cordons,* for their resemblance to ropes. There are many advantages to this form of training, but the two main ones are for decorative value and to save space.

Plants chosen for espaliers are mostly those with attractive flowers or fruits for which training can heighten the decorative appearance. Camellias, firethorn, pears, plums, apples, peaches, nectarines and figs are especially popular because of their pliable branches, which make them easy to train. However, English ivy, Japanese yew and podocarpus are also espaliered because of their evergreen qualities.

A typical espalier is shown in the photo at left. The secret to success is *pruning* and *training*. Although a full-size apple tree may naturally grow 20 feet high with upright branches in its natural state, it can be heavily pruned to keep it dwarf, and the upright-growing branches can be bent at right angles and secured in position with string. The training is best done with young branches called *whips* because they are generally slender and pliable. Dwarf fruit trees cost more than standard sizes, but they are generally easier to keep low.

Espaliers are a great way to save space because they grow flat against a wall or frame. When grown against a wall, care should be taken to match the proper plant with the wall. For example, apples thrive in full sun, but pears will tolerate light shade. Brick walls and wood fences are better than stucco walls for espaliers because plants grown against stucco walls are susceptible to sunscald and damage from high temperatures. On stucco walls, dense evergreens such as ivy and yew have the best chance for survival.

A much higher success rate, especially with apples and pears, can be achieved by growing the espaliers along low wooden railings to edge a lawn area or vegetable plot, where free air circulation and stable temperatures help increase fruit yields.

Many nurseries and garden centers sell ready-trained espaliers already growing on a trellis in a container. These are also available by mail order from Henry Leuthardt Nurseries, Montauk Highway, East Moriches, New York 11940. The owner, Mr. Leuthardt, has been growing espaliers for 50 years.

Parterres and Mazes — The French word, *parterre* (pronounced *PAH-t-air*) in its literal sense means "along the ground," and describes patterns formed by low hedges, usually along a vista. Parterres are popular in both France and England. They are laid out on flat ground so they can be observed from a tower or hill. In some instances, a special mound is made from which to observe the patterns more effectively.

The first parterres were simple designs cut out of turf to reveal white limestone soil. Most had religious symbolism. As they became incorporated into gardens, parterres became more elaborate, in the form of scrolls and flourishes, accentuated by hedges and colored gravel.

The *maze* was developed out of a desire to add a touch of humor. Reproduced at left is a plan of the famous Tudor maze at Hampton Court, England. A life-size replica is made from English holly at the Governor's Palace, Colonial Williamsburg. However, a much better copy is in the privately owned garden of Deerfield, in Rydal, Pennsylvania. Made of English boxwood, it is a half-size replica, created by first making the outlines with string, then digging away the turf to form planting beds.

Though English boxwood is the best choice for mazes and parterres, it grows extremely slow, at only 1 inch a year. For this reason, other plants are more often used, including holly, yew, hemlock, beech and—in the South— podocarpus. The Deerfield maze is kept sheared to a height of 4 feet because it seems esthetically pleasing at exactly that height. Children can get thoroughly lost along its leafy corridors, while adults can peer over its hedges to find the middle with little hesitation.

The maze concept has also been used to spell out words. At the Hershey Chocolate Factory, in Hershey, Pennsylvania, the words *Hershey Cocoa* are spelled out in immense block letters across a sloping lawn in front of the factory. Appropriately, the words are

Beautiful arbor of pleached apple trees in a restored colonial garden at Eleutherian Mills, near Wilmington, Delaware.

planted in *Berberis atropurpurea*, which is the color of chocolate when observed from a distance.

Pleaching—The word *pleach* is derived from the French and Latin words meaning "to weave." In horticulture, the term is used to describe a hedge or double line of trees that have their branches intertwined to form a leafy tunnel, arbor or a covered avenue. Beech and hornbeam are especially favored for creating pleached arbors and avenues. Their branches are pliable and easily woven. They tolerate severe pruning and can be kept shrublike or trained to a stout, single trunk. To create a pleached arbor, a metal or wooden frame is first constructed and the chosen trees planted around the outside.

There are some fine examples of pleached arbors at Colonial Williamsburg. At Old Westbury Gardens, Long Island, there is a pleached tunnel created from Canadian hemlock. It is so dark and eerie it is called *The Ghost Walk*. In this instance, the plants are freestanding, with no frames for support.

Another kind of pleaching requires no frames. Trees are planted along an avenue. The top growth is allowed to intermingle its branches and the trunks are trimmed of all lower branches so they

look like pillars or posts. When a sufficient canopy has developed, the top is usually sheared square so that from a distance it looks like a hedge on stilts. When this kind of pleaching forms a circle around a lawn or fountain, it is called a *rondel* or an *ellipse*. A fine example of a pleached avenue can be seen at Longwood Gardens, Pennsylvania, and a beautiful ellipse can be seen at Dumbarton Oaks, Washington, D.C.

Pollarding—This is the practice of consistently pruning back the main branches (scaffold limbs) on a tree to a single growing point so they produce a flush of new growth. Sometimes all main branches are drastically lopped off right to the crown, and other times several large branches are cut back to mere stumps of varying lengths, each stump producing a top-knot of foliage. This style of pollarding is known as a *poodle cut*.

The practice of pollarding is popular with willows, catalpas, sycamores and similar vigorous trees that have a tendency to sprout a multitude of new branches and leaves from the stumps. Pollarded trees are effective in formal gardens as lawn highlights, street trees, and when paired on either side of gates and entryways.

Trees & Shrubs in the Landscape **31**

Burning bush (Euonymus alatus) grows shrublike when young, as shown here, but eventually becomes a handsome small tree, as pictured on page 99.

LANDSCAPING A BARE LOT

The photograph at right shows a new house on a bare lot. It is typical of tens of thousands of homes built every year in the suburbs and country on square or rectangular lots. The drawing at right shows what can be accomplished within a few years with plantings of trees and shrubs. In addition to creating a beautiful living environment, the relatively small investment in plantings has significantly increased property value.

First, notice how ground covers (A) at the front of the property cut down on mowing and add texture to a dry slope. Here, horizontal junipers or ivy would work well.

A formal hedge (B) runs along the south side of the property on either side of the entrance gateway. This could be yew, holly or boxwood for slow growth and a sharp outline. An informal, unpruned hedge (C) extends along the south boundary line. Forsythia, spirea or azalea might be good choices here. These hedges provide privacy and serve as a barrier against animals and intruders. In the corner where the hedges meet, a flowering tree (D) spreads its branches overhead. A cherry, dogwood, crabapple or magnolia would be perfect here.

Midway along the informal hedge is an arbor (E) to break up the monotony of too much hedging and to create a side entrance. A flowering vine—such as clematis or climbing rose—is trained to cover it.

The driveway to the house is lined with pyramidal evergreens as an avenue or *allée* (F) to create a natural corridor for embellishment. These also help screen the paving from other areas of the garden.

Close to the house are foundation plantings (G)—mostly needleleaf and broadleaf evergreens. Some are spire-shaped and others clipped as spheres. They help soften the expanse of bare walls. An espalier (H) is trained against the south wall for a special sophisticated effect, and to soften the severe architectural lines of the house siding.

The east side of the house has three rectangular flower beds bordered with low hedges (I) to create a simple parterre garden. The large bed has a topiary centerpiece (J) to provide a highlight. The edging could be dwarf boxwood. A brick path separating the flower beds leads to a vine-covered pergola (K), creating a transition from the formal flower garden to a more informal area containing a mixed-shrub border (L). The vine covering the pergola could be wisteria, trumpet creeper or climbing roses.

Though the mixed-shrub border could contain any number of choice flowering shrubs, the main kinds represented here are azaleas and rhododendrons. In the northeast corner is a small rock garden (M), featuring a collection of dwarf evergreens.

Beyond the shrub border are some skyline trees (N)—large specimens of weeping willow, cedar and pine—though buying specimens of significant size may be beyond the means of most homeowners because of high cost.

In the northwest corner is a shade tree (O) with a swing and a paved area for seats and outdoor dining. A maple or oak would be perfect here. A topiary juniper (P) given a "poodle cut" stands in a container for decorative value. A semicircle of unpruned hydrangeas, viburnum or lilacs provide privacy (Q). On a deck overlooking the back lawn, is a containerized bonsai on a table for decorative appeal (R).

SHRUBS INTO TREES AND TREES INTO SHRUBS

Many plants defined as *shrubs* can become trees—either by virtue of age and maturity or by deliberate training. Alternatively, many plants familiar to us as *trees* can become shrublike—either by accidental damage to the leader or by selective pruning. A large number of shrubs will naturally become treelike with age—hollies, burning bush, camellias, boxwood and rhododendrons are familiar examples. Lilacs, viburnums, privets, hydrangeas and azaleas are good examples of shrubs that have a tendency to be multi-stemmed but can, by selective pruning to form a single stem, be trained into a tree form over a period of years. This selective pruning includes the constant removal of any side branches and *suckers* to maintain one strong main trunk. When choosing shrubs from a nursery, it's often possible to buy one that already has its tree form started with a definite main trunk.

Shrubs with potential for training into trees must be pruned with care. Sometimes, pruning a shrub to a single trunk must be done over a period of years, nudging the plant gradually toward taking on a tree form, because excessive removal of branches at any one time could weaken and kill it. When the main trunk thickens and the crown fills out to form a definite overhead canopy, side branches can be removed entirely.

Many times, the removal of side branches will stimulate a shrub into *suckering,* whereby whiplike stems sprout from the roots in an effort to regain a shrublike appearance. These fleshy shoots are best cut off as soon as they emerge, before they have a chance to become woody and drain the main trunk of energy.

Conversely, it is sometimes desirable to encourage a tree to grow shrublike. This is generally done in the tree's juvenile stage by pruning out the *central leader* (main trunk) and keeping it pruned at a set height. Yews, Russian olives and pittosporum make effective hedges when the central leader is not allowed to dominate.

To encourage multiple-trunk growth on older trees, the crown must be *topped.* The main trunk is drastically cut down from the top, usually by means of a chain saw, by as much as a third—or even half—of its original height.

Some trees can be cut down right to the ground because they will sucker profusely from the roots. Examples are poplars, sassafras and magnolias.

LANDSCAPING A BARE LOT

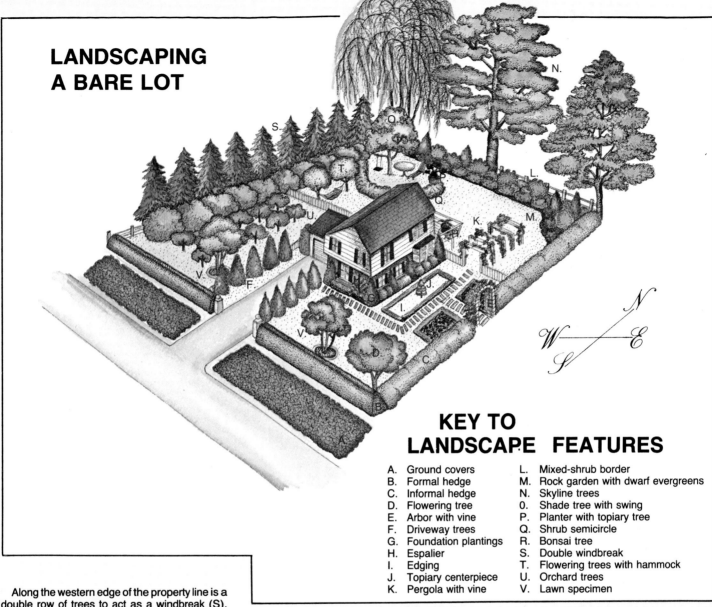

KEY TO LANDSCAPE FEATURES

A. Ground covers
B. Formal hedge
C. Informal hedge
D. Flowering tree
E. Arbor with vine
F. Driveway trees
G. Foundation plantings
H. Espalier
I. Edging
J. Topiary centerpiece
K. Pergola with vine

L. Mixed-shrub border
M. Rock garden with dwarf evergreens
N. Skyline trees
O. Shade tree with swing
P. Planter with topiary tree
Q. Shrub semicircle
R. Bonsai tree
S. Double windbreak
T. Flowering trees with hammock
U. Orchard trees
V. Lawn specimen

Along the western edge of the property line is a double row of trees to act as a windbreak (S). Most prevailing winds in North America come from the west, hence the positioning of this landscape feature. The background trees are evergreens—perhaps blue spruce, while the foreground trees might be gray-foliaged Russian olives for an appealing color combination, in addition to dense habit for screening qualities.

The lawn area running parallel to the windbreak is divided by a fence. On the north side of the fence are two flowering trees (T), such as hawthorns, cherries or crabapples, with a hammock slung between them. On the south side of the fence is an orchard (U) planted with dwarf fruit trees—pairs of apples, peaches, pears, cherries, apricots and plums, each pair representing different varieties to ensure good pollination and maximum fruit set.

The front lawns feature a matching pair of white birch (V) as handsome lawn specimens, each underplanted with a circle of ivy or pachysandra to act as a shade-loving ground cover.

The plants shown in this design are not elaborate, and with the exception of the skyline trees, are within the scope of any homeowner to purchase and plant without the help of a landscape architect. Moreover, the plants suggested in this particular design are easily changed to suit special climatic situations.

House on bare lot is typical of thousands of new homes built every year.

TREES AND SHRUBS FOR DIFFERENT USES

AUTUMN COLOR

Following are some of the best trees and shrubs for autumn color.
Asterisk (*) denotes shrubs.

Botanical Name	Common Name
Acer species	Maples
Amelanchier arborea	Sarvistree
Betula species	Birches
Carya species	Hickories
Cercidiphyllum japonicum	Katsura
Cornus florida	Common Dogwood
Cotinus coggygria	Smoke Tree
*Euonymus alatus	Burning Bush
Franklinia alatamaha	Franklinia
Fraxinus species	Ashes
Ginkgo biloba	Ginkgo
Lagerstroemia indica	Crape Myrtle
Larix species	Larches
Liquidambar styraciflua	Sweetgum
Liriodendron tulipifera	Tulip Tree
Nyssa sylvatica	Tupelo
Oxydendrum arboreum	Sourwood
Pistacia chinensis	Chinese Pistacio
Populus species	Poplars
Pyrus calleryana	Callery Pear
Quercus coccinia	Scarlet Oak
Rhus typhina	Staghorn Sumac
Sassafras albidum	Sassafras
*Viburnum species	Viburnum
Zelkova serrata	Japanese Zelkova

DECORATIVE BERRIES OR FRUIT

Asterisk (*) denotes shrubs.

Aralia spinosa	Devil's Walking Stick
Arbutus unedo	Strawberry Tree
*Berberis thunbergii	Japanese Barberry
*Callicarpa japonica	Beautyberry
*Carissa grandiflora	Natal Plum
Castanea mollissima	Chinese Chestnut
*Chaenomeles speciosa	Flowering Quince
Citrus species	Ornamental Citrus
Cornus kousa	Korean Dogwood
*Cotoneaster horizontalis	Rockspray Cotoneaster
Crataegus species	Hawthorns
Diospyros kaki	Japanese Persimmon
*Ilex species	Hollies
Koelreuteria paniculata	Golden Rain Tree
*Mahonia bealei	Leatherleaf Mahonia
Malus species	Crabapples
*Nandina domestica	Heavenly Bamboo
*Poncirus trifoliata	Hardy Orange
Prunus species	Cherries, Peaches, Plums
*Pyracantha coccinea	Firethorn
*Rosa rugosa	Rugosa Rose
*Skimmia japonica	Japanese Skimmia
Sorbus aucuparia	Mountain Ash
*Viburnum species	Viburnums

DECORATIVE BARK

Asterisk (*) denotes shrubs.

Acer griseum	Paperbark Maple
*Acer palmatum 'Senkaki'	Red-twig Maple
Alsophila cooperi	Australian Tree Fern
Betula papyrifera	White Birch
*Cornus sanguinea	Red-twig Dogwood
*Cornus sericea 'Flaviramea'	Yellow-twig Dogwood
Cryptomeria japonica	Japanese Cedar
Eucalyptus species	Eucalyptus
Lagerstroemia indica	Crepe Myrtle
Pinus nigra	Austrian Pine
Platanus occidentalis	Buttonwood
Prunus serrula	Shiny Bark Cherry
Salix × chrysocoma 'Niobe'	Golden Weeping Willow
Stewartia sinensis	Chinese Stewartia

SKYLINE TREES

Asterisk (*) denotes evergreens.

*Abies species	Firs
Acer saccharum	Sugar Maple
Aesculus hippocastanum	Horse Chestnut
*Araucaria araucana	Monkey Puzzle Tree
*Araucaria heterophylla	Norfolk Island Pine
Carya species	Hickories
*Casuarina cunninghamiana	Australian Pine
Catalpa species	Catalpas
*Cedrus species	Cedars
Cercidiphyllum japonicum	Katsura Tree
*Chamaecyparis species	False Cypresses
Chorisa speciosa	Floss Silk Tree
*Cupressus species	Cypresses
*Eucalyptus species	Eucalyptus
Fagus species	Beech
Fraxinus species	Ashes
Ginkgo biloba	Maidenhair Tree
Gleditsia triacanthos inermis	Honeylocust
Jacaranda acutifolia	Jacaranda
Juglans nigra	Black Walnut
*Juniperus virginiana	Red Cedar
Larix	Larches
*Liriodendron tulipifera	Tulip Tree
*Metasequoia glyptostroboides	Dawn Redwood
Nyssa sylvatica	Black Tupelo
*Palmae	Palms
Paulownia tomentosa	Empress Tree
*Picea species	Spruces
*Pinus species	Pines
Platanus occidentalis	Buttonwood
Populus species	Poplars
Pseudolarix kaempferi	Golden Larch
Quercus species	Oaks
Robinia pseudoacacia	Black Locust
Salix babylonica	Weeping Willow
*Sciadopitys verticillata	Japanese Umbrella Pine
Taxodium distichum	Bald Cypress
Tilia species	Lindens
*Tsuga species	Hemlocks
Ulmus species	Elms
Zelkova serrata	Zelkova

WINDBREAK TREES AND SHRUBS

Asterisk (*) denotes shrubs.

EVERGREEN

Abies species	Firs
Casuarina cunninghamiana	Australian Pine
Chamaecyparis lawsoniana	Lawson False Cypress
Cupressocyparis leylandi	Leyland Cypress
Cupressus macrocarpa	Monterey Cypress
*Escallonia rubra	Escallonia
Eucalyptus species	Eucalyptus
*Ilex species	Hollies
Juniperus virginiana	Eastern Red Cedar
*Ligustrum species	Privets
*Nerium oleander	Oleander
Olea europa	European Olive
Picea abies	Norway Spruce
Pinus strobus	White Pine
Pinus sylvestris	Scotch Pine
Podocarpus macrophyllus	Yew Podocarpus
Taxus species	Yews
Thuja occidentalis	American Arborvitae
Tsuga canadensis	Canadian Hemlock

DECIDUOUS

Acer platanoides	Norway Maple
Carpinus species	Hornbeams
Crataegus species	Hawthorns
Nyssa sylvatica	Black Tupelo
Platanus acerifolia	London Plane Tree
Populus hybrids	Hybrid Poplars
Ulmus parvifolia	Chinese Elm

STREET AND CITY TREES

Asterisk (*) identifies plants noted for spectacular flowering displays.

*Acacia longifolia	Acacia
Acer species	Maples
*Aesculus species	Horsechestnuts
Ailanthus altissima	Tree of Heaven
Carpinus betula	European Hornbeam
Casuarina cunninghamiana	Australian Pine
*Chorisa speciosa	Floss Silk Tree
*Crataegus species	Hawthorns
*Elaeagnus angustifolia	Russian Olive
Eucalyptus ficifolia	Scarlet Gum
Fraxinus species	Ashes
Ginkgo biloba	Maidenhair Tree
Gleditsia triacanthos inermis	Honeylocust
*Koelreuteria paniculata	Golden Rain Tree
Liquidambar styraciflua	Sweetgum
Pinus sylvestris	Scotch Pine
Pinus thunbergiana	Japanese Black Pine
Pistacia chinensis	Chinese Pistacio
Platanus acerifolia	London Plane Tree
*Pyrus calleryana 'Bradford'	Bradford Pear
Quercus species	Oaks
*Sophora japonica	Japanese Pagoda Tree
Tilia cordata	Littleleaf Linden
Ulmus parvifolia	Chinese Elm
Zelkova serrata	Japanese Zelkova

SHADE-TOLERANT TREES AND SHRUBS
Asterisk (*) denotes shrubs.

Acer palmatum	Cutleaf Maple
*Aesculus parvifolia	Bottlebrush Buckeye
Alsophila cooperi	Australian Tree Fern
*Aucuba japonica	Gold Dust Plant
*Buxus species	Boxwood
*Camellia japonica	Camellia
Cercis canadensis	Eastern Redbud
Cornus florida	Flowering Dogwood
Cryptomeria japonica	Japanese Cedar
Enkianthus campanulatus	Red-Vein Enkianthus
*Euonymus alatus	Burning Bush
*Euonymus fortunei	Wintercreeper
Halesia carolina	Silverbell
*Hamamelis species	Witchhazels
*Hedera helix	English Ivy
*Hydrangea macrophylla	Hydrangea
*Ilex species	Hollies
*Kalmia latifolia	Mountain Laurel
*Kerria japonica	Japanese Kerria
*Leucothoe fontanesia	Drooping Leucothoe
*Mahonia species	Mahonias
*Nandina domestica	Heavenly Bamboo
*Pachysandra terminalis	Japanese Spurge
*Parthenocissus quinquefolia	Virginia Creeper
*Pieris japonica	Andromeda
*Pittosporum tobira	Fragrant Pittosporum
*Prunus laurocerasus	Cherry Laurel
*Rhododendron species	Azaleas, Rhododendrons
*Skimmia japonica	Japanese Skimmia
*Taxus species	Yews
Tsuga canadensis	Canadian Hemlock

TREES FOR WOODLAND & GROVES
Asterisk (*) denotes evergreens.

*Abies concolor	White Fir
Acer rubrum	Red Maple
Acer saccharum	Sugar Maple
Amelanchier arborea	Sarvistree
Betula papyrifera	White Birch
Carya species	Hickories
Cercis canadensis	Eastern Redbud
Cornus florida	Flowering Dogwood
Crataegus species	Hawthorns
*Cryptomeria japonica	Japanese Cedar
*Eucalyptus species	Eucalyptus
Fagus species	Beeches
Fraxinus species	Ashes
Gleditsia triacanthos inermis	Honeylocust
Halesia carolina	Silverbell
Juglans nigra	Black Walnut
*Juniperus virginiana	Eastern Red Cedar
Liquidambar styraciflua	Sweetgum
Liriodendron tulipifera	Tulip Tree
*Magnolia grandiflora	Southern Magnolia
*Metasequoia glyptostroboides	Dawn Redwood
Nyssa sylvatica	Black Tupelo
Oxydendrum arboreum	Sourwood
*Picea species	Spruces
*Pinus species	Pines
Platanus occidentalis	Buttonwood
Populus tremuloides	Quaking Aspen

Azalea 'Coral Bells' drapes its flowering branches over stone wall. Partial concealment of architectural structures is one of principal uses for flowering shrubs.

*Pseudotsuga menziesii	Douglas Fir
Quercus species	Oaks
Robinia pseudoacacia	Black Locust
*Sequoia sempervirens	Coast Redwood
*Taxodium distichum	Bald Cypress
*Tsuga canadensis	Canadian Hemlock
Ulmus species	Elms
Zelkova serrata	Japanese Zelkova

HEDGES
Asterisk denotes evergreens.

Abelia × grandiflora	Glossy Abelia
Arundinaria species	Bamboo
Berberis thunbergii	Japanese Barberry
*Buxus sempervirens	English Boxwood
*Buxus microphylla	Japanese Boxwood
*Carissa grandiflora	Natal Plum
Chaenomeles speciosa	Flowering Quince
*Chamaecyparis lawsoniana	Lawson False Cypresses
Crataegus phaenopyrum	Washington Hawthorn
*Cupressus species	Cypress
Elaeagnus angustifolia	Russian Olive
*Escallonia rubra	Escallonia
Euonymus alatus	Burning Bush
Fagus sylvatica	European Beech
Forsythia × intermedia	Forsythia
Gardenia jasminoides	Gardenia
*Hibiscus rosa-sinensis	Chinese Hibiscus
Hibiscus syriacus	Rose of Sharon
*Ilex species	Hollies
*Juniperus species	Junipers
Ligustrum species	Privet
Lonicera species	Honeysuckles
*Myrica species	Wax Myrtles
*Nerium oleander	Oleander
*Osmanthus species	False Hollies
*Photinia × fraseri	Red Tip Photinia

*Pinus mugo mugo	Mugo Pine
*Pinus strobus	White Pine
*Pittosporum species	Pittosporum
*Podocarpus macrophylla	Fern Pine
*Prunus laurocerasus	Cherry Laurel
Pyracantha species	Firethorn
*Raphiolepsis indica	Indian Hawthorn
*Rhododendron species and hybrids	Azaleas, Rhododendrons
Rosa species	Roses
Spiraea species	Spireas
Syringa vulgaris	Lilac
*Taxus species	Yews
*Thuja species	Arborvitaes
*Tsuga species	Hemlocks
Viburnum species	Viburnums
Weigela florida	Weigela

VINES AND CREEPERS

Bougainvillea spectabilis	Bougainvillea
Campsis radicans	Trumpet Creeper
Celastris scandens	Bittersweet
Euonymus fortunei	Wintercreeper
Ficus pumila	Creeping Fig
Hedera helix	English Ivy
Hydrangea anomala	Climbing Hydrangea
Jasminum nudiflorum	Yellow Jasmine
Lonicera hallii	Hall's Honeysuckle
Parthenocissus quinquefolia	Virginia Creeper
Polygonum aubertii	Silver Lace Vine
Rosa banksiae	Lady Banks Rose
Rosa laevigata	Cherokee Rose
Trachelospermum jasminoides	Confederate Jasmine
Wisteria floribunda	Wisteria

3
Buying, Planting
& Aftercare

Planting trees and shrubs is largely a one-time investment capable of returning tremendous benefits to the owner, not only by beautifying a home, but also by increasing property values. Ornamental shade trees and attractive foundation plantings using decorative shrubs can add *thousands* of dollars value to a home.

If you select trees and shrubs adapted to local climate and soil conditions, take some extra care when planting them. Give them a moderate amount of aftercare and they will likely outlive you, becoming even more beautiful and valuable with age. Detailed planting instructions for trees and shrubs start on page 44, tree and shrub care on page 47.

SELECTING TREES AND SHRUBS

Careful initial selection of varieties—and matching the right tree or shrub to the site—are vital in creating a successful landscape. Some of the factors that should be considered when choosing trees include climate, soil type, nutrient needs, drainage, growth rate, flowering and fruiting habits, and resistance to pests and diseases.

FIT FORM TO FUNCTION
This is the very first consideration in selecting a tree or shrub. Particularly

Left: Tree farms are excellent outlets for quality plants. This one specializes in evergreen conifers.

important in your decision process should be the mature size of the tree or shrub. A common mistake is to plant potential giants in a relatively small area or in close proximity to power lines or underground cables and drains. This can lead to site conflicts and high maintenance costs later, especially when a tree specialist needs to be hired to correct the problem. Similar problems can occur when large shrubs overgrow beds and borders, crowd walkways and block windows.

Also consider other habits that may or may not make a tree or shrub suitable to a particular site. For example, excessive shedding of twigs and small branches (willows), or messy or malodorous fruit (female ginkgo, walnut, fruiting mulberry), may make a tree undesirable for high-traffic areas.

Arborists, landscape architects and local nurserymen can provide valuable assistance in selecting trees and shrubs compatible with a given site. The encyclopedia, starting on page 65, can help in this selection. Also, it pays to visit local arboretums, parks, botanical gardens and even golf courses to see first hand the kinds of trees and shrubs that do well in your area. State or county extension services can also offer advice.

Although selecting the right tree or shrub for the site will avoid future complications and maintenance, all desirable landscape plants will require periodic care to ensure survival and preserve their esthetic value. Watering, fertilizing, pruning and pest control are the most important cultural practices necessary to maintain healthy trees and shrubs.

Work conducted by tree specialists may be necessary from time to time, especially for large or very old trees. This can include installing structural support cables to correct a leaning tree, or adding bracing supports to prop heavy limbs in danger of breaking under their own weight. Lightning protection, storm-damage repairs and cavity filling are other jobs that may require a tree specialist.

CLIMATE
Many climatic conditions determine whether a plant will survive in a given area. Seasonal temperature extremes, available sunlight, humidity, rainfall patterns and prevalence of winds are all factors that can influence the adaptability of plants to a given location.

Some trees and shrubs are amazingly adaptable. I have seen varieties of hybrid poplars green and leafy in the suburbs of Tucson, Arizona, when other vegetation was parched and dry, and the same varieties growing contentedly on the icy, windswept shores of Lake Michigan.

For such a large body of land, North America has a fairly predictable climate. This is because the main mountain ranges run north and south—the Rocky Mountains in the west and the Appalachians in the east. They create a "funnel" that channels cold arctic air far south in winter. Areas of warm influence—the Gulf of Mexico, the Pacific Ocean and the Gulf of California—hold back this cold air mass in some locations. Coastal California, the Pacific Northwest, the Gulf states, the Colorado River Basin and Southern

California generally remain mild enough in winter to grow many tender and even tropical plants. But the rest of North America experiences pronounced seasonal changes characterized by hot, dry summers and cold, wet winters.

Cold Hardiness—Freezing temperatures are the biggest influence in determining adaptability. Broadly speaking, trees and shrubs can be classified as *hardy* and *tender*. Hardy trees and shrubs can survive winters where temperatures drop below freezing (32F/0C). Tender trees and shrubs cannot tolerate freezing weather. Many tender woody plants can tolerate occasional light frosts, but prolonged periods of sub-freezing temperatures—especially frozen soil—will kill them.

A cold-winter region is any area where winter temperatures consistently drop below freezing. Most of these areas also experience snowfall. This seems to be the critical distinction that sharply defines the adaptability of tender trees and shrubs. Though North America has a wide range of climates, ranging from sub-arctic to sub-tropical, more than three quarters of the continent has snow cover in winter, requiring most gardeners to limit their plant selections to hardy kinds.

There are also *degrees of hardiness* among hardy plants. That is, some plants can withstand lower minimum winter temperatures than others. The USDA Plant Hardiness Zone Map on the facing page divides North America into 10 climate zones, based on average minimum winter temperatures. It is the standard reference used by North American plantsmen for defining a plant's hardiness. For instance, if a plant is said to be hardy to Zone 7, it can be expected to survive a minimum winter temperature between 0F and 10F (-18C and -12C).

Of course, this does not mean that a plant that is cold-hardy to a given zone will necessarily grow in all zones warmer than that. As mentioned, adaptation is also limited by other factors, such as summer heat, humidity and rainfall patterns. For example, portions of the arid Sonora Desert and humid central Florida both fall into Zone 9, yet a vastly greater range of tender plants can be grown in central Florida because of its high rainfall.

Also, there are many *microclimates* within the broad geographic areas represented on the zone map, where minimum winter temperatures may vary greatly from the overall region. This is particularly true where temperate coastal plains change to high hills and mountains, where arctic-type weather can prevail. For example, Bear Meadows, Pennsylvania is a high-elevation glacial swamp teeming with hardy native trees and shrubs. It is in the middle of Zone 5, where the last frost date in spring is usually May 10. Yet Bear Meadows has frost *every month of the year*.

Proximity to the ocean and large bodies of water also have a big influence on temperatures. Coastal or lakeshore areas within a given region may not experience the late-spring frosts that occur several miles inland, which can cause damage to newly emerging flower buds. For example, varieties of *Camellia japonica* will bloom sucessfully in sheltered locations along the New Jersey shore and on Long Island, New York, but usually not in the rest of these two states.

Despite these factors, the USDA climate map can be useful for selecting plants if it is treated only as a general guide to hardiness. To make the map even more useful, zone designations for plants listed in the plant encyclopedia of this book include a range of zones—from coldest to warmest—in which the plant will most likely grow.

Rainfall—Both the amount of rain and when it comes are factors in determining plant adaptability. Rainfall patterns—as opposed to total annual rainfall—have a much greater influence on adaptability. Much of the Midwest, Southwest and Southern California are subjected to dry summers, making it difficult to grow many kinds of moisture-loving plants. In areas where precipitation comes mostly as snow in winter, the choice of woody plants is severely restricted unless supplemental water is provided during summer. On the other hand, areas like the Pacific Northwest may be *too wet* for trees and shrubs that naturally grow in drier climates.

Generally speaking, most established garden trees require at least occasional, periodic deep waterings during the dry summer months. For more on watering, see page 48.

Winds—Much of the Great Plains is devoid of trees because of the ceaseless winds that sweep across the land. Only grasses and a few other small plants grow with ease. Coastal clifftops are also difficult planting sites, due not only to high winds but also the salt spray that is carried with them. Before any realistic landscaping with trees and shrubs can be attempted in these locations, windbreaks must be provided to create *shelter belts* for plantings.

In some cases, a double or triple row of trees and shrubs is needed to sufficiently break the force of the wind to create a shelter belt for ornamental plants. Temporary windbreaks must be devised to protect young windbreak trees and shrubs until they become established.

Heat and Humidity—Although Southern California is warm enough to grow coconut palms, they refuse to succeed there because the climate is too dry. South of Vero Beach, Florida, mild winters and humid summers combine to create an ideal climate for the coconut palm.

The Pacific Northwest has high humidity from coastal fogs and abundant rainfall, but relatively cool summer temperatures. There, gardeners can grow the huge Himalayan tree rhododendrons, plus a wide range of heaths and heathers that are impossible to establish in other parts of North America.

A plant's ability to adapt to various degrees of heat and humidity are directly related to its *transpiration rate,* or the amount of water it loses through its leaves. Even if given plenty of water, plants adapted to humid conditions will quickly become desiccated and die in a dry climate because their leaves transpire water faster than the root system can absorb it. Conversely, dry-climate plants with slow transpiration rates may rot in humid climates, and are often more prone to various fungal and bacterial diseases.

Cloud Cover—In areas that have plenty of cloud cover during summer, like the Pacific Northwest, plants recommended for shade can be grown out in the open. Over the rest of North America, absence of cloud cover in summer generally means that shade-loving plants must be protected. Newly planted trees and shrubs often require some kind of shade

PLANT HARDINESS ZONE MAP

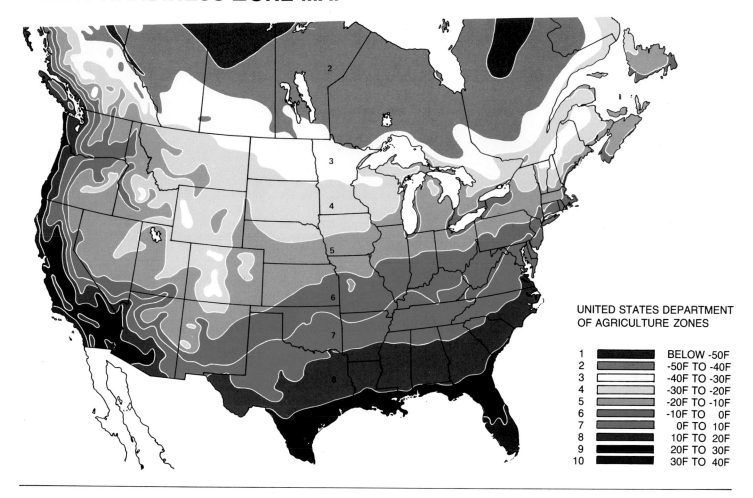

UNITED STATES DEPARTMENT
OF AGRICULTURE ZONES

1		BELOW -50F
2		-50F TO -40F
3		-40F TO -30F
4		-30F TO -20F
5		-20F TO -10F
6		-10F TO 0F
7		0F TO 10F
8		10F TO 20F
9		20F TO 30F
10		30F TO 40F

protection to prevent sunburn and survive their first summer.

GARDEN MICROCLIMATES

Every garden surrounding a home has one or more *microclimates*. These are spots where the climate is slightly different than the surrounding area. Exposure to sun, changes in elevation, bodies of water and slope of the land create microclimates. If you take a walk around your house you can often feel subtle differences. A northern exposure that does not receive afternoon sun will be cooler and moister than a southern exposure.

The warmest places in a garden are generally on the south side of a house or garden wall, or beside paving or masonry where heat is reflected during the day and retained at night. Large trees, roof overhangs and patio overheads also help retain heat at night.

Northern exposures offer cooling shade in summer, but are also more susceptible to frost. Also, frost pockets are created when cold air flows down valleys and slopes, reducing temperatures at the lowest level. Plants situated on higher ground have a better chance of survival.

Star and saucer magnolias are hardy to Canada, but their gorgeous flowers are badly damaged by frost. A warm spell in early spring can stimulate blooming, only to have flowers turn into brown mush by an untimely frost. This can often be avoided by locating such a tree in a frost-protected area such as the south side of a house or masonry wall.

When siting trees and shrubs, look for suitable existing microclimates on your property. You can also use trees and shrubs to *create* microclimates for other plants, such as to provide shaded or wind-protected areas.

Where there is no choice but to put cold-tender trees and shrubs in vulnerable locations, you can provide cold protection during winter, as described on page 54.

SITE SELECTION

The most important conditions to consider when selecting a planting site are:
- Sun or shade.
- Drainage.
- Shelter from wind, cold or salt spray.

The type of soil in your garden may also influence your choice of sites. More often, though, you'll be dealing with the same kind of soil no matter what site you choose, unless soil has been previously amended in some locations and not in others. Many gardeners are fortunate enough to have the ideal soil for growing the trees and shrubs they've selected, but in some cases the soil will need conditioning. For more on soils and soil amendments see page 41.

Sun or Shade—When trees and shrubs are offered for sale, they are generally recommended for planting either in sun or shade. However, this is somewhat simplistic because the intensity of sunlight varies across the country, and there are different kinds of shade.

HOW TO CORRECT POOR DRAINAGE

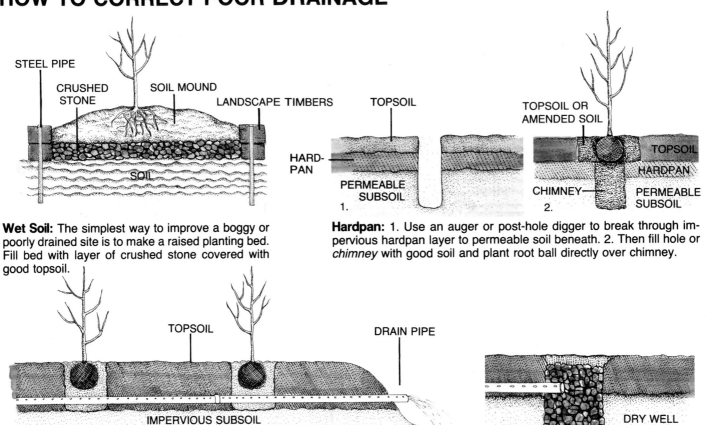

Wet Soil: The simplest way to improve a boggy or poorly drained site is to make a raised planting bed. Fill bed with layer of crushed stone covered with good topsoil.

Hardpan: 1. Use an auger or post-hole digger to break through impervious hardpan layer to permeable soil beneath. 2. Then fill hole or *chimney* with good soil and plant root ball directly over chimney.

Shallow Soil: If only a shallow layer of topsoil exists over impervious subsoil, lay perforated drain pipe leading to lower grade (left) or rock-filled dry well (right).

Plants such as camellias and rhododendrons are almost always recommended for shaded areas. But they will grow perfectly well in the open in areas like the Pacific Northwest where frequent cloud cover, ample rainfall and cool temperatures in summer create a different environment from the cloudless summer skies over most other areas of North America. Similarly, in some coastal valleys where ocean fogs are common, the question of sun or shade may not be so critical.

Shade can take many forms, including light shade, deep shade, high shade and low shade. Even azaleas and camellias recommended for shade may grow tall and spindly in deep shade. Many flowering plants actually retain better petal colors in light shade, but completely fail to bloom in too much shade.

There are also differences between morning, noon and afternoon shade. Plants that grow well in noon shade may find morning or afternoon shade insufficient because of the strength of the noon-day sun and its high light intensity.

It's often possible to alter existing shade conditions without difficulty. Pruning just a single branch from an overhanging tree may be enough to stimulate flowering on understory shrubs. Painting an adjacent wall white and mulching the ground with white landscape stone can dramatically improve the light intensity of a heavily shaded area. Light is such a critical factor that just 1% more light can mean 100% improved plant performance, as demonstrated time and again under controlled tests at light laboratories.

Shade is often more important when trees and shrubs are small and vulnerable to sunscald. Indeed, many trees and shrubs begin life in the forest shaded by tall trees, but once past their juvenile years—with a well-established root system—the need for shade becomes less important.

When a tree or shrub is growing in the nursery it is generally planted in close proximity to other trees, so it is shaded by its neighbors. However, when that same tree is planted in an exposed sunny location, it becomes susceptible to *sunscald*. This can kill the outer layers of bark. The lower regions of tree trunks are especially susceptible. To avoid sunscald, protect the lower one third of the trunk with a tree wrap, such as plastic, burlap, or with white interior latex paint for the first year after planting.

Drainage—Relatively few trees and shrubs will survive in permanently waterlogged soil. The magnificent bald cypress, prevalent in swamps along the Atlantic seaboard, is a beautiful exception. The dark, eerie "water forests" they create are a unique environment, little changed since the age of dinosaurs. But the vast majority of woody plants need good drainage, and even the bald cypress thrives on well-drained sites.

The most common drainage problem is a low-lying site that remains waterlogged for long periods. To improve this situation, you can lay down a system of underground drainage pipes to direct water to a lower grade or dry well, as shown in the drawing above. Or else lay down a foundation of crushed stones and make a raised bed with landscape ties, mounding the middle with good topsoil.

Another type of drainage problem exists where a thin layer of topsoil is underlaid with an impervious soil layer, called *hardpan*. This is common in the Southwest, where calcium deposits build up a cement-hard layer, called *caliche*. Hardpan is also common in new housing developments where the site has been graded and the subsoil compressed by heavy trucks and machinery before the topsoil was replaced.

If the hardpan layer isn't too thick, you can correct the problem by boring a hole through it with an auger to the permeable subsoil beneath, creating a drainage *chimney*. The chimney is then filled with topsoil and the root ball placed directly over it so roots can penetrate deep and surface moisture can drain down.

It is becoming more and more common for trees to be planted in areas where they are surrounded by paving or masonry. To allow rainwater to penetrate to the roots, a *tree grate* should be installed. These are made of cast iron and fit around the trunk. The surrounding paving is sloped or channelled so water flows toward the grate, giving the tree ample moisture.

Shelter — For the majority of ornamental trees and shrubs, exposed sites should be avoided. Constant winds can cause windburn and winterkill unless a windbreak is established. Scotch pines, Monterey cypress, hollies, *Casuarina* and pittosporum are examples of tough evergreens that will resist both high winds and heavy salt spray, and can be planted first to provide a windbreak for other trees and shrubs.

Cold winds are one of the biggest killers of newly planted trees, due to rapid dehydration. Such being the case, you might wonder how it is possible to establish a windbreak of trees in the first place. In extremely exposed sites it may first be necessary to erect a temporary fence of wood, reed matting or burlap until young windbreak plants have become well established. A wall of straw bales is also commonly used to help shelter windbreak plants through their early years.

SOIL AND SOIL AMENDMENTS

Good soil is the foundation of

Metal tree grate in brick patio allows natural rainfall and fertilizer to penetrate to tree roots.

successful tree and shrub growth. You can water and feed a plant all you like, but if the soil is poor the plants are unlikely to do well. Soil anchors plants and supplies them with nutrients and moisture. Because nutrients are absorbed by plant roots in *soluble* form (dissolved by moisture) soil should have good moisture-holding capacity. This is created by air spaces between soil particles. Air also provides oxygen to roots, allows their free passage through the soil and prevents rot. A good soil holds enough moisture to satisfy plant requirements, yet allows excess moisture to drain away.

Avoid compacting soil, which leaves little space between soil particles for air and moisture.

Soil Types—Garden soil comes in three basic types—*clay, sand* and *loam*. These terms describe a soil's texture and consistency. *Sandy soil* is composed of large mineral particles. It drains quickly and has a tendency to dry out. If you squeeze a handful of moist, sandy soil, it crumbles when released. It holds plenty of oxygen.

Sandy soil is actually a good growing medium for most plants because plant roots can penetrate it freely. The drawback of sandy soil is that water and nutrients drain away quickly. Also, sandy soils tend to be alkaline, which many trees and shrubs dislike. You can improve the texture and moisture-holding capacity of sandy soil by adding *organic matter*—the more, the better. Compost,

leaf mold, well decomposed manure, peat moss and ground bark products are common oganic soil amendments.

Clay soil is difficult to work with. It is composed of small mineral particles that tend to pack tightly together. If you squeeze a handful of moist clay it feels slimy and sticky, and compacts into a thick, heavy mass. Clay soil is heavy and cold in spring and can bake into a hard crust in summer. It drains slowly and acts as a barrier to plant roots. Water tends to form puddles on its surface.

You can improve the texture of clay soil by adding organic matter—the same as for sandy soil. Sometimes the addition of sand is recommended for clay soils, but sand alone will not improve clay soil without also adding organic matter. Sand particles are hard and granular, and merely stick to the clay, while organic matter is light and fluffy, and improves aeration.

Loam soil is the best garden soil. It contains proportionate amounts of large and small mineral particles, and usually lots of organic matter. Loam soil retains moisture and nutrients in the root zone, yet drains well. If you squeeze a handful of loam, it forms a loosely packed ball in your hand. In loam soils, beneficial soil bacteria can work most efficiently in converting soil particles and organic matter into plant nutrients.

Soil pH—Before you can make an intelligent choice of plants appropriate to your soil, you must know whether it has an *acid, alkaline* or *neutral* pH. The

Azaleas prefer acid soil, which is usually found in forests or areas with high rainfall.

term pH literally means *potential hydrogen* and determines the acidity or alkalinity of a substance or material. The pH scale extends from 1 to 14. A reading of 7.0 is neutral. Readings below 7.0 are considered acid, and above 7.0, alkaline.

Acid and alkaline soils tend to be distributed through wide geographic areas. Sections of the country with high rainfall tend to have acid soils. Desert areas tend to be alkaline. Most trees and shrubs prefer a soil that is moderately acid, with a pH of 6 to 7, though certain acid-loving plants such as dogwoods, rhododendrons, azaleas and camellias like it even more acid, in the 5 to 6 range. Trees adapted to arid or semi-arid climates, such as European olive, California pepper, aleppo pine *(Pinus halepensis)* and mesquite will tolerate alkaline soils. Alkaline-tolerant shrubs include bottlebrush, Texas ranger *(Leucophyllum frutescens)* and cassia. For a more complete selection of plants that tolerate alkaline soils, see *Plants for Dry Climates* by Mary Rose Duffield and Warren Jones, published by HPBooks.

Prior to planting acid-loving plants in alkaline soils, it is best to create either a raised bed with a suitable soil mix mounded in the middle, or add plenty of organic matter to the planting holes—particularly peat moss or garden compost. For established plantings in alkaline soil, the area can be treated with aluminum sulfate, ferrous sulfate or sulfur at amounts specified on the package. These applications should be followed immediately by heavy mulching with peat moss or compost. To prevent the soil from turning alkaline again, feed plants with fertilizers marked *for acid-loving plants*, such as Miracid. Lime, usually in the form of dolomitic limestone, is used to reduce soil acidity (raise pH). Apply lime by raking it into the upper soil surface at rates recommended on the package.

If you are in any doubt about the pH of the soil in your garden, you can contact your state extension service, usually located at a state university. Most extension services conduct soils tests and offer recommendations for improving soil. In California and Illinois, where the service is not provided by the state, you will receive a list of private soil-testing laboratories to contact.

Also, many nurseries, garden centers and horticultural suppliers sell inexpensive kits for testing soil pH. Although the readings may not be as accurate as those provided by a laboratory test, they do provide a general indication of soil pH, so you know whether or not it needs to be corrected, and approximately how much amendment is required to do so.

Soil Nutrients—A fertile soil provides 13 of the 16 basic nutrients necessary for plant growth. They are *nitrogen, potassium, phosphorus, calcium, sulfur, iron, copper, magnesium, manganese, zinc, molybdenum, boron and chlorine.* The remaining three nutrients, *carbon, hydrogen and oxygen,* are provided by air and water.

Most soils contain these nutrients in varying proportions. However, the three primary nutrients—nitrogen, potassium and phosphorus—are used by plants in the largest amounts, so they need periodic replenishing by means of a general-purpose fertilizer that provides these nutrients. The secondary nutrients—calcium, sulfur and magnesium—are used to a lesser degree and may need periodic replenishing if plants show signs of deficiency. The remaining nutrients, called *trace elements,* are used by plants only in minute quantities and usually are only added to the soil if plants show specific signs of a nutrient deficiency.

Because plants can only absorb nutrients in a soluble form, good soil structure, correct pH and adequate moisture must exist to make these nutrients available. For more on fertilizers and fertilizing, see page 50.

BUYING TREES AND SHRUBS

Trees and shrubs can be purchased from mail-order suppliers, local garden centers, nurseries and tree farms. Mail-order is generally the least expensive way to purchase plants, and it allows you to choose from a greater selection. But you must be careful to read the catalog description to understand what you are buying and only buy from reputable companies.

Young trees and shrubs are sold *bare-root, balled-and-burlapped* and *container grown.* Bare-root trees and shrubs are sold in a dormant state when the plant is not actively growing. The roots are usually packed in moist sawdust or moss. Mail-order trees and shrubs are generally sold this way because bare-root plants are lighter in weight so shipping costs are less. Some mail-order sources also offer seeds and unrooted cuttings—6- to 8-inch dormant sticks capable of rooting and leafing out when inserted into soil.

Plants sold through local retail outlets are generally balled-and-burlapped or container-grown. The sizes available are much larger than bare-root plants offered by mail. Bare-root stock is also available through most nurseries during the dormant season. Though the selection at local nurseries may be limited, you have the advantage of examining the tree or shrub before you buy it.

The best way to buy a tree or shrub is from a specialty nursery or tree farm. For instance, there are nurseries that specialize in dwarf conifers, others in azaleas and rhododendrons. Camellias and fuchsias are other popular specialty items, planted out in fields or under shade, ready for digging. If you want a weeping Norway spruce with a particular outline, or a red maple with a particular intensity of fall coloring, you can walk the rows, point to a plant you want, have it tagged and dug with a root ball for transporting to your property. This is the true connoisseur's method of selecting plants. It's also the most expensive. There is an increasing number of tree specialists who tour old estates and defunct arboretums to collect particularly fine tree specimens for resale. As much as $50,000 has been paid for a single tree, and another $10,000 paid to move it, with no guarantee of survival!

Selecting Healthy Plants—When buying bare-root stock by mail, you don't have the advantage of choosing what you get and must rely on the reputation of the mail-order company to send you a healthy plant. You almost always have the opportunity to send back plants you are not satisfied with and get a replacement or refund, but this can be a nuisance.

If you order plants by mail, immediately open the package when it arrives and examine the stems and roots of the plant. If a few small branches or roots are broken, they can be pruned away without harm to the plant. However, if the roots have signs of mildew or tiny fungus pustules, return the plant.

Buying bare-root stock from a local nursery allows you to pick and choose. The most important thing to look for is a vigorous root system. Scaffold branches should be well spaced, and buds should be plump, never shriveled and dry. Shriveled, dried-out buds that flake apart in your fingers indicate the plant may be too dehydrated to survive planting.

Balled-and-burlapped trees are waiting to be shipped to retail garden centers. Balled-and-burlapped is the safest way to buy trees and shrubs.

Because bare-root plants should be planted while dormant or when just breaking dormancy, avoid plants with leaves that have already sprouted. A few buds breaking dormancy and showing a little green is okay—and it tells you the plant is alive—but too much advanced leaf growth may already be placing the root system under excessive stress. If you have no choice but to accept a bare-root plant that is already green, prune away about one third of the branches before planting.

Sometimes bare-root stock is purchased to make economical mass plantings—I know a homeowner who once purchased 10,000 bare-root azaleas by mail. Although this is an extreme example, with any large purchase it is best to make a temporary nursery bed to keep plants in until they are acclimatized and you know how many survivors you have to work with. Provide light shade until plants are more mature and ready for moving to permanent positions.

Determine if the plants you're buying are *seedling stock* (seed-grown plants),

grafted stock or a named variety grown *vegetatively* (such as cuttings). Seedling trees and shrubs are generally the least expensive, but can be variable in quality. If a tree or shrub has been grafted it will have a large swelling near the soil line, where the top of a special variety has been joined to the root system of a different variety or species noted for root hardiness. This swelling, called the *bud union* or *graft union*, should be located above the soil line of the container and it should be examined closely for strength.

Always check for rodent and deer damage. Deer damage is fairly obvious—the bark is usually shredded in long strips. Rodent damage is easily overlooked because it occurs close to the roots and might consist of a narrow band of bare wood girdling the trunk.

Plants sold in containers and balled-and-burlapped at garden centers are usually big enough to plant directly in the garden. In the case of flowering shrubs, they may already be flowering size, some in full bloom. Optimum planting times are determined by the kind of tree or shrub you've bought and the climate in which you live.

Always check the soil before taking home a containerized or balled-and-burlapped plant. Some nursery personnel are careless about watering. If soil is dust-dry, chances are the plant is already dehydrated and on the verge of dropping its leaves. Weeds growing in containers also indicate a lack of care. Feel the leaves to test if they are brittle. Look for good color—leaves should be a healthy green. There should be no curling, yellowing or blemishes such as browned tips or spots. Wilted leaves indicate that the plant is either dehydrated or diseased.

With needleleaf evergreens, look for signs of localized browning. Rub your hand over the needles. If they feel brittle and fall from the branches easily, don't buy the plant. Needles that shatter or drop at the touch of your hand indicate the tree may be on the verge of dehydration and will probably worsen after transplanting.

Check for pest damage, including chewed or discolored leaves. Examine the underside of leaves for signs of mites — detected by a lackluster appearance and presence of fine webs. To check mite damage on needleleaf evergreens, part the branches and look inside the canopy. Look for blisters on branches, leaves and trunk — signs of fungus infections. Small holes or gummy sap deposits on the trunk or branches are signs of borer infestation.

PLANTING

A moderate amount of care taken in planting is well worth the small amount of time and expense involved. This includes conditioning the soil, if needed, *before* you set the tree or shrub in the hole. The old maxim, "Dig a ten-dollar hole for a five-dollar tree" says it succinctly.

The actual method of planting depends on whether the plants are *bare-root, balled-and-burlapped* or *containerized*. General planting procedures common to all three types are covered here. Specific planting instructions for bare-root plants and balled-and-burlapped plants are on page 46, and containerized plants on page 47.

WHEN TO PLANT

Containerized and balled-and-burlapped plants can be planted virtually any time the soil can be worked and watered. For bare-root deciduous trees, the best planting times are early spring or late fall when the plants are dormant. Bare-root needleleaf evergreens in exposed situations are best planted in spring because of their high moisture needs and susceptibility to dehydration from winter conditions.

Though most home gardeners think in terms of spring planting, fall is actually a good planting season for many trees and shrubs. In the South, where winters are mild, fall planting makes especially good sense because it avoids the heat and drought stress of hot summers, and gives newly planted stock an extended cool, moist period in which to become well established.

Though deciduous trees enter a dormant period in winter when the top growth loses its leaves, the roots remain active until the ground actually freezes. Winter dormancy is also induced by day length, so that trees in frost-free sections of the country may lose their leaves and go dormant, even though temperatures are favorable for normal growth. Generally speaking, it is safe to plant hardy trees and shrubs up to 6 weeks before the ground freezes. This is not only true of broadleaf deciduous trees and shrubs, but also of certain deciduous needleleaf conifers, such as larches, dawn redwood and bald cypress. Only during the depths of winter will the roots stop growing, and they will revive at the return of a warm spell long before the top breaks dormancy and leafs out.

The success rate of evergreens can be improved by planting in spring in Northern states. Because they continue to transpire large amounts of moisture during winter, they are more susceptible to dehydration during dry, windy or severely cold winters. However, if supplemental watering can be provided, and if the site is not too exposed, evergreens can safely be planted in fall.

I once planted three new evergreen azaleas in spring on an exposed stream bank and lost them all from summer drought. I planted three more on the same site in fall, and though some leaves were browned by a sudden early freeze,

they all revived spectacularly in spring and I didn't lose one.

Also, I've had similar success with containerized and balled-and-burlapped needleleaf evergreens, especially live Christmas trees. Every year prior to the ground freezing, I dig a hole where I want the tree to grow after it does its duty as a Christmas tree. I save the soil in a wheelbarrow, keeping it in a garage area to prevent it from freezing. While the tree is in the house decorated with lights, the root ball remains in its burlap or container, but is placed in a plastic trash bag so it can be watered whenever the soil feels dry, without puddling onto the living room rug.

Three weeks after Christmas, I move the tree from the living room to the garage for 2 weeks to acclimatize it, then move it outdoors into the hole. It is watered with at least 2 gallons of water whenever a week goes by without natural rainfall. I have never lost a tree yet. There was one year when a Douglas fir started to show severe browning on one side, but I doused it with a hose almost daily and sprayed its needles weekly with a liquid fertilizer and it greened up beautifully.

DIGGING THE HOLE

In the case of bare-root stock, you need to dig a hole 6 inches deeper than the roots extend. As you dig, separate the good soil (topsoil) from inferior soil (subsoil). After the hole is dug, break up the bottom with a spade, fork or crowbar. Then put about 6 inches of topsoil into the bottom so the new roots will have fertile soil in which to grow. Mixing an amendment such as peat moss or compost with the planting soil at the rate of 1 part amendment to 3 parts soil will improve soil structure, particularly if the soil is clay or sand.

In the case of stock that is balled-and-burlapped or containerized, the planting procedure is a little different. If the soil is good and well-suited to the particular plant—for example, planting azaleas or rhododendrons in a woodsy or high-humus soil—dig your hole the same size as the root ball and lower the root ball into the hole.

If, however, the site has poor soil, it's better to improve soil over the whole site or at least dig a bigger-than-normal

PLANTING A TREE

1. Dig hole twice the width of the root ball. To keep tree from settling in hole, do not dig hole deeper than height of root ball.

2. Add thin layer of good topsoil or compost to bottom of hole. Sprinkle fertilizer into bottom of hole and stir into soil.

3. Gently lower balled-and-burlapped tree into hole. Use a plank to slide heavy root ball to avoid straining yourself by lifting it.

4. Untie string from around trunk and loosen burlap flaps. Remove any nails.

5. Fill around sides of root ball with topsoil or compost. Pack soil to settle it.

6. Untie strings from around branches. Prune away any of the branches that are broken or appear dead.

7. Wrap trunk with tree wrap to avoid sun scorch and to deter pests such as rodents and deer.

8. Apply at least 5 gallons of water to roots. Water same amount weekly in the absence of rainfall.

9. Apply mulch of wood chips or similar organic material to deter weeds and conserve moisture.

BARE-ROOT PLANTING

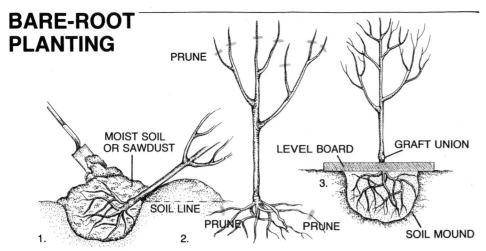

PRUNE

MOIST SOIL
OR SAWDUST

LEVEL BOARD

GRAFT UNION

SOIL LINE

3.

PRUNE

PRUNE

SOIL MOUND

1.

2.

1. If you can't plant bare-root stock immediately, dig a shallow hole in a protected location and cover roots with sawdust or topsoil and keep moist. This is called *heeling-in*. 2. If top seems too large in relationship to roots, prune back excessive topgrowth. Also prune off any damaged roots or ones too long to fit into planting hole. 3. Use level board to position tree at correct level. With grafted trees, graft union should be above soil line. Spread out roots over soil mound in planting hole, then backfill hole.

planting hole. For example, when planting azaleas and rhododendrons in a heavy clay or stony soil, it might be advisable to haul in leaf mold to thoroughly amend the soil structure before digging planting holes. Or, with larger shrubs and trees, dig a generous hole and backfill with leaf mold before planting. To determine whether or not your soil needs amending before planting, refer to the section Soil and Soil Amendments, starting on page 41. A light application of a general-purpose fertilizer may also be beneficial right after planting.

As the planting hole is filled, create a *catchment* or *catch basin* around the tree or shrub to hold water, by mounding soil to form a rim. Make the catch basin so the perimeter is positioned around the root mass. After 6 to 8 weeks, extend the perimeter directly below the plant's *drip line*, or outer edge of the leaf canopy.

Fill the basin with water and allow the soil to settle. If the plant settles too much, gently raise it back to the original planting depth, adding more soil, if necessary. Never plant more deeply than the level at which the plant grew originally. Next, cover the soil with an organic mulch to retain moisture and deter weeds. Wood chips or shredded leaves are ideal. See Mulching on page 48.

BARE-ROOT PLANTS

All bare-root trees and shrubs need to be planted as soon as possible after you receive them—preferably the same day. Bare-root evergreens have green leaves

year-round and it's easy to determine the health of plants on arrival. Bare-root stock of deciduous trees is generally sold in *dormant* condition with no leaves showing, for spring or fall planting. As the plants enter their winter dormant period in autumn—and before they break dormancy in spring—many kinds can be efficiently shipped and planted. To prolong the dormant state in spring and extend the selling season for bare-root stock, some mail-order nurseries will hold deciduous trees in cold storage.

The roots of bare-root stock are generally wrapped in moist sphagnum moss or damp newspaper to prevent their drying out during transit. Before planting, remove this packing material carefully and immerse the roots in a bucket of water for 2 to 3 hours.

There are five *Don'ts* when planting bare-root stock:

1. *Don't* let plants dry out. Keep the roots moist.
2. *Don't* let the roots freeze. Store plants in a frost-free area.
3. *Don't* let plants mold in storage. If planting is delayed beyond 10 days, spray with Captan or Benlate to discourage mold.
4. *Don't* handle plants roughly. Roots and branches are usually brittle and will break easily.
5. *Don't* store plants too long. It is better to risk planting too early than storing too long.

Do not delay planting a day longer than absolutely necessary. If you cannot

plant the same day bare-root stock is received, lay the plants down in a cool basement or other cool, sheltered, shaded place. Cover the roots with damp newspaper or a damp cloth to prevent drying out.

Pruning is sometimes desirable even before you plant. For example, with bare-root stock, if any roots are broken, the damaged portions should be pruned away. Similarly, if the leader or any side branches are broken, the damaged portions should be pruned clean.

Do not plant a bare-root tree on which the top growth is disproportionate to the bottom. If the tree is *top-heavy*, with more branches than the root system appears it can support, prune back the branch ends and allow the root system to produce new growth according to its own ability. As mentioned earlier, if bare-root plants have already started to leaf out, prune the top growth back by one third to avoid stressing the tree.

BALLED-AND-BURLAPPED PLANTS

These are generally field-grown in well-spaced planting rows. A machine is used to dig up the plant with a rounded or cone-shaped root ball. The root ball is wrapped in burlap to keep it from falling apart, and bound secure with string. This is a popular way for many nurseries, tree farms and garden centers to sell trees and shrubs, though it is the most expensive because considerable labor is needed to dig the trees, wrap and transport them. The ball should be intact and solid when purchased and should not show signs of breakage, which could damage the fine roots.

Balled-and-burlapped trees are often planted as is, with no attempt to remove the string or the burlap, because the theory is that these materials will quickly decompose once the root ball is covered with soil. However, some root balls are bound with plastic string which does *not* decompose, and may strangle the tree as the girth of the trunk expands. Even if the root ball is bound with natural fibers, it is best to cut or loosen the string from around the trunk.

There is wide disagreement over whether the burlap itself should be removed. The best policy is to simply loosen the top, but not until you have lowered the root ball into its hole. If you try to remove the burlap completely, the root ball will generally fall apart, breaking delicate root ends in the process, which destroys the advantage of paying a premium price for a balled tree. However, when you backfill the hole, make sure the edges of the burlap are well covered with soil. Any exposed burlap will act like a wick, drawing moisture away from the root ball.

CONTAINERIZED PLANTS

These are generally grown in metal or plastic containers, peach baskets or peat pots, usually varying in size from 1-gallon to 15-gallon capacity. This is a popular way for nurseries and garden centers to sell trees and shrubs. They are generally more expensive than bare-root stock, but less expensive than balled-and-burlapped plants. With peat containers and peach baskets, it is generally sufficient to cut away the bottom of the container and plant the whole package. The peat decomposes quickly once covered with soil, and the thin wood of the peach basket soon rots away to release the side roots.

With both metal and plastic containers that don't decompose, use a sharp knife or sheet-metal shears to cut away the sides and release the root ball. Alternatively, you can cut out the bottom and push the root ball up out of the container. In some cases, the container can be tipped upside-down and the plant will slip out easily. The whole idea is to keep as much soil as possible around the roots.

If the plastic container is large and heavy, cut out the bottom and slide the tree into its planting hole. Then, when the root ball is well seated in the hole, remove the sides of the container with a hatchet, heavy duty can opener or sheet-metal shears. In most cases, a tree or shrub in a 1- to 5-gallon plastic or corrugated-metal container will easily slip out, if you tap the container several times and upend it. Large plants are best handled by two people. In all cases, be careful not to shatter the root ball.

Sometimes, if the tree or shrub has been in the container too long, it will be *rootbound*, that is, the roots have become crowded and taken on the shape of the container. After the root ball is in the planting hole, loosen or cut any matted or encircling roots so they can spread out into the surrounding soil. Otherwise, severe problems with girdling roots may develop in future years.

CONTAINER PLANTING

1. With metal and plastic containers, trim away any roots protruding through drainage holes to facilitate removal of container. 2. Tilt plastic container on its side and gently slide it off root ball, tapping container lightly to loosen, if necessary. 3. Cut metal container on opposite sides with shears and spread container apart. 4. Pull loose any encircling or matted roots and prune off broken or damaged ones. Plants in peach baskets (5.) and peat pots (6.) can be planted as-is. Peat pots and flimsy wood sides of peach basket quickly decompose in moist soil.

AFTERCARE

The basics of tree and shrub care are watering, mulching, fertilizing, pruning, protection from pests and diseases, and protection from weather extremes. Newly planted trees and shrubs are much more vulnerable than established ones, so some of these chores will have to be done on a more frequent basis until the plant is better able to fend for itself.

Most shrubs and bare-root trees are small and do not need staking. But large balled-and-burlapped and container-grown trees will require staking if they cannot stand on their own or will be exposed to high winds. This is especially true of trees that have grown tall and spindly because they have been crowded in the nursery row. Staking methods are described at right.

During the summer months, newly planted trees and shrubs generally require more frequent watering than established ones—at least weekly for most kinds. For more on watering, see page 48. Young trees and shrubs are also susceptible to weather extremes, especially sunscald during summer and freezing during winter. Methods of winter protection are described on page 54.

STAKING

Some trees need support to help get them established. This is particularly true of open-branched evergreens such as Atlas Cedars and any deciduous trees with long, straight trunks. *Bare-root* stock is generally too small to stake, but trees that are *balled-and-burlapped* or *containerized* often require staking.

Even in sheltered locations where wind is unlikely to snap the trunk or blow a newly planted tree over, even slight winds can rock a newly planted root ball and either break feeder roots or tilt the tree out of alignment.

The best way to stake a tree to anchor the roots is with three sets of guy wires. Loop one end around a main branch where it meets the trunk, about two-thirds up the tree, cushioning the area of contact with strips of cloth or rubber hose. Extend the other wires out on opposite sides of the tree and secure to stakes driven into the ground, like tent pegs.

To stake a tall, spindly tree, use two

HOW TO STAKE A TREE

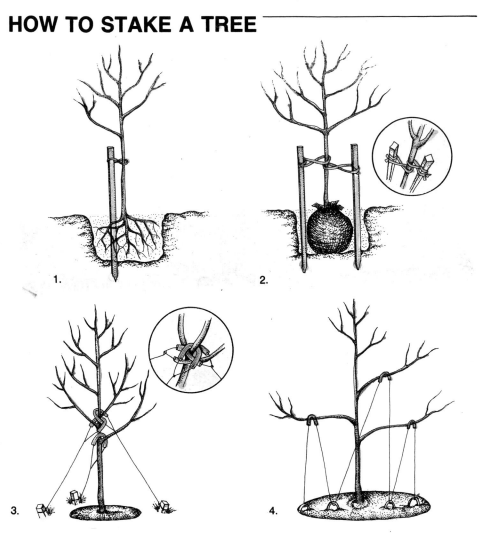

1. One-stake method for support of bare-root trees. Drive stake before planting tree to avoid damaging roots. 2. Two-stake method for support of tall, spindly balled-and-burlapped or container trees. Tie tree loosely to stake to allow some trunk movement. Use cloth strips or padding where ties contact trunk. 3. Guy wires are used to support larger trees and prevent movement of root ball. Use sections of flexible rubber hose or other padding to protect branches where wires contact them. 4. Wires woven through bent-wire pins driven in ground splay out tree branches to make a spreading outline and also to support tree. Pieces of flexible rubber hose or other padding is used where wires contact branches. This technique is used to direct branch growth on flowering and fruiting trees to allow maximum air circulation for improved blossom and fruit production.

Wire guys are used to stake tree. To prevent guys from cutting into bark, loops are cushioned with rubber hose.

tall stakes, positioned on opposite sides of the trunk, as shown in the drawing above. The trunk should be tied to the stakes with a non-abrasive material such as cloth or rubber strips. Tie strips loosely enough to allow some trunk movement in the wind, but not so loose that the trunk will be abraded by contact with the stakes. If the tree is staked too rigidly, it will develop a weak, thin trunk.

WATERING

Newly planted trees and shrubs need to be watered generously. During the first 6 months of active growth, if a week goes by without natural rainfall, trees and shrubs should be watered. As a rule of thumb, water at least twice a week for first 2 months after planting.

Do not keep trees and shrubs constantly swamped with water. Unlike small plants such as annual flowers and vegetables that require almost daily watering during dry weather, trees and shrubs benefit more from a deep, thorough watering once or twice a week. This allows soil to dry out slightly between waterings so air can reach the roots. Only a few swamp plants—such as bald cypress—will tolerate constantly wet conditions. Adequate drainage is vital for most trees and shrubs.

Because sandy soils lose moisture more quickly than clay soils, adding large amounts of peat moss, leaf mold or similar organic amendment is recommended to help retain moisture.

Although most mature trees and shrubs can endure longer periods of drought than smaller plants, and need not be watered as frequently, they still require adequate moisture. If a tree or shrub goes too long without water, it will become stressed, making it vulnerable to diseases and pests.

Frequent shallow waterings during a dry spell in an attempt to save a tree will have little effect. This kind of emergency relief can work with small plants, which recover quickly, but once the ground is dry and a tree or large shrub has started to dehydrate, it requires copious amounts of water to save it.

MULCHING

A mulch is any type of soil covering used for the purpose of conserving moisture, suffocating weeds and stabilizing soil temperatures. Mulches can be organic—shredded bark or licorice root, for example—or inorganic, such as gravel, decorative rock or black plastic. Organic mulches are popular for placing around trees and shrubs because most tend to be highly decorative. Those made from wood and vegetable byproducts are especially desirable because they decompose and enrich the soil. Also, they tend to keep the soil cool for improved plant growth. However, some organic mulches deplete the soil of nitrogen while decomposing, so it is desirable to use them in conjunction with a nitrogen fertilizer.

Care should be taken when using landscape stone around acid-loving plants such as hemlocks, dogwoods, hollies, azaleas and camellias, because rain can leach alkaline salts from the stone into the soil and change the pH balance. Feeding these plants with fertilizers marked "for acid-loving plants" can help prevent this.

Black plastic has a tendency to overheat the soil if it is not covered with a layer of organic mulch. Also, it has an unnatural appearance that many people find objectionable. Black plastic of at least a 5-mil thickness is mostly used as a weed barrier under decorative mulches such as stone and bark chips.

Mulch materials should be chosen according to cost and local availability. At one time, licorice root was a popular mulch throughout North America, but in

Heavy mulch of shredded bark in azalea bed not only deters weeds, conserves moisture and keeps soil cool, but helps establish a *mowing strip* so grass can be cut without the mower touching branches.

MULCHING MATERIALS

Material	Thickness for Weed Control	Advantages	Disadvantages	Comments
Aluminum foil	1 layer.	Reflective surface increases light intensity in areas. Helps control aphids. They become disoriented by it.	Tears easily. Looks unnatural. Expensive for large areas. May reflect too much heat in warm-summer areas.	Cools soil. Allow soil to warm before using around new plantings. Best for short-season areas.
Bark chips and ground bark	2 to 3 inches.	Attractive, natural appearance.	Harbors ants, ticks and termites. Expensive for large areas.	Cools soil. Allow soil to warm before using around new plantings. Bark products available in a variety of sizes.
Compost	3 to 4 inches.	Adds nutrients to soil. Usually attractive, natural appearance. One of the best organic mulch materials.	If compost is not made properly, it may harbor weed seeds.	Cools soil. Allow soil to warm before using around new plantings.
Corncobs, ground	3 to 4 inches.	Attractive, natural appearance.	Takes nitrogen from soil as it decomposes. Compensate with high nitrogen fertilizer.	Cools soil. Allow soil to warm before using around new plantings.
Cottonseed hulls	3 to 4 inches.	Attractive, natural appearance. Adds some nutrients to soil.	Lightweight—blows away when dry. Possible contamination from chemical sprays.	Cools soil. Allow soil to warm before using around new plantings. Available in South and parts of Southwest.
Grass clippings	2 to 3 inches.	Commonly available. Decomposes quickly to add organic matter and nutrients to soil.	Sometimes contains weed seeds. May need additional application midseason to be effective as a weed control. Thick layers will mat.	Cools soil. Allow soil to warm before using around new plantings. Best applied when dry. Don't use clippings treated with weed-killers.
Hay and straw	6 to 8 inches.	Attractive, natural appearance. Adds nutrients to soil. Commonly available.	May contain seeds. May need additional applications midseason if used for weed control.	Cools soil. Allow soil to warm before using around new plantings.
Leaf mold	3 to 4 inches.	Attractive, natural appearance. Adds nutrients to soil. The best organic-mulching material.	Takes time to make. A lot of leaves are needed to make a small amount. Turns soil acid. Compensate with lime.	Cools soil. Allow soil to warm before using around new plantings. Good moisture-holding capacity.
Newspapers	1/4 inch.	Commonly available. Decomposes quickly.	Unnatural appearance, but can be covered with other, more attractive mulch.	Cools soil. Allow soil to warm before using around new plantings.
Peanut hulls	3 to 4 inches.	Adds nutrients to soil. Decomposes quickly to add organic matter to soil.	Lightweight. Blows away when dry. Not readily available outside Southern states.	Cools soil. Allow soil to warm before using around new plantings.
Peat moss	2 to 3 inches.	Attractive, natural appearance. Adds organic matter to soil.	Expensive for large areas. Better as soil amendment.	Cools soil. Allow soil to warm before using around new plantings. Good moisture-holding capacity.
Pine needles	3 to 4 inches.	Natural appearance. Readily available. Gradually adds organic matter to soil.	Slightly acidic, but no problem when lime is used prior to planting.	Cools soil. Allow soil to warm before using around new plantings.
Plastic, black	1 layer. Use 1-1/2 mil thickness.	Excellent for weed control. Maintains warm soil temperatures.	Unnatural appearance.	Warms soil. Use under other mulches, especially stone, for permanent weed barrier.
Plastic, clear	1 layer. Use 1-1/2 mil thickness.	Maintains higher soil temperature than black plastic, encouraging earlier establishment of sub-tropicals.	Unnatural appearance. Weeds grow underneath.	Warms soil. Best used in conjunction with an irrigation system.

recent years has become less available in many parts of the country and is somewhat high priced. Organic mulches of wood byproducts, such as wood chips and shredded bark are more-common, less expensive alternatives.

Extended use of organic mulch can have the disadvantage of depleting nitrogen in the soil due to the accelerated activity of decay microorganisms. This condition can be corrected through periodic additions of a high-nitrogen fertilizer.

In the Southwest, gravel and rock is not as expensive as bark and other wood mulches, while on the West Coast cedar chips are becoming a popular choice for their ability to repel slugs and other pests. In agricultural areas, locally available agricultural byproducts are used as mulches. Examples are corncobs, cottonseed hulls, various nut hulls, grape pomace and mushroom compost. See page 49 for list of mulches with comments on their use.

FERTILIZING

There are many misconceptions about the need to fertilize trees and shrubs. Because trees in the wild are not given applications of commercial fertilizers, the general notion is that trees don't need feeding. But that is not the case.

In the wild, trees shed their leaves and the leaf litter is allowed to build up on the forest floor. It decays and forms leaf mold, which provides the tree with vital nutrients and trace elements as it breaks down further. This life-giving humus also acts as a mulch, covering the soil to conserve moisture, stabilize soil temperatures and discourage weeds. In most home landscapes, leaves are not allowed to remain on the ground. They are raked up and either burned or otherwise disposed of. For this reason, supplemental feedings of fertilizer is *essential* to healthy tree and shrub growth.

There is a great deal of conflicting information about fertilizing trees and shrubs. Some experts warn not to fertilize until after the first year of planting, others recommend applications immediately after planting. There is also disagreement as to whether high-nitrogen formulas or high-phosphorus formulas are best. However, without a soil test to determine the precise makeup of your soil, and an understanding of a particular plant's nutrient requirements, specific recommendations are difficult, but here are some general guidelines:

The first year a tree or shrub is in the ground, all we should ask of it is to survive through its first winter. At the time of planting, a mild application of a high-phosphorus fertilizer, such as 5-10-5, can be mixed in with the soil. High-phosphorus fertilizers are recommended for initial applications because they stimulate root development. The best time to make subsequent applications of fertilizer is in the fall. Tree roots continue to function in winter whenever the soil temperature is above 40F (4C). Limb and trunk development in the spring is largely derived from food stored in the roots during fall and winter. Commercial fertilizers applied in the spring do not generally benefit a tree that same spring. However, fertilizer applied to a tree in the fall as it slows down its metabolism will benefit the tree remarkably the following spring and summer.

Tree fertilizers are usually sold in granular form for applying to the soil. Fertilizer may be applied directly on the soil surface because most feeder roots are in the upper few inches of soil. According the the U.S. Forest Service, except where slow-release fertilizers are used and on sloping sites, there is little advantage to using fertilizer *tree spikes* or injecting other fertilizer formulations into the soil by boring holes in the ground or by other means.

Because trees and shrubs can also absorb nutrients through their leaves, liquid fertilizers can be applied to leaves in a fine spray. Called *foliar feeding,* this application method is usually used only as a quick "pick-me-up" or booster to stimulate growth at a particular time of need—such as when flower buds are forming on flowering shrubs, or when fruit is forming on fruiting trees.

There are three primary nutrients essential to healthy plant growth. *Nitrogen* is the most important of these, because it is responsible for healthy leaves. *Phosphorus* is the next most important nutrient because it promotes flowering, fruiting and healthy root development. The third major nutrient *potassium* (potash) promotes cold-hardiness, disease resistance and overall vigor.

The primary nutrients are sometimes abbreviated to N-P-K on the fertilizer package, with the amount of each nutrient given as a percentage, such as 20-10-10. In this case, the numbers mean that the formula is composed of a total of 40% nutrients—20% nitrogen, 10% phosphorus and 10% potassium. Usually, the rest of the formula is filler—water or sterile granules that serve as a distributing agent—though the fertilizer may also contain small amounts of other nutrients, depending on brand.

As mentioned on page 42, a good soil provides 13 of the 16 plant nutrients necessary for healthy growth. In addition to the three primary nutrients discussed above, plants require the others, called *trace elements*, in varying amounts. The three most important for healthy tree and shrub growth are *calcium, iron* and *boron*. Lack of calcium, for example, is evident in some species of *Prunus* when the trunk or branches crack and ooze a gummy resin. This condition, called *gummosis*, can also indicate the presence of borers. If the resin is clear, lack of calcium is usually the cause; if the gum is mixed with sawdust, then a borer is the culprit.

Lack of boron will cause new growth at branch tips to shrivel and die. Lack of iron is the most common cause of *chlorosis*, a condition indicated by yellowed leaves with predominately greener leaf veins. Chlorosis can also be caused by lack of copper. These and other trace elements are usually not applied on a regular basis, but only if the tree or shrub shows a specific deficiency in one of them. If you suspect a nutrient deficiency, describe the symptoms to a local nurseryman, tree specialist or extension agent. They are generally familiar with soil conditions and nutrient deficiencies common to your area. For instance, lack of iron is common in areas with alkaline soils.

However, the ability of a tree or shrub to use fertilizer depends on other factors besides nutrient content. Good soil texture—a crumbly loam soil, for example—helps a plant's roots penetrate freely and absorb the nutrients efficiently. The other vital factor is pH—a measurement of acidity and alkalinity. Some trees and shrubs demand a highly acid soil. Plants such as rhododendrons, azaleas, camellias, hollies and andromeda demand such high levels of acidity that special fertilizers are avail-

SCHEDULE FOR TREE AND SHRUB CARE

This chart shows the recommended times for the various basic tasks required to maintain healthy trees and shrubs. However, specific problems may arise that require immediate attention, such as storm damage to a tree or an untimely outbreak of a certain pest or disease. In some cases, you may have to call in a professional tree-care service to correct the problem. Appropriate timing for many of these tasks will depend on location and plant species. Check with local extension services for recommendations.

TYPE OF CARE	Jan	Feb	Mar	Apr	May	June	July	Aug	Sept	Oct	Nov	Dec
Transplanting Large Trees	■	■	■						■	■	■	■
Transplanting Small Trees and Shrubs		■	■	■					■	■	■	
Pruning Flowering Trees and Shrubs		■				■					■	■
Pruning Foliage Trees (Shade Trees)	■	■									■	■
Fertilizing			■	■	■	■	■	■	■	■	■	
Aerating and Conditioning Soil			■	■	■	■	■	■	■	■		
Spraying For Control of Scale on Dormant Plants		■	■	■								
Spraying Evergreens (Pest and Disease Control)				■	■	■	■	■	■			
Spraying Fruit Trees (Pest and Disease Control)				■	■	■	■	■				
Spraying Shade Trees (Pest and Disease Control)						■	■	■	■			
Gassing Borers									■			
Irrigation				■	■	■	■	■	■	■	■	
Removing Undesirable Trees	■	■	■	■				■	■	■	■	■
Winterizing Trees and Shrubs	■									■	■	■

□ Most Important   ■ Also Recommended

able, marked "for acid-loving plants." Miracid is a familiar example.

Though modifying soil pH is practical for flower beds and vegetable plots, it is much more difficult to accomplish for trees and shrubs. In areas of the country where a particular soil pH predominates—acid soils are prevalent in the Northeast, alkaline soils in the Southwest—the easiest solution is to create a raised bed, using landscape ties to form the sides, and filling the center with an appropriate soil mix. Smaller trees and shrubs can be grown in containers. Easier yet would be to grow species adapted to local conditions. For more on correcting soil pH, see page 42.

Leaf Mold—Adding leaf mold in spring and fall will benefit mixed-shrub borders and trees with a circle of turf cleared around the base of the trunk. Mrs. Lena Caron, director of gardens at the famous Ladew Topiary Gardens, near Monkton, Maryland, feels that the value of leaf mold cannot be overrated in maintaining healthy plants. It wasn't until the garden's caretakers started stockpiling it to use around their trees and shrubs that they began to see a remarkable improvement in the general health and flowering ability of the plants.

Rich, black leaf mold is a kind of compost. It has long been valued as an amendment to improve soil texture, but it also makes an excellent fertilizer. Leaf mold can be dug up directly from the forest floor, but the best source of the material is from storing fallen leaves in special compost piles. Form a circular bin with chicken wire to hold the leaves together. The leaves will decompose much faster if they are shredded with a lawn mower before loading into the bin. You can also speed up decomposition by adding nitrogen. The nitrogen provides food for the microorganisms responsible for decay. Nitrogen is available naturally in animal manure and in green plant parts such as fresh green leaves and fresh grass clippings.

A general compost is a good alternative to leaf mold. It is made from all kinds of general plant or vegetable waste, biodegradable kitchen scraps and other decomposable organic matter. Large scale composting is best done in square or rectangular wooden bins treated against rot.

The key to making good garden compost is to maintain a balance between *green material* and *dead material*. Technically, this is a nitrogen (green) to carbon (dead) ratio that must be maintained for efficient decomposition of organic materials in the pile. So when you add a batch of fresh grass clippings or hedge trimmings (green material) to the pile, cover it with a layer of sawdust or wood chips (dead material).

Although compost is excellent for improving texture and moisture-holding capacity, it does not always provide adequate amounts of soil nutrients. Periodic soil tests are recommended as a check on soil nutrient levels.

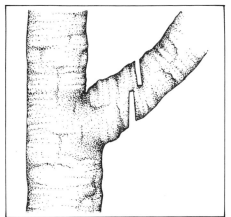

First, undercut branch until saw begins to bind. Make second cut from top, slightly to outside of undercut, to remove branch. Third cut close to tree eliminates stub. Make cut just outside bark collar. Cut may be sealed with orange shellac.

PRUNING

Pruning is considered by most tree experts to be the most important phase of tree care. Although there are trees and shrubs that require less pruning than others—particularly trees in a naturalized setting—some pruning is advisable, if only to remove dead or diseased branches and to keep pathways clear. Landscape trees are pruned mostly to improve their appearance and health. Correctly done, pruning is an invigorating process that channels the plant's energy into the remaining branches. Pruning also helps limit plants to a specific size, improves flowering and fruiting and eliminates wayward branches that might interfere with power lines or structures.

Pruning is mostly done to shape a tree or shrub to a particular form. Prune a tree along the sides and it will tend to grow spirelike or columnar. Prune out the leader and it will tend to grow outward until a new leader has a chance to grow, which in turn can be pruned out again, and so on, to keep the tree bushy.

There are two basic kinds of pruning techniques—*heading* and *thinning.* Heading involves cutting back branches to a side branch or lateral bud. This results in a denser, more compact form. Heading is most often done to control the overall size of a tree or shrub. Thinning interior branches increases the amount of light and air penetration to the crown, improving vigor and wind resistance.

Generally speaking, shrubs can take much heavier pruning than trees. Some

BASIC PRUNING TECHNIQUES FOR TREES

TOPPING A TREE

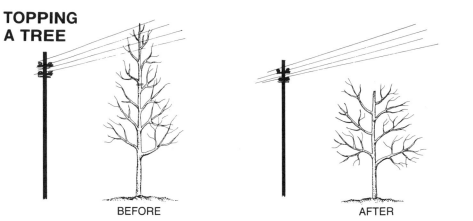

BEFORE

AFTER

Topping central leader of tree stimulates side branching.

LOWER-BRANCH PRUNING

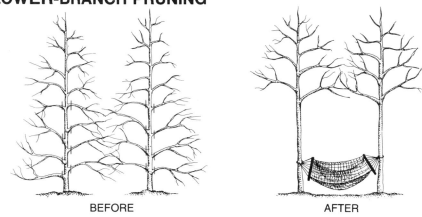

BEFORE

AFTER

Lower side branches are pruned away to leave slender, straight trunks and overhead leaf canopy.

SCULPTURAL PRUNING A CONIFER

BEFORE

AFTER

All branches except selected few are pruned back to main trunk. Stakes and wires are used to bend trunk and remaining branches, forcing tree to grow to desired form.

BASIC PRUNING TECHNIQUES FOR SHRUBS

REJUVENATING A SHRUB

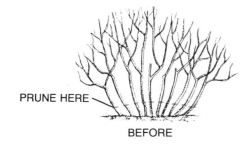

PRUNE HERE

BEFORE

AFTER

Heavy pruning to just above soil level stimulates bushy new growth.

THINNING

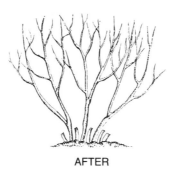

BEFORE

AFTER

Prune away suckers and intermediate stems on multi-stemmed shrub to open up interior. This allows more light penetration and air circulation.

LOWER-BRANCH PRUNING

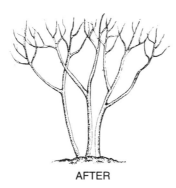

BEFORE

AFTER

Lower side branches are pruned away to leave only main, upright stems.

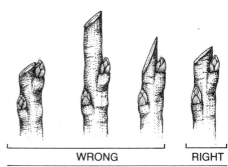

WRONG   RIGHT

Correct cut is made at a slight angle about 1/4 inch above bud.

Loppers allow you to cut through thick branches up to 3 inches in diameter.

Bow saw is suitable for cutting through thick branches.

Electric hedge shears make easy work of shaping shrubs.

shrubs benefit from pruning right down to the ground. For instance, when forsythia has established itself, it is often a good policy to prune it down to the ground immediately after flowering. This stimulates growth of new stems and a more vibrant flowering display the following spring on a compact plant.

If you want a tree with a trunk that's clear of limbs so you can walk under it, prune off undesirable lower limbs.

Some trees to send up sprouts at the soil line, called *suckers*. If you want a single-stemmed tree, remove these.

Always prune on a slant so cut ends of branches shed water, and make the cut at least 1/4 inch above a bud on shrubs and 1 inch above a bud on trees.

Avoid pruning flowering trees or flowering shrubs other than immediately after flowering. For example, pruning a rhododendron late in the year, such as fall or winter, will deprive the plant of flowers in spring. Pruning other deciduous trees and shrubs is best done

Boxwood shrub is protected from cold winter winds by a wood frame covered with burlap. In exposed situations in cold climates, boxwood leaves will turn brown unless protection is provided.

Plastic tree wrap helps protect a newly planted tree from *sunscald.* Wrap also protects bark from rodents and deer.

Fig tree is protected from freezing by wire cylinder filled with leaves. Tree has been pruned short so it is completely encased, or *mummified.*

in fall, winter or early spring while plants are dormant.

The four most-useful pruning tools are: hand pruners for cutting small branches up to 1/4 inch in diameter; two-handled lopping pruners for cutting thick branches up to 2 inches in diameter; a curved pruning saw or bow saw for cutting through thicker branches, and electric hedge shears to trim shrubs to a smooth, clean outline. A chain saw can be used to cut very large limbs, but this work is best done by a tree surgeon.

When using a pruning saw on large branches, always make the initial cut on the underside of the branch before cutting through the branch from above. That way the branch will not tear on its underside, but come away clean. See drawing on page 52.

For more about pruning trees and shrubs, refer to *Pruning, How-To Guide for Gardeners,* by Robert L. Stebbens and Michael MacCaskey, published by HPBooks. The book contains specific pruning instructions for 350 different trees and shrubs.

WINTER PROTECTION

Many hardy trees and shrubs can survive freezing weather provided they stay dormant during the entire cold spell and have sufficient moisture in the root zone to prevent dehydration from cold winds and winter sun. A tree or shrub subjected to alternate thawing and freezing is easily damaged. One way to help keep a plant dormant is to pile mulch material over the root zone *after*

the ground freezes. This helps *keep* the ground frozen until a definite spring warming trend has started.

Similarly, if a tree or shrub has insufficient moisture in autumn through lack of natural rainfall, it can die unless supplemental water is provided through irrigation. This is especially true of evergreens that continue to transpire large amounts of moisture during winter.

Burlap can be used to protect special plants—especially newly planted trees—in exposed locations. Trees can be protected with burlap trunk wraps, shrubs by surrounding the entire plant with a burlap shelter. In addition to burlap, suitable screens can be made from reed matting and wire cylinders wrapped with tar paper. Anti-dessicants are sprays that apply a thin coating of wax or plastic to exposed leaves and branches to protect woody plants from moisture loss.

Heavy snowfall and freezing rain can cause tremendous damage. If snow is left to freeze on many kinds of evergreens—boxwood especially—ugly brown patches will result. In severe cases, this condition, known as *winterkill,* can kill the entire plant.

Freezing rain can be devastating, and there is not much that can be done after the fact. Usually the rain falls in the night and freezes as it touches limbs. It can be a beautiful sight the following morning, but if a sudden strong wind comes up, the sound of crashing limbs will fill the air within minutes. The best remedy is prevention.

Prior to the snow season, columnar

trees should have their branches bound close to the trunk with twine. This prevents the snow or ice from pulling the branches out of alignment and snapping them. Immediately after snow falls and before it has a chance to freeze, use a broom to sweep off the snow covering from low shrubs and reachable tree branches.

Cracks or splits in bark can occur when the west or south side of a tree trunk is warmed excessively by winter sun. When the sun sets and the temperature drops drastically, the cells on the exposed side of the tree can be killed. The bark then cracks or splits. If severe enough, this damage can kill the top, particularly in the case of young trees unprotected by tree wrap. To minimize the risk of bark cracks from frost, either wrap the trunk with a white reflecting tree wrap or paint the trunk with white latex paint.

Fruiting fig is a particularly vulnerable tree in Northern climates. Though the roots are reasonably hardy, the top is easily damaged by cold. The best way to get a fruiting fig—and other small, tender trees and shrubs—through the winter is to prune back excessive topgrowth and make what nurserymen call a *mummy.* Form a wire cylinder around the trunk and fill the air space between the trunk and the wire with leaves or straw, as shown in the photo above.

An alternative method for small shrubs is to prune the top to within 12 inches of the ground and cover the plant with a "Wall-O-Water" plastic cone. The cone is formed by cylinders of water that will freeze and create a warm microclimate around the plant.

In addition to figs, tender plants such as hibiscus, bamboos and jasmines can be nursed through the winter in regions where the plants are at the coldest limits of their recommended hardiness zones.

Another important technique for providing winter protection involves bareroot plants purchased in autumn. Sometimes you may find you have insufficient time to get them planted before winter arrives and must hold them over until spring. You can protect them using a technique called *heeling-in*. This is done by digging a shallow trench in a sheltered location, inserting the roots at an angle into the trench and covering them with loose soil. The trunks protrude at an angle to present a low profile to damaging winds. In spring, before active growth begins, the heeled-in plants can be easily dug up and moved to their permanent sites.

If a containerized or balled-and-burlapped plant is left above ground over winter, chances are it will die from freezing temperatures. To save these plants until spring planting, sink them into pits with loose soil or mulch piled to the top of the container or burlap. Alternatively, build up a raised area of landscape ties, set your plants in the center and mound loose soil or wood chips several inches above the container rim or burlap.

PESTS AND DISEASES

Trees and shrubs suffer much less from pests and diseases than other forms of cultivated plants, such as vegetables. Also, the evidence is clear that maintaining plants in vigorous condition is by far the best protection. Adequate amounts of fertilizer and moisture, and timely pruning are especially important. When trees are weakened from neglect, competition from other plants, or by a long summer drought, they become highly vulnerable to attack.

The common lawn mower and filament-line grass trimmers are also a major causes of pest and disease problems. Careless use of these and other garden implements can cause bark wounds that provide a point of entry for pests and disease organisms.

Most shrubs and small trees can be treated with many of the same pest controls used on other garden plants. Descriptions of specific pests and diseases, starting at right, include recommended controls. However, it is usually not practical for a homeowner to administer these and other cures for pest and disease problems of large trees. Cures rely heavily on chemical poisons and specialized equipment to reach the extremities of a tree. It's better to call in a tree-service company. Certain preventative measures can be taken by homeowners, including use of traps and biological controls, such as predatory insects and bacterial products. Also, the use of tree wraps on young trees can prevent sunscorch and rodent damage.

PESTS

The bigger the pest, the easier it is to control. Deer and rodents, for example, are easily discouraged from eating bark and girdling a tree simply by using protective plastic tree wraps. Infestations by sap-sucking scale insects, caterpillars and wood-eating borers are much more difficult to control, often requiring professional tree services to eliminate them.

Controls can be classified as *preventative* and *curative*. Many pests that can be prevented may be impossible to eradicate once they have a foothold. For example, oils sprayed on trees while dormant can kill eggs of overwintering insects, especially aphids and mites.

On the other hand, it simply isn't practical to take preventative measures against every potential tree pest. However, some problems can be pinpointed as potentially disastrous. Gypsy moth is an example. Most trees can survive defoliation through one season, but won't make it through two.

If you live in an area where a specific pest is a problem, it might be worth getting together with neighbors to take preventative action through a large-scale spray program. If you are new to an area, a good way to pinpoint potential pest problems is to check with your county extension agent.

Here are some of the most common pest problems afflicting trees and shrubs:

Aphids are tiny, soft-bodied insects about 1/8 inch long that form colonies on tender parts of trees and shrubs, sucking their juices. Though infestations are seldom serious enough to kill a tree or shrub, they are carriers of diseases. Also, they excrete a substance called *honeydew*, which attracts sooty-mold fungus that coats leaf surfaces with a black deposit.

Look for aphid colonies at the tips of branches and on newly sprouted leaves. They are usually green, but can vary in color from white to black. Viburnums and roses are especially vulnerable.

Control: Jets of water directed at the infested branch tips can dislodge them. Sprays of insecticidal soaps or a mild solution of dish detergent in water are also effective. Malathion, Sevin and pyrethrum-based insecticides are common chemical controls.

Bagworms are the caterpillar larvae of a night-flying moth, widely dispersed from New England to Texas. The larvae hatch from eggs and build around themselves cone-shaped bags made from pieces of leaf, particularly evergreen needles. Spruce, arborvitae and cedars are especially susceptible to attack. The pest can cause severe defoliation, stress and death.

Control: Bags can be hand-picked from infested trees. Winter is a good time to remove the bags because they contain the eggs of the next generation. The bacterial disease *Bacillis thuringiensis* is effective while larvae are small. Sprays of diazinon, malathion and Sevin are effective chemical controls, applied every 7 to 10 days during spring and whenever re-infestation occurs.

Borers include the larvae of a number of different kinds of beetles and moths. They are capable of burrowing through even the toughest wood, causing branches to wilt and trees to die. Eggs are deposited by the adult female on the bark of the trunk. These hatch, and the larvae immediately penetrate the bark. Once inside the wood, they are virtually impossible to control. Among many trees, such as flowering peach and cherry, the tree bleeds a gummy brown or white substance from holes made by the borers. A similar condition, caused by lack of calcium in the soil, is known as *gummosis*.

Control: Borer infestation is prevalent among newly transplanted trees. Any kind of barrier wrapped around the

Peach-borer damage is evident by gummy sap oozing from holes made by the borers.

Japanese-beetle trap is one of the few non-chemical controls to combat pests. Sex attractant lures beetles into disposable bag.

trunk will deter the pest, particularly a commercially available plastic tree wrap, which should remain in place for at least 2 years. Sprays of malathion and methoxychlor will kill the adult female moths before they have a chance to lay eggs. These sprays need to be applied at regular intervals to be effective, particularly from midsummer into autumn when the female is actively laying eggs. Moth balls heaped around the base of trunks during this period is an effective control practiced by organic gardeners. Pheromone traps designed to attract the adult moths of several borer species can be used to pinpoint mating and egg-laying periods.

For severe infestations, the services of a professional tree service should be considered. The commercial pesticide *Borerkil* is effective against small infestations. It is a paste that is squeezed into the holes to asphyxiate the borers.

Gypsy Moths were accidentally introduced into New England from Europe in the 1880's and have gradually spread throughout most of the Northeast. The female is a flightless moth that lays its eggs in elongated tan egg cases that are deposited in the fissures of bark. Oaks are particularly susceptible. The larvae hatch as tiny black worms that grow rapidly into 2-inch, long-haired caterpillars. In some years, they are so numerous they can completely defoliate trees. When defoliation occurs 2 years in a row, the tree usually dies.

Control: Sprays of Sevin are the most common chemical control, applied in spring after eggs have hatched. The bacterial disease *Bacillis thuringiensis* is an effective biological control. Once infected, the caterpillar stops eating and starves to death. *B. thuringiensis* is sold under the brand names Thuricide, Dipel and Biotrol.

Japanese Beetle is a widespread insect pest. In its adult stage, it is a serious problem of many trees and ornamental shrubs. These beetles feed on the upper leaf surfaces, leaving the leaves skeletonized. Trees most susceptible to Japanese beetles include linden, elm, maples, horsechestnut, birch, black walnut, apple, cherry, plum, and mountain ash. Trees in full sun are particularly prone to attack. From fall through spring the larvae—large, white grubs—live in the soil, feeding on the roots of lawn grasses.

Control: A bacterial spore disease *Bacillus popillae*—also known as milky spore—is effective in killing 70% to 80% of resident populations. Traps using sex attractants that lure adult beetles into disposable bags are less effective, even though they are capable of trapping large numbers. Most of the chemical controls recommended for Japanese beetles are only partially effective, owing to the ability of the pest to build up resistance rapidly. Sevin and diazinon offer partial control if applications are repeated at intervals of 7 to 10 days during periods of heavy infestation.

Leaf Miners are the larval stage of numerous insects, including flies, moths and beetles. Adults lay their eggs inside the leaves of specific trees and shrubs. When the young hatch, they begin burrowing through the leaf, leaving snaking patterns and blotches. Leaf miners are especially serious pests on birches, but also attack holly, beech, elm, boxwood and many conifers.

Control: Once the pest is inside the leaf, it can only be controlled by a systemic insecticide such as Orthene. In their adult stage, the insects are more easily controlled by spraying with malathion, diazinon or Sevin.

Mites are colonies of tiny spiderlike arachnids no bigger than grains of pepper. Usually colored red or brown, they build webs among leaves and stems and suck plant juices. Infestations can be so severe they will kill trees and shrubs—even tough plants such as junipers. On broadleaf plants mite feeding damage is most severe toward the interior of the tree. Symptoms include curling of leaf edges and a dusty appearance to the underside of the leaves. On evergreens, needles look dull and lack luster—ugly patches of brown needles disfigure the plants and eventually kill them. The presence of delicate white webs is a sure sign of mites.

Control: Once infestations are heavy, control may be impossible. Kelthane is an effective mite spray, applied on upper and lower leaf surfaces when mites first appear. Insecticidal soap is also effective.

Rodents and Deer can cause major damage to trees and shrubs, especially during winter. Mice and other rodents will gnaw the bark and cambium layer of young trees and shrubs, girdling the tree and killing it. Deer are also fond of stripping bark from young trees, and eating tender shoots as well. Male deer like to rub their horns on the trunk of a young tree, scraping off the bark and cambium layer and killing the tree.

Control: Use a commercial tree wrap on young trees to protect the trunk. Plastic tree guards are particularly effective. Forming flexible spiral cylinders, they expand freely as the tree grows. Keep fresh mulch away from base of tree to discourage mice from nesting around base of plant.

Scales are sucking insects that attach themselves to branches like limpets. Some are hard-bodied and well camouflaged to resemble lumps of bark. Others are soft bodied, white and quite conspicuous. Symptoms of scale injury are wilt, dieback and chlorosis. Some scales excrete *honeydew,* a moist sticky substance that can develop an ugly, destructive fungus disease called sootymold, which forms a black, powdery covering on leaf surfaces.

Control: Apply a dormant-oil spray in early spring, or a scalecide in early spring and summer. Remove and burn badly infested branches.

Webworms and Tent Caterpillars attack trees in spring and fall. The branches become covered in flosslike webs or tents containing colonies of voracious caterpillars. Tent caterpillars emerge from their tents in spring and can eat considerable quantities of leaves. The fall webworm lives on leaves encased in its tent and does little damage. The tents themselves are unsightly and are mostly attached to species of cherry, hawthorn and crabapple.

Control: The bacterial disease *Bacillis thuringiensis* is an effective biological control when applied as a spray. Effective chemical sprays include Sevin, diazinon and malathion.

DISEASES

Relatively few diseases of trees and shrubs are lethal. Exceptions such as *Dutch elm disease* and *oak wilt* can be both lethal and fast-acting. Diseases of trees and shrubs usually occur when the plant has become weakened by environmental conditions, such as pest attacks, strangulation by vines, dehydration from drought or lack of nutrients.

When diseases do occur, they can normally be diagnosed early and corrected. However, some symptoms, such as leaf spots and branch dieback, may need an expert to identify the particular disease organism responsible so that a suitable cure or control can be administered. Good sources for expert advice include the horticulture department of your state university, or the state or county extension service.

Diseases are generally classified as *infectious* and *non-infectious.*

Infectious diseases are commonly caused by fungus, bacteria or viruses. Fungus diseases cause the greatest amount of damage to trees and shrubs. Fungus organisms are unable to manufacture chlorophyll, so many obtain

Anthracnose disease on dogwood. This particularly destructive strain is known as *lower branch dieback.*

their nourishment from living plant tissue. They reproduce by means of microscopic spores that are dispersed by wind or rain, or carried on the bodies of insects.

Bacteria and viruses also obtain their nourishment from living plant tissue. They reproduce by cell division, and are easily transmitted from one plant to another by wind or insects.

Non-infectious diseases are mostly caused by environmental conditions such as nutrient deficiencies, but also by chemical or mechanical injury to plants. For example, mineral deficiencies in soil can cause *chlorosis,* or leaf yellowing. Lack of iron is one of the most common causes of chlorosis. Lack of calcium in the soil can cause *gummosis,* whereby the bark splits and bleeds a gummy sap. Excessive exposure to sun turns leaves brown, a condition referred to as *sunscorch.* On some trees, such as horse chestnut, sunscorch looks hideously lethal, turning leaf margins an ugly brown, but it rarely kills a tree.

Diseases of trees and shrubs can also be classified as *leaf diseases, stem diseases, vascular diseases* and *root diseases,* referring to the part of the tree that is mostly infected.

Leaf diseases include *powdery mildew, leaf spot, leaf blotch, leaf blight, leaf sunscorch, rust* and *chlorosis.* Of these, powdery mildew is probably the most common. Prevalent during periods of high humidity, it occurs mostly in mid-summer and fall, coating leaf surfaces with gray or powdery white patch-

Orange spots with dark centers are evidence of cedar-apple rust on crabapples.

es. Though generally not lethal, it can weaken a tree or shrub and leave it vulnerable to attack by more serious diseases.

Stem diseases include *anthracnose, cankers, galls, dieback, witches broom* and *rot.* Cankers are dead areas on branches or trunks. They may be sunken or raised and show cracking or flaking. Fruiting bodies of fungi may frequently break through the diseased area. Cankers can completely girdle a branch, killing it.

Gall diseases appear as growths on branches or trunks caused by fungi, bacteria or viruses that enter the tree through wounds. The growths are exceedingly ugly, but rarely lethal. Some insects also cause galls.

Root diseases include *shoestring root rot,* a fungus that attacks tree roots of weakened trees, causing severe branch dieback and death.

Vascular diseases include *Dutch elm disease, verticillium wilt* and *oak wilt.* They attack the inner sapwood, causing branch dieback and death.

Here are some of the most common diseases that attacks trees and shrubs:

Anthracnose includes numerous strains of a fungus disease that attacks trees and shrubs. An especially destructive form is currently causing widespread death to dogwoods throughout North America. Also called *lower branch dieback,* it first shows itself when branch tips die, followed by dieback of entire lower branches. Leaves shrivel, turn brown and remain attached

Crown galls disfigure main trunk and branches of weeping willow.

Powdery mildew on lilac. Though it rarely kills plants, powdery mildew is unsightly and weakens them.

to the tree, even through winter.

Trees in shaded locations are especially susceptible. Death can occur within 3 years of infection. Other trees susceptible to special forms of anthracnose include sycamore, ash, elm and maple. With these trees, the disease is not lethal but causes some leaf drop and scattered twig dieback. The severity of anthracnose is determined by the weather, with a cool, moist spring favoring disease development.

Control: Once a tree is heavily infected, controls are ineffective. Sprays of Benomyl or Maneb can control mild infections, if properly administered by a tree-service company. Infections generally follow a period of stress, such as drought. The best preventative method is to keep trees healthy by regular watering and fertilizing.

Cankers are stem diseases that affect the branches and trunk of many trees. They are caused by fungi and bacteria. Infected areas start to crack or flake away, turn dark and become sunken. Some will form a ridge of raised bark around the canker. When a canker girdles a branch, it cuts off the flow of sap and the branch dies. When the trunk is girdled by a canker, the tree will die. Some cankers produce colorful fruiting bodies of fungus — red and yellow slimy masses that emerge through a crack.

Control: Keep plants in good health. Prune away infected branches and burn. Between each cut, sterilize the cutting tool with rubbing alcohol. When cankers occur on trunks, they can be removed by routing out the diseased area back to living wood, then painting the wound with shellac.

Cedar Apple Rust is widespread throughout the Northeast wherever junipers and apples grow in close proximity. It needs two kinds of trees to complete its destructive life cycle. First it overwinters on species of junipers, forming corky brown galls. Then, in spring, the galls radiate slimy yellow fingers like the arms of an octopus. These produce spores that must land on species of apple trees, where they infect leaves, twigs, fruit and stems. This stage of the disease is called *rust*. It is first evident as yellow or orange spots on leaves, then as swollen lesions on new growth. The spots thicken to produce small, black fruiting bodies that disperse spores to infect junipers.

Control: Plant only disease-resistant varieties, or avoid planting crabapples in close proximity to junipers. Fungicidal sprays, such as Zineb, can be used on junipers or crabapples. On crabapples, make four to five applications of spray, spaced at 10-day intervals, after buds open in spring. On junipers, make four applications at 7-day intervals in mid-summer.

Chlorosis is a general term used to describe nutritional deficiencies of plants. Typical symptoms are a yellowing of leaves, usually leaving the veins deep green. Any imbalance of plant nutrients can cause chlorosis, but it is mostly associated with a deficiency of iron. It is especially common among acid-loving plants planted in alkaline or neutral soil.

Control: With acid-loving plants, the addition of organic matter to the soil will help. For more immediate results, the use of a fertilizer marked 'for acid-loving plants' is best. Or use an iron-chelate, either in the soil or sprayed on leaves. Sulfur added to soil is also an effective control.

Crown Galls are caused by bacteria that produce ugly, warty swellings on trunks, branches or roots, particularly on willows and poplars. Cherry, walnut and roses are also susceptible. Galls usually cause little damage, but can spoil the ornamental value of specimen plants.

Other kinds of galls — caused by fungi — commonly infect the leaves or twigs of oak trees and look like huge tumors.

Control: A common source of gall infection is through a trunk injury caused by a lawn mower or other implement.

Fireblight is common on crabapples, hawthorn, firethorn, cotoneaster and mountain ash. It is prevalent throughout all areas of North America with hot, humid summers — particularly the Northeast and Midwest. Blossoms, shoots, branch tips and fruit turn brown or black and appear scorched. Fireblight completely destroys a plant's ornamental value and will sometimes kill the plant. Infected branches are scarred by conspicuous cankers and rough, scaly areas of bark.

Control: Plant only disease-resistant varieties in areas where the disease is a problem—control is extremely difficult. Prune away all branches and twigs showing evidence of the disease, disinfecting the pruning tool *after every cut* by dipping in rubbing alcohol.

Powdery Mildew attacks the leaves of many ornamental trees and shrubs, particularly lilacs, crabapples, hawthorns and roses, and most broadleaf evergreens, such as rhododendrons and azaleas. It appears as a gray or dirty white powdery coating on leaf surfaces. On plants that are infected early in the season, severe growth distortions can result. Though it usually does not kill the plant, powdery mildew looks ugly and weakens it by inhibiting photosynthesis. High humidity favors the disease because the spores will only germinate in warm, saturated air.

Control: Spray leaf surfaces with benomyl whenever the fungus appears and at 10-day intervals as needed. Other fungicides such as sulfur, karathane, chlorothalonil and triflorine are also effective controls.

Scab is the most common disease among crabapples and hawthorns, prevalent in all areas of North America except desert regions. It also attacks mountain ash and pyracantha. The disease begins with olive-colored, velvety leaf spots that become larger and turn dark brown. The center of each spot bulges upward, giving the appearance of a scab. Severely infected trees can lose their leaves by midsummer, and any fruits that form generally shrivel up and turn black. The disease is prevalent during wet weather. Though scab is an unsightly disease and can severely weaken a tree or shrub, it does not kill it.

Control: Use scab-resistant varieties of crabapples and pyracantha. Chemical controls require four applications of benomyl or zineb at 14-day intervals from the time the buds open in spring.

Woodrot diseases are caused by fungi that gain a foothold in a wounded part of a tree and cause decay. The decay can produce a "hollow tree," destroying the heartwood, but will not infect actively growing layers of wood. The fungi responsible for woodrot are usually the *shelf fungus* type or *toadstools*.

Control: Wounds and pruning cuts should be shaped properly to facilitate rapid healing. Fertilizing and watering as needed can also encourage tree vigor and prompt wound closure. In severe cases the infected area can be routed out to living wood and filled with cement, like a tooth filling. However, the filling of cavities should be practiced only as a last resort because it often results in new pockets of rot underneath. Also, rigid columns of cement can cause trunks to snap off in a wind.

TREES AND SHRUBS IN CONTAINERS

Trees are generally not the easiest plants to grow in containers, yet certain varieties are well worth considering. Indeed, special dwarf varieties of conifers and fruit trees are eminently suited to container gardening. In fact, many trees make far better container plants than shrubs, because most shrubs tend to remain squat and less appealing than the upright, pyramid and spire-shaped forms of many trees.

Apart from ornamental value, there are several advantages to planting trees and shrubs in containers. Although it's a good way to bring trees and shrubs close to the house—on decks, patios, terraces and entryways—it's also good for locations with unsuitable soil. For example, rhododendrons, azaleas and camellias that won't grow in alkaline garden soil can be grown in containers filled with a suitable acidic soil mix. Some trees and shrubs also make excellent decorative indoor house plants, notably Norfolk Island pine, ornamental citrus, gardenias and camellias.

The bigger the container, the wider variety of trees and shrubs you can grow—unless you want to grow bonsai specimens. In the case of bonsai, special root pruning and shaping of the plant will allow it to be grown in a small pot or *bonsai dish*. Bonsai culture is described on page 29.

Adaptability—Left outdoors, trees and shrubs in containers are highly susceptible to drying out in summer and freezing in winter—much more so than plants in the ground. To avoid drying out during summer, container plants may need to be watered daily. Plants sensitive to sunscald can be moved to shaded locations during the hottest months. To avoid freezing in winter, containerized trees and shrubs are best moved to a sheltered location or a greenhouse where frost can be excluded. Because containers *are* portable, they allow you to grow many kinds of trees and shrubs that otherwise won't survive your climate.

Container Choices—The choice of container is important to the successful growing of trees and shrubs. In metal or plastic containers, for example, roots are prone to burning from the soil overheating. Wood and clay containers keep soil temperatures cooler than plastic or metal ones. Plants in clay containers will need watering more frequently than those in wood containers because clay has a tendency to soak up water and evaporate moisture though its sides.

All containers will need adequate drainage. This should be provided by holes in the bottom, covered by a screen or broken clay pieces to prevent the soil mix from washing out.

Wooden half barrels and *wooden tubs* make excellent planters. Redwood and cedar resist rot better than other woods. Beware of wood preservatives that may be toxic to plants. Even so, it is a good policy to line them with a sheet of plastic to prevent rot. A coat of asphalt emulsion can also be used as a rot-resistant barrier. Raise wooden containers several inches above the ground to prevent the base from rotting. Fitting large containers with casters will accomplish this and also make the container easier to move.

Unglazed clay pots, stone troughs, concrete and *terracotta urns* make excellent planters and are readily available at garden centers, ceramics dealers and stone quarries.

Wire baskets lined with sphagnum moss are also readily available from garden centers. Though unsuitable for displaying trees, there are certain kinds of cascading evergreens and tropicals that make striking displays, including cascading types of azaleas, gardenias and bougainvilleas.

With hanging-basket plants, exposure to sun and wind is a problem, causing dehydration, sunscald and overheating. If sphagnum moss is kept moist, it helps create a humid airspace around the root zone.

Baskets should be at least 16 inches wide and extra deep. To fill a wire basket, place it on a flower pot or bucket to hold it in place. Line bottom and sides with moist spaghnum moss to a thickness of at least 1 inch. This creates a planting nest. Fill the center area of the basket with potting soil, or make a mix of equal parts peat, sifted garden topsoil and sand. Position plants and bend branches around the sides of the pot, securing them to the outer wire frame with twist-ties to begin the cascading effect. Water plants daily. Feed with diluted liquid fertilizer at least once a week.

Soil for Containers—Container soil should provide plants with three basic necessities: adequate anchorage, moisture and nutrient-holding capacity, and drainage. Brands of specially formulated soilless mixes are available from garden centers. They are called soilless because they do not contain garden soil. They are made up of materials such as peat moss, ground bark and other organic materials. Usually, these materials are sterilized, and fertilizer and micronutrients (trace elements) are added to the mix.

Two ingredients commonly included in potting soils are *vermiculite* (a lightweight, expanded mica) and *perlite* (a porous, volcanic rock). Both are granular materials capable of holding many times their own weight in moisture. Because of their structure they also add valuable air space to the mix.

Although these mixes can be used as-is from the bag, they are expensive, if used in large quantities. In some instances, they are too light and plants can be toppled by gusts of wind. Like many gardeners, I prefer to add some garden loam to the mix. This gives plants better anchorage and reduces moisture evaporation. It also makes the mixes go further.

Be aware that when you add garden loam the mix is no longer sterile. In addition, soil drainage is reduced. Consider the plant's requirements for soil drainage and water requirements before adding garden loam. The amount of loam to add depends on its composition, but in most situations 1/3 loam to 2/3 soilless mix is a good ratio.

Making Your Own Soil Mix—The most popular container mixes are available in two basic formulations. One has been developed for the East, where peat moss is relatively inexpensive. The other is more common in the South and West, where ground bark or redwood sawdust is more readily available.

Cornell mixes are formulated for the East. After many years of research, Cornell University developed several lightweight soil mixes, primarily for professional growers. Many planter mixes available to gardeners today are based on the Cornell formula. A typical Cornell mix contains by volume 1 part coarse sphagnum peat moss to 1 part vermiculite, size No. 2, 3 or 4.

Add *chelated micronutrients* (trace elements) to the water used for moistening the mix. Lightly moisten ingredients and mix thoroughly. It helps if water is warm. Allow to stand in a pile for 24 to 48 hours so the dry peat will soak up moisture.

Fertilizer should be added to the mix before using, so you'll need to include the following *starter ingredients:* 5 pounds ground limestone, preferably dolomitic limestone, which contains both calcium and magnesium; 2 pounds single superphosphate fertilizer, 1 pound calcium nitrate or 1/2 pound ammonium-nitrate fertilizer.

U.C. mixes were developed by the University of California for growers in the West and South, primarily for container use. A typical U.C. mix consists of: 2 parts fir or pine bark, with particles less than 1/2 inch in diameter; 4 parts aged or composted redwood sawdust, or *forest mulch*, which is a sawmill mix of fine and coarse sawdust composted with a small amount of nitrogen fertilizer; 1 part graded, 30-mesh, fine sharp sand. Do not use beach sand because of its high salt content. If the weight of the mix will be a problem, omit the sand or substitute perlite.

To a cubic yard of U.C. mix, add chelated micronutrients and the same fertilizer starter ingredients as for Cornell mix.

Mixing Tips—For small lots, keep in mind that a *cubic foot* fills about seven to ten 1-gallon cans. Count on about a 15% to 20% loss of volume when you mix ingredients because the small particles will fill in between the larger ones.

To keep the soil mix sterile, blend materials on a plastic sheet or concrete pad that has been washed with a solution of 1 part chlorine bleach and 10 parts water. Use clean, sterile tools for mixing. To mix thoroughly, shovel ingredients into cone-shaped piles. Drop the material on top of the pile so it cascades evenly down the sides. Rebuild the cone three times to ensure a complete mix. Store unused mix in plastic garbage cans or heavy-duty plastic bags to prevent contamination.

Moisten the soil mix before adding it to the container so it is thoroughly saturated. Dry potting soil is difficult to moisten after it's in the container. Don't rely on available fertilizer to last through the season. After 3 months, feed regularly with diluted liquid fertilizer every 2 weeks.

Watering—Watering may be necessary every day, depending on the size of the container. Test for soil moisture by taking a pinch of the soil mix and rubbing it between your fingers. Hanging-basket plants are more exposed than container plants to heat and wind, so are especially susceptible to drying out. They may need watering as often as three times a day to keep plants from wilting.

Viterra Hydrogel is a product that can be added to soil mixes to prevent rapid dehydration. It is a granular material capable of absorbing up to 20 times its own weight in water. This product is useful when added to soils for hanging baskets and seed flats, which tend to dry out rapidly.

Drip-irrigation systems are well adapted to container gardening. Systems with *spaghetti hoses* work well. These have small, numerous hoses projecting from a main hose. Each small hose supplies water to individual containers or hanging baskets. Emitters at the end of each small tube supply water slowly to soil around the root area.

Fertilizing Container Plants — Most plants in containers require regular amounts of fertilizer. Nutrients, especially nitrogen, are continually being washed out of the soil. A timed-release fertilizer distributes plant nutrients for an extended period. But you will probably have better results by adding a diluted liquid fertilizer about once a week when you water. Plant foods designed to be mixed with water can be purchased in concentrated form as a liquid or crystals.

Raised Planting Beds — Raised beds are planting areas elevated above the normal soil level. They help create a neat, tidy appearance in the home landscape. Many are bordered by wood, brick or stone. Because they are above ground level, the soil warms faster in spring and drainage is improved. Soil depth is increased, providing extra room for root growth.

The heartwood of redwood and red cedar are good materials for building raised beds, as is lumber that has been treated with a non-toxic wood preservative. Sturdy railroad ties are popular for a rustic appearance. For long raised beds, telephone poles laid on their sides work well. Raised beds can either be island beds or butted against a fence or wall.

PROPAGATING TREES AND SHRUBS

There are four main methods of propagating trees and shrubs—*seeds, cuttings, layering and grafting.* Each method has advantages and disadvantages, and the recommended method varies, depending on the kind of tree or shrub you're trying to propagate.

SEEDS

Some tree and shrub seeds germinate reliably as soon as they ripen on the tree, and the fresher the seed, the higher the germination rate. For example, a high germination rate can be expected from rhododendrons and camellias. Other seeds may need a period of *chilling* to simulate winter conditions before they will break dormancy. These include the seeds of many of the conifers.

To start seeds of trees and shrubs that require no chilling, scatter the seeds over moist, sterile potting soil in a seed tray. Place the tray under a bright light at room temperature and keep the soil moist. To prevent the seed tray from drying out, avoid direct sunlight and enclose the tray in a plastic bag. The plastic covering helps maintain a humid environment and prevents moisture loss.

For trees and shrubs that require chill-

TAKING AND ROOTING CUTTINGS

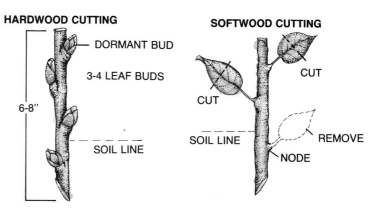

HARDWOOD CUTTING — DORMANT BUD — 3-4 LEAF BUDS — 6-8" — SOIL LINE

Cut bottom at slant just below bud.

SOFTWOOD CUTTING — CUT — CUT — SOIL LINE — REMOVE — NODE

Cut at slant just below node.

Hardwood cuttings (left) are taken from previous season's growth when plant is dormant. Cut pencil-thick piece with three to four buds; insert in soil as shown. Softwood cuttings (right) are taken from new growth with leaves attached. Cut pencil-thick piece with three or four leaves, just below leaf node. Remove bottom leaf, dust bottom end with rooting hormone and insert in soil as shown. If leaves are large, cut tops off to reduce moisture loss.

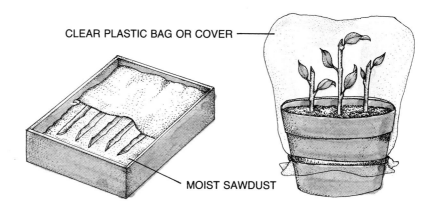

CLEAR PLASTIC BAG OR COVER

MOIST SAWDUST

Left: Hardwood cuttings taken in winter can be stored in moist sawdust until spring planting. Right: Plastic sandwich bag or clear-plastic cup placed over pot keeps cuttings moist while rooting.

ing to break dormancy, the seed tray can be placed in the vegetable bin of a refrigerator for the required chilling period (6 weeks to 6 months, depending on species.) Or, the seeds can be sown outdoors into a specially prepared seed bed in fall, for the seeds to germinate in spring. Outdoor seed beds are best located under a lath covering to provide light shade, otherwise seed beds will be subjected to drying out, and the seedlings may suffer from sunscald. Cold frames are also useful for starting seeds, allowing seedlings to be protected during severe weather.

Seeds chilled in a refrigerator should be timed so they are removed in early spring. Germination will usually occur within 3 weeks, and the comforts of

spring weather will help the seedlings become established.

After seeds have germinated and formed a true set of leaves, they can be transferred from their seed trays into individual pots, or into temporary nursery beds, to make further strong growth before being moved to their permanent planting location.

Seeds collected from trees and shrubs will not always produce progeny identical to the parent. This is especially true of seeds taken from a hybrid or named cultivar, such as the 'Bradford' pear. Such seed will either be sterile or will produce a large percentage of inferior plants. Seeds taken from the *species*—or the plant as it is found in the wild—are more likely to come true to type. Unless

GRAFTING

CLEFT GRAFTING

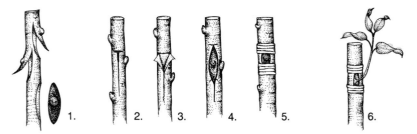

1. Cut cleft in understock with blade. 2. Cut scions and taper ends as shown. 3. Insert pair of scions into cleft, making sure cambium layers of both scions are aligned with cambium layer of understock. Bind tight with rubber band or grafting tape, and cover with grafting wax. 4. When one scion leafs out, remove second scion. Graft has taken.

BUD GRAFTING

1. Cut shield-shaped bud slips from scion with sharp blade. 2. Make "T" shaped slit in bark. 3. Peel back bark. 4. Insert bud slip into "T" cut. 5. Bind with rubber band or grafting tape. 6. When bud leafs out, graft has taken.

you know that a particular tree or shrub will reproduce true from seed, the only way to be assured of producing offspring identical to the parent is to make cuttings, layers or grafts.

CUTTINGS

Most trees and shrubs can be increased by cuttings. Those considered difficult are fir, pine, hemlock, locust, mimosa, redbud, ginkgo, mountain laurel, golden rain tree and pieris.

Cuttings are usually made of newly formed wood taken in spring or summer. These are known as *softwood cuttings* and generally take 4 weeks to form a root system. Some trees and shrubs can be rooted satisfactorily from *hardwood cuttings*, on old growth usually taken in fall. For example, holly, yew, arborvitae and juniper will root best in fall after new growth has toughened up and has been subjected to frosts. Hardwood cuttings generally take 2 to 3 months to form roots.

The easiest way to root cuttings is in a flower pot covered with a plastic bag. The plastic cover creates a humid microclimate that prevents moisture loss.

Once the plastic cover is in place, the cuttings need not be watered again until they are well rooted.

A mixture of equal parts peat and sand makes an ideal rooting medium, though this can be varied. For acid-loving plants like rhododendrons, azaleas and camellias, a mix of 1 part sand to 3 parts peat can improve the rooting percentage.

Cuttings should be 6 inches long wherever possible, pruned on a slant. Score the bark with a sharp blade 2 inches from the tip and strip away all lower leaves for two-thirds of the length of the cutting. Dip the base of the cutting in a root stimulant such as Rootone. This is essential. Without a rooting stimulant the success rate can be zero. Then press the cutting for half its length into the moist rooting medium, spacing each cutting at least 1-inch apart. A 6-inch flower pot can comfortably hold 12 cuttings. Spray the cuttings with water, place the pot in a clear plastic bag and close the top with a twist-tie.

Set the pot in a bright location, but avoid direct sunlight which can kill the cuttings from overheating. Bottom heat from a heating duct is beneficial.

Cuttings from most woody plants will form roots within 2 months. After they have been in the pot that length of time, you should see roots poking through the drainage hole. If not, lift one of the cuttings and see if any root development has started. If not, replace the cutting and continue periodic inspection until the roots appear or until the cuttings turn black and die.

After cuttings are well rooted, they can be transferred outdoors to a cold frame or temporary nursery bed, shaded from direct sunlight. The cuttings should remain in temporary nursery beds for 1 year before moving to permanent locations. Preferably, they should spend their first winter in a cold frame with a glass or plastic cover that can be closed to protect them during severe weather. Cold frames must be opened up on sunny days, even in winter—otherwise plants can overheat and die.

GRAFTING

Trees and shrubs that are difficult to root from cuttings can be grafted to produce plants identical to the parent. Many weeping evergreens, such as 'Sargent's' weeping hemlock and 'Pendula' weeping spruce will not come true from seed and are virtually impossible to reproduce from cuttings. But portions of healthy wood (called scions) are easily grafted onto the rooted stem of a compatible plant (called an *understock)*, which is usually a seedling of a closely related tree. For example, a scion from 'Sargent's' weeping hemlock will graft onto the understock of a Canadian hemlock and the top will be weeping. Graft a pink dogwood scion onto a white dogwood understock and the top will produce pink flowers.

Many kinds of grafts are possible, but the two most commonly used are *bud grafts* and *cleft grafts*.

Bud Grafts—Only one leaf bud is needed to make a bud graft onto the understock branch, called a *bud stick*. A sharp knife is used to cut a shield-shaped section of bark with each bud. These sections are usually 1 inch long, 1/4 to 1/2 inches wide, and tapered at each end. The cut section of bark must be deep enough to include the green cambium layer and just a small sliver of wood. Choose a scion with plump buds that are dormant. If the bud is in a leaf axil with the leaf still attached, cut off the leaf, leaving about 1/4 inch of stem showing, because this helps in handling the scion and offers some protection for the bud.

You can use seedlings or rooted cuttings for understocks. In either case, the understock should be about the thickness of a pencil.

Use a sharp knife or razor blade to make a T-shaped cut in the bark of the understock. The stem of the T should be 1-1/2 inches long and positioned about midway down the stem of the understock. The crosscut of the T should be about 1/2 inch wide and extend one third the way around the understock. Cut only into the bark and cambium. Do not cut into the wood.

Using the point of your blade, lift the bark along both sides of the vertical cut to create flaps and insert the bud scion so it fits snuggly under the flaps, flat against the bare wood. Wrap grafting tape or a rubber band around the stem, above and below the bud.

In 3 to 5 weeks the bud should be united with the understock and the wrapping can be removed. Buds will remain dormant until the following season. To encourage the bud to sprout in spring, cut off the top of the understock about 1/2 inches above the grafted bud. All growth from the bud graft will be identical to the bud-source parent.

Cleft Grafts—With a cleft graft, the scion is usually a piece of branch about 3 inches long with several buds along its length. The lower end is cut to form a wedge shape, with the bottom of the wedge 1 inch above the lowest bud. The scion wood should be taken from the previous year's growth. It should be hard, woody and dormant.

To prepare the understock, cut it level, as shown in the drawing on the facing page. Use a chisel or knife to split the end open, then pry open the split to make a V. Insert the wedge-shaped end of the scion into the V of the understock. Position the scion at one edge of the cut so its cambium layer touches the cambium layer of the understock. The cambium is the green area under the bark.

The scion should be firmly seated in the cut. If it feels loose, tighten it with a rubber band. Keep the graft shaded until a good union has been established. To prevent the graft from drying out, coat the cut surfaces with grafting wax avail-

LAYERING

SOIL LAYERING

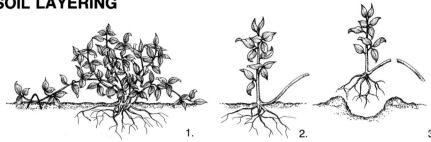

1. Select flexible stem and bend to soil. Scrape bark from underside of stem where it contacts soil, and secure stem with wire pin or stone. 2. Stem will sprout roots where it contacts soil and top will sprout new leaves. 3. When layered stem is large enough to transplant, cut from parent plant and transplant.

AIR LAYERING

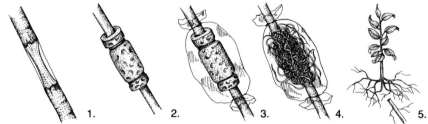

1. Scrape bark from 1-inch section of stem. Dust wounded area with rooting hormone. 2. Wrap moist kitchen sponge around scraped section. Secure with rubber bands. 3. Cover sponge with plastic sandwich bag or clear plastic wrap and secure with rubber bands. 4. Examine for root formation every 2 weeks. 5. When roots have filled bag, cut layer from parent plant and transplant.

able from garden centers.

Usually, two scions are wedged into each understock. At the end of the first growing season the weaker graft is pruned off and the cut treated with grafting wax.

LAYERING

Many woody plants—particularly shrubs with pliable branches—can be reproduced by layering. There are two kinds of layering—*soil layering* and *air layering*.

Soil layering is achieved by taking a pliable branch and bending it to the ground. A scratch or wound is made on the underside of the branch with a penknife, and the scratched section is pegged against the ground with a forked stick. Cover the scratched section with a layer of loose organic material such as peat or compost and keep the area of contact moist. Rubbing the wound with rooting hormone encourages rooting.

After the branch has rooted it can be detached and transplanted.

Layering is most successful when done in spring or early summer. New plants should not be removed from the parent until the following spring. After cutting the rooted plant free of the parent, leave it in place 2 to 3 weeks before digging it up for transplanting.

Air layering can be done with container plants or with branches that cannot be bent to the ground. This method is particularly successful when practiced on indoor trees such as rubber plants.

With air layering, the simplest method is to select a healthy branch and girdle it with a knife, creating a notch all the way around the stem at a point midway between a pair of leaf nodes. Dab the notch with rooting hormone and wrap a moist household sponge around the cut portion, somewhat like wrapping a hot-dog bun around a hot dog. Use a rubber band to hold the sponge in place.

Or, you can wrap the cut with moist sphagnum moss. Cover the sponge or sphagnum with plastic wrap and tie the ends above and below the cut. When a healthy mass of roots has developed, sever the stem below the root mass, unwrap the plastic, soak new root mass in water for 6 hours and plant.

Encyclopedia of Ornamental Trees & Shrubs

The following encyclopedia includes more than 200 separate species or distinct varieties of trees and shrubs. They are arranged alphabetically by botanical (Latin) name, with the exception of azaleas, bamboo and palms. Although azaleas belong to the genus *Rhododendron,* they are a large, distinct group of plants within that genus, so it seemed best to list them by their common name (page 74). Members of the palm family are represented by several genera, but most have similar habit and landscape uses—most are confined to frost-free areas or grown indoors—so selected garden-worthy palms are grouped together on pages 126-127. Bamboo describes a large group of woody members of the grass family, also represented by several genera. These are described on page 75.

If you know a tree or shrub only by its common name—oak or boxwood, for example—refer to the index on page 158 to find its botanical name. In botanical nomenclature, plants are identified by the *genus* name and the *species* name. For instance, the genus name for all oaks is *Quercus*. The California live oak is identified by the botanical name *Quer-*

cus agrifolia. Plants are further divided into varieties or cultivars within the species, such as *Aucuba japonica* 'Variegata'. Acuba japonica identifies the gold dust plant (species) and 'Variegata' describes a particular variety of gold dust plant that has smooth, green leaves with yellow spots. Botanical nomenclature and plant classification is discussed in more detail on page 66.

Hardiness—This term refers to a plant's ability to survive cold temperatures—the lower the minimum winter temperature a plant can survive, the hardier it is. Generally speaking, a *hardy* plant is one that can survive temperatures below freezing (32F/0C), while a *tender* plant cannot.

Though most trees and shrubs listed in this encyclopedia are hardy, some of them are tender, such as crape myrtle and bougainvillea. These plants may tolerate light frosts, but generally grow well only in mild-winter climates such as coastal California and the South. A few are so tender they will survive only in frost-free areas, such as Southern California and the Gulf Coast, but they are such spectacular plants that they deserve to be featured in this book.

The *zones* listed for each plant correlate with the USDA plant-hardiness zone map on page 39. The map defines climate zones in the United States and southern Canada, based on minimum winter temperatures. For instance, if a

particular plant is cold-hardy to Zone 4, that means it can survive a minimum winter temperature between -30 to -20F. This does not mean that the plant will necessarily grow in *all zones* with higher minimum temperatures than this because other factors, such as summer heat, humidity and soil conditions, also determine a plant's adaptability to a particular area.

In this encyclopedia, rather than simply listing the coldest zone in which a certain plant will survive, a range has been given that also indicates the *warmest zone* in which that plant will grow. Still, the zone allocations should be used as a general guideline only, due to the factors mentioned above. For example, much of the Gulf Coast and portions of the Southwest desert are both in Zone 9, but growing conditions are radically different, due to the extreme contrasts in humidity and rainfall patterns between the two regions.

Height and Size—The size of a plant is determined by its height and spread at maturity. However, within important plant groups, especially conifers, there are many dwarf varieties that are suitable for small spaces. Also, the size of many trees and shrubs can be controlled by pruning. Soil type, rainfall and other climatic factors can have an influence on size. The sizes given in this encyclopedia are those attained under average growing conditions. Under ideal con-

Left: Like a beacon of fire, sugar maple *(Acer saccharum)* undergoes one of the most beautiful color changes in fall. See page 69 for description.

Flowers of *Abelia* ×*grandiflora*.

BOTANICAL NOMENCLATURE

Horticulturists identify plants by their scientific or botanical names. A plant is identified by both its genus and species name, set in italics. Cultivar names within a species are set off in single quotes. The system of identifying and classifying plants by botanical names is called *taxonomy*.

Genus (plural genera)—This term defines a large group of plants that share certain basic characteristics. For example, there are about 450 kinds of oak trees and all belong to the genus *Quercus*.

Species—This describes a distinct type of plant within a genus. For example, *Quercus robur* (English oak) is a species native to Europe, particularly England.

Variety—In the strict botanical sense, the term *variety* denotes a natural variation within a species. For example, the common white dogwood (species) is known botanically as *Cornus florida,* but the pink-flowering dogwood is considered a natural variation identified as *Cornus florida* var. *rubra.*

Cultivar—When a variety has resulted from selection among cultivated plants, then the term *cultivar*—meaning cultivated variety—

is sometimes used instead of the term *variety.* For example, the red-flowering dogwood 'Cherokee Chief'—a selection from the pink variety—is considered a *cultivar* and is written botanically as *Cornus florida* 'Cherokee Chief'. In this and other modern books, the term variety is used to mean both natural varieties and cultivars, although cultivars are readily identified by the name set off in single quotes, as in 'Cherokee Chief' above.

Hybrids—These are plants that result from crossing two distinctly different plants. They can be crosses between plants of different genera *(bigeneric hybrids),* different species, between a species and a hybrid or between two hybrids. To denote a hybrid, the botanical name includes the symbol "×." For example, ×*Cupressocyparis leylandi* denotes a cross between two genera, in this case between *Cupressus macrocarpa* (Monterey cypress) and *Chamaecyparis nootkatensis* (Nootka false cypress). When the × appears in the middle of a name, it denotes a hybrid within the same genera, usually between two species, cultivars or hybrids. For example, *Cytisus* ×*praecox* denotes hybrid between two species of *Cytisus,* in this case a hybrid variety of Scotch broom.

Strain—A group of plants, usually within a species, with common lineage.

ditions, trees and shrubs may grow bigger than the sizes given here, and under adverse conditions—poor soil in particular—they may grow smaller.

Growth Rate—General terms such as *fast growing, medium-fast growing* and *slow growing* are sometimes used for describing growth rates of trees and shrubs. Trees tend to be fast growing in their juvenile years (the first 3 or 4 years especially) then slow down and spread out. A tree that grows 4 feet or more a year during its juvenile years, such as tulip poplars and paulownias, would be considered fast growing. Trees that grow 2 to 4 feet a year are medium-fast growing, those that grow less than 2 feet a year are slow growing.

A different scale of reference applies to shrubs. Slow-growing shrubs are those that put on less than 1 foot growth a year—boxwood is considered extremely slow-growing at only 1 inch a year. Medium-fast growing shrubs grow 1 to 2 feet a year, fast-growing shrubs 2 or more feet a year. Vining shrubs capable of growing 6 to 10 feet or more a year—such as trumpet creeper—are considered extra-fast growing.

Variety Recommendations—Some descriptions give specific variety recommendations, with an explanation for why they are considered superior for landscape use. The 'Bradford' form of Callery pear and 'Sargent's Weeping' form of hemlock are examples of trees that are so outstanding that they rate special mention.

It is impossible in a book of this scope to feature every species and variety deemed "garden worthy." The primary criteria used in the following selection is *ornamental value*—plants that are either attractive and useful as *shade* trees or ones that have decorative flowers, leaves or berries. However, you'll find a broad range of trees and shrubs for many landscape uses. The selection represents a cross-section of trees and shrubs suitable to a wide range of climates and soil conditions. In the following listing, symbols identify plants as trees or shrubs:

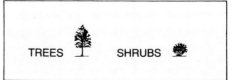

TREES   SHRUBS

ABELIA X GRANDIFLORA
Glossy Abelia

Reasonably hardy semi-evergreen flowering shrub hybridized from species native to Asia. Plants grow 3 to 6 feet high and equally wide, creating a spreading, dense rounded habit. The shiny green, oval leaves turn bronze by late summer, making a bold contrast to the pinkish-white, trumpet-shaped flowers that are 3/4 inches wide, held in clusters and persisting all summer.

How to Grow—Plant from containers. Propagated mostly from softwood cuttings. Prefers moist, well-drained, acid soil in full sun or partial shade. Grows from Zones 6 to 10.

Landscape Use—Excellent flowering hedge. Mass plantings good for erosion control on slopes.

Abies concolor (white fir) growing as a grove.

ABIES CONCOLOR
White Fir

Firs consist of about 40 species of evergreen conifers, widely dispersed throughout the Northern Hemisphere, including North America. White fir is native to Colorado and high-elevation areas of California. Conical in habit, it is slow growing to 100 feet and spreads 40 feet. Numerous related species and varieties are popular as landscape plants, including prostrate and pendulous forms. Two widely planted species are Balsam fir *(A. balsamea)*, valued for its fragrant balsam odor, and Fraser fir *(A. fraseri)*, which is popular as a Christmas tree. Douglas fir belongs to a different genus *(Pseudotsuga menziesii)* and is described on page 138.

How to Grow—Plant balled-and-burlapped or from bare-root stock. White fir tolerates summer heat and drought but must have some winter chill. Fraser and balsam firs prefer moist, well-drained, acid soil that is rich in humus. Grows from Zones 3 to 7.

Landscape Use—Lawn highlight, skyline tree and windbreak.

ACACIA LONGIFOLIA
Sydney Golden Wattle

Tender evergreen flowering shade trees native to Australia, popular in frost-free locations such as Florida and California. Trees grow to 25 feet high, spread 25 feet, have graceful willowlike blue-green leaves. Weeping branches erupt into a billowing mass of yellow pompon flowers in early spring. A related species, *A. baileyana*—known as Bailey acacia or Cootamondra Wattle—is very similar in appearance, but with greener, fernlike foliage. Plants are reasonably fast growing, shallow rooted and not long lived.

How to Grow — Plant from containers or balled-and-burlapped.

Propagated mostly from seeds and softwood cuttings taken in summer. Can be pruned after flowering to main-

Acacia longifolia (Sydney golden wattle tree) in flower under glass at Longwood Gardens, Pennsylvania.

Acer palmatum 'Dissectum Atropurpureum' (Japanese threadleaf maple) showing purple summer foliage.

Acer platanoides (Norway maple) in summer on the author's lawn.

tain a compact shape. Prefers sandy, moist soil. Tolerates salt spray. Susceptible to scale pests (see page 57 for controls). Grows in Zones 8 to 10.

Landscape Use — Sensational street tree and lawn highlight. In Northern states often grown in tubs under glass for winter flowers.

ACER
Maples

About 115 species of maples are distributed worldwide, in Europe, Asia and North America. They range in size from the silver maple—a large forest tree—to the low, bushy Japanese maples, which are valued as ornamental shrubs. The large winged seeds, called *keys,* are readily dispersed by the wind. With most species, the fall foliage is extremely colorful. Following are the most popular maples for home gardens:

JAPANESE MAPLE *(Acer palmatum* and *A. japonicum)*

Though two species of maple are commonly called Japanese maple, it is *A. palmatum*—also known as cutleaf maple—that is familiar to most people and more widely planted. *A. japonicum,* also known as full-moon maple, generally has broader, less-indented leaves, and grows slightly higher. Culture is generally the same for both species. The following description applies to *A. palmatum.* The variety 'Senkaki' has red branches, excellent for winter color.

Reasonably hardy deciduous ornamental shrub or small tree native to Japan. Superb landscape plant for many situations. Very graceful foliage and plant habit. Grows to 20 feet, spreads 20 feet or more. Beautiful rounded shape, sharply indented leaves that are usually purple or limegreen in color, depending on the variety, changing to orange in fall. Small, purple, inconspicuous flowers are followed by small, paired winged seeds formed in clusters. Plant is slow growing, shallow rooted, long lived. Numerous varieties are available. 'Dissectum' is a strain known as lace-leaf and thread-leaf maples, for their finely cut, feathery leaves.

How to Grow—Best planted from containers or balled-and-burlapped. Propagated from seeds and from bud grafts. Prefers fertile, acid loam or sandy soil in full sun or filtered light, sheltered from wind. Grows from Zones 5 to 9 and parts of Zone 10 on the West Coast.

Landscape Use—Superb lawn highlight. Popular for bonsai and sculptural pruning. Also widely used as container plants for decorating decks and patios.

NORWAY MAPLE *(Acer platanoides)*

Hardy deciduous shade tree native to Europe. Vigorous, pollution resistant, growing 50 to 60 feet high, spreading 35 to 45 feet. Five-lobed, dark green leaves have sharp tips, and change to yellow and orange in fall. Clusters of small, greenish-yellow flowers appear in spring as the leaves start to unfurl and are more conspicuous than those of most other maples. Large bunches

of winged seeds change color from green through pink to brown, dispersing by wind in fall. Billowing, rounded habit, medium-fast growth, shallow rooted, long lived.
How to Grow—Plant balled-and-burlapped or from bare-root stock. Propagated by seeds, which germinate at low soil temperatures (40F/4C). Does well in a wide range of soils, including alkaline soil. Tolerates dry conditions better than most maples. Needs full sun. Grows from Zones 3 to 7.
Landscape Use—Lawn highlight, street tree, windbreak. Good choice for creating a wooded lot, though it casts such dense shade few plants can grow under its canopy.

RED MAPLE (Acer rubrum)

Hardy deciduous shade tree native to eastern North America. Derives its name from the rich, red flowers that appear in early spring even before the leaves unfold. Also called swamp maple because of its natural distribution along stream banks and areas subjected to periodic flooding. Grows 50 to 80 feet high, spreads 40 to 60 feet. Attractive oval or rounded habit. Dark green leaves are typical maple-leaf shape, turning orange or scarlet-red in fall. Dull, red-winged seeds turn brown before dispersal by the wind. Medium-fast growth, fairly deep rooted, long lived.
How to Grow—Plant balled-and-burlapped or from bare-root stock. Propagated from seeds, cuttings and grafts. Prefers fertile, moist, acid soil that is rich in humus, but also thrives in many poor soils. Grows in sun or partial shade. Grows from Zones 3 to 9.
Landscape Use—Good lawn highlight and windbreak. Superb for lining vistas and driveways. Popular choice for creating a wooded lot. Not highly pollution tolerant.

SILVER MAPLE (Acer saccharinum)

Hardy deciduous shade tree native to eastern North America. Flexible branches sway in the wind, flashing the bright, silvery undersides of the otherwise medium-green leaves. Grows 60 to 90 feet, spreads 50 to 80 feet. Upright, oval habit. Small, inconspicuous, greenish-yellow flowers are borne before the leaves unfold in spring. Seeds are winged, but not showy. Fast growth, fairly deeply rooted, long lived.
How to Grow—Plant balled-and-burlapped or from bare-root stock. Propagated mostly from seeds, but also layering and cuttings. Prefers deep, moist, acid soil though it tolerates poor soils. Grows in sun or partial shade. Grows from Zones 3 to 9.
Landscape Use—Lawn highlight, windbreak. Some experts consider this a "weed tree" because of its greedy roots and ability to self-seed, but it is popular in suburban gardens and admired for its leaves that sway in the slightest breeze, reflecting sunlight off their silvery undersides.

SUGAR MAPLE (Acer saccharum)

Hardy deciduous shade tree native to eastern North America. Source of maple syrup, produced by tapping the trees for their watery sap during winter months. Grows 70 to 80 feet, spreads 40 to 60 feet. Beautiful rounded or oval

Acer rubrum (red maple) showing fall colors.

Acer saccharinum (silver maple) flashes silvery leaves when the wind blows.

Aesculus hippocastanum (European horsechestnut) in full flower.

habit. Medium-green leaves are typical maple shape, sharply pointed, changing to yellow and orange-red in fall. Greenish-yellow flowers appear in early spring before the leaves unfold, followed by winged seeds. Fairly slow growing, fairly deeply rooted, long lived.

How to Grow—Plant balled-and-burlapped or from bare-root stock. Propagated mostly from seeds, budding and layering. Prefers fertile, moist, acid loam soil in sun or light shade. Leaf scorch is a problem in dry soils. Grows from Zones 3 to 8.

Landscape Use—Favorite choice for creating a wooded lot. Good lawn highlight and windbreak.

AESCULUS HIPPOCASTANUM
European Horsechestnut

Hardy deciduous flowering shade tree native to Greece and Albania. Grows 60 to 70 feet, spreads 40 to 60 feet. Beautiful upright, rounded habit. Oval, serrated leaflets are arranged in groups of five or six, splayed out like a hand. White flowers appear in spring, borne in long, conical clusters known as *candles,* up to 12 inches long. Red and pink flowering varieties are available. Flowers are followed by spiny, round nut cases that split open to release a single, shiny brown nut in fall. Grows moderately fast, deep rooted, long lived.

How to Grow—Best planted balled-and-burlapped. Propagated from seeds except for named varieties, which are budded or grafted. Thrives in any deep, fertile, moist soil in full sun. Bagworm and borers can be serious pests (see page 55). Grows from Zones 3 to 7.

AILANTHUS ALTISSIMA
Tree of Heaven

Hardy deciduous shade tree native to China. Grows 40 to 60 feet high, spreads 30 to 50 feet. Compound dark green leaves resemble those of sumac. Yellowish-green flowers are borne in large clusters, males and females on separate trees. Female flowers are followed by reddish-brown winged seeds borne in clusters, persisting into fall. Rate of growth is very fast—up to 6 feet a year in its juvenile years. Roots run deep.

How to Grow—Plant from containers or from bare-root stock. Propagated from seeds and cuttings taken from female plants, because the odor from male flowers is unpleasant. Plants tolerate a wide range of soils, even poor soil, though they do best in light, moist, sandy soil. Prefers full sun. Grows from Zones 4 to 10.

Landscape Use—Extremely tolerant of industrial pollution. Widely used as a street tree. Takes heavy pruning. Some experts consider Tree of Heaven a "weed tree" because of its ability to naturalize on vacant city lots and come back even after being cut back to the ground. However, it does have its admirers, and is often planted for fast shade in extremely poor soils.

Ailanthus altissima (tree of heaven) at Paso Robles, California, in 110F heat.

ALBIZIA JULIBRISSIN
Silk Tree

Reasonably hardy deciduous flowering shade tree native to Asia, where more than 100 related species are distributed from Iran to Japan. Also known as mimosa tree. Plants grow to 30 feet high, spread 40 feet, creating an airy canopy of feathery, fernlike leaves made up of small, oval, overlapping leaflets. The pink powderpuff flowers appear in midsummer, followed by long, slender seed pods filled with bean-size seeds.

'Tyron' (light pink) and 'Charlotte' (deep pink) are outstanding disease-resistant varieties.

How to Grow — Plant from containers. Propagated mostly from seeds. Prefers a sandy or loam soil in a sunny, open location. Tolerates drought and pollution. Grows from Zones 6 to 10.

Landscape Use — Light, airy tree for tropical effect. You can let grass grow right up to trunk. Excellent for shading lawns and patios. Good skyline tree.

ALSOPHILA COOPERI
Australian Tree Fern

Tender evergreen shade tree native to Australia. Plants grow to 20 feet high, with a slender, fibrous, palmlike trunk and a crown of light green fronds that cascade like a fountain. Similar widely grown species include West Indian tree fern *(Cyathea arborea),* Hawaiian tree fern *(Cibotium glaucum)* and Tasmanian tree fern *(Dicksonia antarctica).*

How to Grow — Best planted from containers. Propagated from spores or offsets. Plants need a humid atmosphere and acid, humus-rich soil in sun or light shade. Grows in Zones 9 and 10.

Landscape Use — Mostly grown in clumps in atriums and courtyards where irrigation is readily available to meet their high moisture requirements. Outdoors it is restricted mostly to coastal California and southern Florida. Popular container plant for conservatories in Northern climates.

AMELANCHIER LAEVIS
Sarvistree

Hardy deciduous flowering tree native to North America from Maine to South Carolina. Also called serviceberry, shadblow and Juneberry, it is among the first trees to flower in early spring, covering itself in snow-white blossoms resembling those of crabapples. These are followed by small, purple, edible fruits. Forms a rounded crown and multiple trunks, but can be pruned to a single trunk. Grows to 30 feet, spreads 20 feet. The oval, pointed leaves turn yellow, orange and red in fall.

How to Grow — Plant from containers or bare-root stock. Propagated from seeds, suckers and grafts. Plants tolerate poor soil and prefer sun or partial shade. Grows from Zones 3 to 8.

Albizia julibrissin (silk tree) showing silky pink flower plumes.

Amelanchier laevis (sarvistree) in full flower. Edible fruits resemble blueberries.

Aralia spinosa (devil's walking stick) has tropical-looking foliage.

Araucaria araucana (monkey puzzle tree) towers above a home near San Francisco.

Landscape Use — Good lawn highlight. Looks attractive in mixed-shrub borders. Especially lovely planted as a grove of three or more trees at the edge of a lawn.

ARALIA SPINOSA
Devil's Walking Stick

Small, hardy deciduous tree native to North America from Pennsylvania to Florida and east to Iowa. Also known as Hercules' club because the trunk and branches are armed with vicious spines. Plants grow 10 to 20 feet high. Leaves have a tropical appearance, growing from multiple slender trunks. Panicles of white flowers cover the topmost branches in summer, followed in fall by purple- black fruit clusters resembling huge bunches of elderberries, which are relished by birds. A taller-growing related species from Japan *(A. alata)* has variegated leaves.

How to Grow — Plant from containers. Mostly propagated from root division. Tolerates a wide variety of soils, even poor and alkaline soil in full sun or partial shade. Grows from Zones 4 to 9.

Landscape Use — Good background plant, forming an impenetrable thicket of tropical-looking foliage. Many experts consider it a "weed tree" too aggressive for most outdoor situations, but it can be effective when confined to an atrium or bordering a patio.

ARAUCARIAS

Three kinds of *Araucarias* are popular in mild-climate areas of North America — mostly Southern California and Florida. They are the bunya-bunya tree, the monkey puzzle tree and Norfolk Island pine. All are tender, evergreen trees.

BUNYA-BUNYA *(A. bidwillii)*

Evergreen conifer native to Australia. Plants are moderately fast growing, with a dense, billowing, pyramidal shape, to 60 feet high, spreading 35 feet. Has upward-curving branches and coarse, dark green, scalelike needles. Produces very large cones (up to 20 pounds).

How to Grow — Plant from containers. Tolerates dry and alkaline soil, making it popular in desert areas. Prefers full sun. Grows in Zone 9 and parts of 10.

Landscape Use — Good lawn highlight. Excellent windbreak.

MONKEY PUZZLE *(A. araucana)*

Slow-growing, evergreen conifer native to Chile. Plants are pyramidal-shaped in their juvenile stage, maturing into giant trees 60 to 70 feet high with a 30-foot-wide domed canopy. Female trees bear large coconut-size cones. Knifelike, dark green scales point upward so that animals—such as monkeys—can climb up but cannot shinny back down.

How to Grow—Plant from containers. Prefers moist, sandy or loam soil in a sunny location. Grows from Zone 7 to 10.

Landscape Use—Good lawn specimen. Not for confined spaces. Marvelous skyline silhouette.

NORFOLK ISLAND PINE (A. heterophylla)

Evergreen conifer native to Norfolk Island in the South Pacific. Popular throughout North America as house plants because of their low light tolerance. Popular outdoors in frost-free areas, particularly Southern California and Southern Florida but will take light frosts. Moderately fast growing to 80 feet high, spreading 20 feet. From a distance, mature plants look like slender feathers. Branches sweep upward, coming to a sharp point.

How to Grow—Plant from containers. Plants tolerate a wide range of soil conditions, including sandy and alkaline soil in sun or partial shade. Grows in Zones 9 and 10.

Landscape Use—Excellent lawn specimen. Popular container tree to decorate patios and atriums. Excellent for coastal gardens. Magnificent skyline silhouette.

ARBUTUS UNEDO
Strawberry Tree

Tender broadleaf evergreen bush capable of becoming a small tree. Native to Europe. Derives its common name from the clusters of strawberrylike fruits that ripen in summer. White flowers are decorative, small and urn-shaped. New growth of green leaves exhibits a reddish cast. Slow growing to 20 feet high, spreading 20 feet. 'Compacta' and 'Elfin King' are good dwarf forms. A related species, *A. menziesii*, (madrone) is native to the Pacific Northwest and California, and is noted for its attractive, peeling red bark.

How to Grow — Plant from containers. Propagated from seeds. Prefers sandy or loam soil in full sun, and regular moisture. Needs lower branch pruning to form an attractive tree. Does best in coastal gardens. Grows from Zones 7 to 10.

Landscape Use — Attractive lawn highlight. Good for mixed-shrub borders.

AUCUBA JAPONICA
Gold Dust Plant

Hardy slow-growing broadleaf evergreen shrub native to Japan. Derives its common name for the variegated leaves that are flecked with yellow. Grows to 10 feet high, spreads 8 feet, but generally kept shorter by shearing. Different varieties have different variegation but the common 'Variegata' has smooth, shiny green leaves covered with golden spots. 'Picturata' has golden yellow centers and green leaf margins.

Araucaria heterophylla (Norfolk Island pine) is a favorite spire-shaped evergreen for frost-free areas.

Arbutus unedo (strawberry tree) showing close-up of ripe, edible fruits, for which it gets its common name.

Aucuba japonica 'Variegata' (gold dust plant) is a hardy evergreen with broad, gold-flecked leaves.

How to Grow—Plant from containers. Cuttings root easily taken any time of year. Prefers moist, humus-rich, acid soil in a sheltered, lightly shaded location. Grows from Zones 6 to 10.

Landscape Use—Popular for foundation plantings, especially in shrub borders combined with rhododendrons and dwarf conifers. Beyond its hardiness range it can be grown indoors in containers.

AZALEA
Rhododendron Species

At one time azaleas and rhododendrons were thought to belong to different plant genera, but botanists have decided azaleas are really a small-leafed, compact type of rhododendron. There are two basic kinds of azaleas—evergreen and deciduous. The evergreen species are mostly native to Asia, and the deciduous species mostly native to North America.

Azaleas are much more popular as landscape plants than true rhododendrons, chiefly because they are less demanding of cool temperatures and high rainfall. In the Deep South and Southern California it is the evergreen *R. indicum* (Southern Indian azalea) that is most popular because of its large, showy flowers. In the North, the evergreen Kurume azaleas are preferred for their hardiness. Kaempferi hybrids, Gable hybrids and Glenn Dale hybrids are other popular evergreen groups.

Hardy deciduous azaleas include the *R. mollis* types, Exbury hybrids and Knap Hill hybrids.

Flowers on evergreen azaleas are mostly star-shaped and come in white and shades of pink, red and purple. Many of the deciduous azaleas have funnel-shaped flowers, like honeysuckle, and the color range includes yellow. Height ranges from 1 foot to 10 feet high depending on variety, but most plants normally are kept pruned to 3 to 6 feet high.

How to Grow—Plant from containers. Propagated mostly from seeds and cuttings. Plants prefer acid, humus-rich soil in light shade. Should be protected from direct sun and drying winds.

The majority of azalea varieties have exacting climate requirements. Native azalea-growing areas include the mid-Atlantic coast, Pacific Northwest, Southern Appalachian Mountains and swampy areas of the South. The best way to choose varieties for your area is to visit a specialist azalea grower or check with your local university or county extension agent. Though no single variety is adaptable to all areas of North America, by careful selection, azaleas can be grown from Canada to southern Florida.

Landscape Use—Undoubtedly the most popular of all flowering shrubs for foundation plantings. Excellent for mass plantings on slopes, in island beds and mixed-shrub borders.

Azalea stewartstonian has evergreen foliage, creates dome of brick-red flowers in spring. It is kept compact by shearing.

BAMBOO
Arundinaria and Phyllostachys Species

Native mostly to Asia, bamboos comprise a large number of genera, including *Arundinaria, Bambusa, Phyllostachys* and *Sasa*—the four most widely planted groups in North America. They are woody, evergreen members of the grass family, and though dwarf kinds suitable as ground covers are available, bamboos mostly form tall canes topped with willowy leaves. Some are *clump-forming* and stay within bounds. Others are *running,* using vigorous underground rhizomes to spread in all directions.

Most bamboos are tender plants, but a few are sufficiently hardy to withstand temperatures of -20F (-29C) and even lower in sheltered sites.

Arundinaria variegata (dwarf white-stripe bamboo) grows a low mounded clump of striped green and white leaves, 3 to 4 feet high. *Phyllostachys aureosulcata* (yellow groove bamboo) grows to 30 feet high, has beautiful green canes striped golden yellow. Both are hardy, and though tops may be damaged by freezing, they recover quickly.

How to Grow—Transplant from containers. Propagated by division. Bamboos grow in most soils, except heavy clay and waterlogged soil. All need full sun, tolerate high heat and humidity. Hardy bamboos will grow in zone 5, but bamboos generally are most prevalent in Zone 8 south.

Landscape Use—*Arundinaria variegata* makes a fine specimen shrub for tubs and mixed-shrub borders. *Phyllostachys aureosulcata* forms runner-type clumps and is best used as a grove.

Yellow groove bamboo *(Phyllostachys aureosulcata)* is more cold-hardy than most other bamboos and grows up to 30 feet.

BAUHINIA BLAKEANA
Hong Kong Orchid Tree

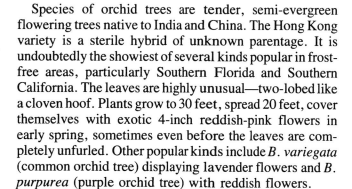

Species of orchid trees are tender, semi-evergreen flowering trees native to India and China. The Hong Kong variety is a sterile hybrid of unknown parentage. It is undoubtedly the showiest of several kinds popular in frost-free areas, particularly Southern Florida and Southern California. The leaves are highly unusual—two-lobed like a cloven hoof. Plants grow to 30 feet, spread 20 feet, cover themselves with exotic 4-inch reddish-pink flowers in early spring, sometimes even before the leaves are completely unfurled. Other popular kinds include *B. variegata* (common orchid tree) displaying lavender flowers and *B. purpurea* (purple orchid tree) with reddish flowers.

How to Grow—Plant from containers. Propagated by cuttings, the species mostly from seeds. Tolerates a wide range of soils, particularly dry, sandy soil, in full sun or partial shade. Temperatures below 25F (4C) will kill the tree. Grows in Zone 10 and frost-protected areas in Zone 9.

Landscape Use—Good lawn highlight and street tree.

In frost-free areas, *Bauhinia blakeana* (Hong Kong orchid tree) flaunts orchidlike flowers in early spring.

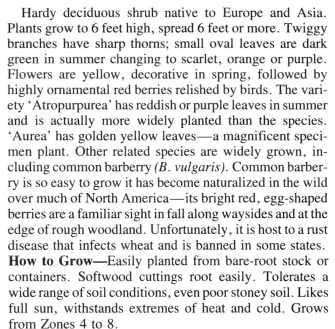

BERBERIS THUNBERGII
Japanese Barberry

Hardy deciduous shrub native to Europe and Asia. Plants grow to 6 feet high, spread 6 feet or more. Twiggy branches have sharp thorns; small oval leaves are dark green in summer changing to scarlet, orange or purple. Flowers are yellow, decorative in spring, followed by highly ornamental red berries relished by birds. The variety 'Atropurpurea' has reddish or purple leaves in summer and is actually more widely planted than the species. 'Aurea' has golden yellow leaves—a magnificent specimen plant. Other related species are widely grown, including common barberry *(B. vulgaris)*. Common barberry is so easy to grow it has become naturalized in the wild over much of North America—its bright red, egg-shaped berries are a familiar sight in fall along waysides and at the edge of rough woodland. Unfortunately, it is host to a rust disease that infects wheat and is banned in some states.

How to Grow—Easily planted from bare-root stock or containers. Softwood cuttings root easily. Tolerates a wide range of soil conditions, even poor stoney soil. Likes full sun, withstands extremes of heat and cold. Grows from Zones 4 to 8.

Landcape Use—Good specimen plant for mixed-shrub borders. Excellent hedge. Dwarf forms such as 'Crimson Pygmy' make good ground covers.

BETULA
Birches

About 40 species of birches are widely dispersed throughout North America, Europe and Asia. The two most widely planted in North American gardens are paper birch and silver birch (European white birch). The term "white birch" is used fairly indiscriminately to describe any species of birch with white bark.

PAPER BIRCH *(Betula papyrifera)*

Hardy deciduous shade tree native to North America. Also called canoe birch because the bark is waterproof and was used by Indians to make birch-bark canoes. The smooth, brilliant white bark peels in paperlike layers. Grows 50 to 70 feet high, spreads 30 to 55 feet. Upright habit when young, rounded crown when mature. Dark green leaves are rounded, sharply pointed and serrated, turning bright yellow in fall. Flowers are small, yellowish catkins, forming small nutlets. Moderately fast growth, fairly deep rooted, short lived.

How to Grow—Plant balled-and-burlapped. Propagated from seed. Prefers acid sandy or loam soil in full sun. Needs good drainage but likes moisture. More resistant to borers than other birches. Grows from Zones 2 to 6.

Landscape Use—Excellent lawn highlight. Looks especially attractive when the top is pruned to a rounded shape to make a *pollarded* tree.

Berberis thunbergii (Japanese barberry) displays bright red berries that persist into winter, long after the leaves have fallen.

Betula papyifera (canoe birch) is a popular lawn highlight.

SILVER BIRCH *(Betula pendula)*

Hardy deciduous shade tree native to Sweden. Also known as European white birch. Grows 40 to 50 feet, spreads 25 to 40 feet. Decorative bark is silvery white, blackens with age. Graceful, rounded habit, branches weeping. Medium green leaves are deeply lobed and serrated. Has poor fall color. Flowers are small, yellowish catkins that form small nutlets. Medium fast growth, fairly deeply rooted, short lived.

How to Grow—Plant balled-and-burlapped, though bare-root stock is available. Succeeds in poor soil, including sandy soil. Needs full sun. Susceptible to borers and leaf miners (see pages 55-56). Grows from Zones 3 to 5.

BOUGAINVILLEA SPECTABILIS
Bougainvillea

Native to South America, this vigorous evergreen flowering vine is one of the most spectacular flowering plants for relatively frost-free areas of the United States, such as Southern Florida and California. Most are sprawling plants that can be used as ground covers or trained to climb so their sharp thorns can hook onto a trellis. Some varieties grow as mounded shrubs. Colors include magenta, orange, gold and white.

'San Diego Red' is one of the hardier vining varieties and recovers quickly from frost. The color does not actually come from flowers, but papery *bracts*, which are specialized leaves that enclose a flower. As vines, plants can grow to 10 feet or more.

How to Grow—Plant from containers. Propagated from cuttings and layering. Tolerates a wide range of soil conditions in sun or partial shade, though best growth is assured from soils with high humus content. Frequent pruning will stimulate plants to flower continuously all year, since flowers are produced on new growth. Tolerates salt spray. Widely used in coastal gardens. Grows in Zones 9 and 10.

Landscape Use—Can be planted to form a dense hedge, though most often used as a flowering vine to climb up a trellis against walls. Good to cover dry slopes. Excellent for tubs and even hanging baskets. 'La Jolla' with red bracts and other shrublike varieties can be used as foundation plants and lawn specimens. 'Crimson Jewel' is a dwarf form that is excellent for hanging baskets.

BUDDLEIA DAVIDII
Butterfly Bush

Hardy flowering deciduous shrub native to China. As the common name suggests, it is attractive to butterflies. It grows to 10 feet high and 10 feet wide, producing a thicket of slender, arching stems. Fragrant flowers have a lilac-like scent and appear in midsummer on new growth. Colors include pink, purple, magenta and white. The variety 'Dubonnet' has extra-large, dark purple flowers up to 10 inches long.

Bougainvillea 'San Diego' creates a beautiful mounded shrub at the South Coast Botanical Garden near Los Angeles, California.

Buddleia davidii (butterfly bush) has fragrant, lilac-scented flower spikes attractive to butterflies.

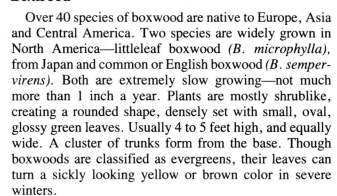

Buxus sempervirens (English boxwood) creates clean, sharp lines for this horticultural maze at Deerfield Garden, near Philadelphia, Pennsylvania.

How to Grow—Easily planted from bare-root stock and containers. Propagated from seeds and cuttings taken in summer. Prefers fertile loam soil in full sun. Can be pruned back to the soil line in early spring to rejuvenate plants. Grows from Zones 5 to 9. Usually, top growth is killed back to the roots during winter in Zone 5.

Landscape Use—Mostly used singly in mixed-shrub and perennial borders. Good container plant for tubs and half-barrels.

BUXUS
Boxwood

Over 40 species of boxwood are native to Europe, Asia and Central America. Two species are widely grown in North America—littleleaf boxwood *(B. microphylla)*, from Japan and common or English boxwood *(B. semper-virens)*. Both are extremely slow growing—not much more than 1 inch a year. Plants are mostly shrublike, creating a rounded shape, densely set with small, oval, glossy green leaves. Usually 4 to 5 feet high, and equally wide. A cluster of trunks form from the base. Though boxwoods are classified as evergreens, their leaves can turn a sickly looking yellow or brown color in severe winters.

Numerous varieties are available. The littleleaf box variety '*Koreana*' is extra hardy (to Zone 4) and faster growing than other varieties. 'Suffruticosa' is a dwarf form of common boxwood, popular as an edging plant. In Italy, there are plants have been kept regularly pruned under 3 feet high for over 100 years.

How to Grow—Plant from containers. Propagated from seeds and cuttings. Likes well-drained, acid loam soil, full sun or partial shade. Protect from cold winds. Do not cultivate too deeply around plants as they are shallow rooted. Reliably grows from Zones 6 to 9, though some varieties will survive to Zone 4.

Landscape Use—There is no finer plant for hedges, topiary, mazes, edging and parterres. Boxwood forms such a dense mass of foliage, grows so slowly, and its lines are so clean and sharp, it is indispensible in formal gardens. Boxwood parterres are particularly popular in some of the great plantation gardens of Virginia and other Southern states.

CALLICARPA JAPONICA
Beautyberry

Native to Japan, beautyberry is a hardy deciduous shrub grown for its berries. A related species, *C. americana*, is native to North America. In autumn, the long, arching branches are crowded along their entire length with shining reddish-purple fruits, which persist for several weeks after the leaves fall, intensifying the ornamental effect. The leaves themselves are decorative—each oval pointed leaf perfectly placed on opposite sides of the branch, almost a carbon copy of the other. Plants grow 4 to 6 feet high, spread 4 to 6 feet, with a rounded habit.

Callicarpa japonica (beautyberry) displays lovely shiny reddish-purple berries along arching stems.

How to Grow—Plant from containers. Softwood cuttings root readily in moist sand. Also easily grown from seeds. Prefers sandy soil in full sun or light shade. Pruning each spring to within 6 inches of the soil heightens the berry display, as the flowers are produced on new growth. Grows from Zones 5 to 8.

Landscape Use—Good for mixed-shrub borders and foundation plantings.

CALLISTEMON CITRINUS
Bottlebrush

This tender evergreen tree or shrub is native to Australia and popular in frost-free areas such as Southern Florida and Southern California. Profuse red flowers resemble bottlebrushes, up to 6 inches long. Grows to 20 feet high, spreads 8 feet. Though flowers occur abundantly in spring, flowering can be continuous all summer. The weeping bottlebrush (*C. viminalis*) is also a fine garden plant, producing smaller flowers than *C. citrinus*.

How to Grow—Plant from containers. Propagated from cuttings. Tolerates a wide range of soils, including alkaline soil. Prefers full sun, moderate amounts of moisture. Survives dry spells, does well in desert areas. Grows in Zones 9 and 10—takes temperatures to 20F (-7C).

Landscape Use—Lawn specimen and informal hedge. Good for tubs to decorate decks, patios and conservatories.

CALLUNA VULGARIS
Scotch Heather

Hardy evergreen ground-hugging plant native to Europe. Derives its common name from its similarity to *Erica cinerea,* which covers the highlands and heaths of Scotland. Calluna is slow growing to 2 feet high, spreads to 4 feet or more. Leaves are needlelike, and flowers are highly ornamental—mostly pink—appearing in late summer and fall. There are hundreds of varieties from Europe. One of the best for North America is 'H.E. Beale', a profuse blooming pink.

How to Grow—Plant from containers. Demands moist, acid soil and high humus content—preferably peat—in full sun sheltered from winds. Grows from Zones 4 to 6.

Landscape Use—Though heath and heather gardens are one of the highlights of European garden tours, they are difficult to maintain over most of North America because of summer heat. Select varieties such as 'H.E. Beale' make good ground covers, mostly used in rock gardens and among dwarf conifer collections.

Callistemon citrinus (lemon bottlebrush) in full flower near Orlando, Florida.

Calluna vulgaris (Scotch heather) variety 'H. E. Beale' is one of the best for North American conditions.

Calycanthus floridus (sweet shrub) showing fragrant, rusty red flowers.

CALYCANTHUS FLORIDUS
Sweetshrub

Also known as Carolina allspice, this hardy deciduous shrub is native to North America, from Virginia to Florida. Its best attribute is the delightfully fragrant, dusky, reddish-brown flowers that permeate the air with a strawberrylike scent in May and June. Though the flowers are small (up to 2 inches across) and rather inconspicuous, the fragrance is reason enough to grow it. Stems and branches are also aromatic when bruised or dried. Grows 6 to 9 feet high and up to 9 feet wide. Slow-growing, dense, bushy and rounded—though highly variable in habit and size of flowers. A rare, yellow-flowered form is available, called 'Katherine'.

How to Grow—Plant from containers. Propagated mostly from cuttings rooted in moist sand. Also from seed. Tolerates a wide range of soils, but prefers moist loam, in full sun or partial shade. Grows from Zones 4 to 9.

Landscape Use—Mostly grown near doorways and outdoor-living areas where the fragrant spring flowers can be best appreciated. Pick the flowers and crush the petals into a bowl for an especially heady fragrance indoors or out.

CAMELLIA JAPONICA
Camellia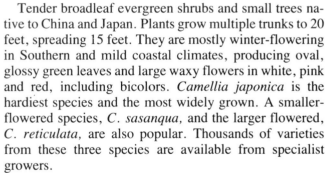

Tender broadleaf evergreen shrubs and small trees native to China and Japan. Plants grow multiple trunks to 20 feet, spreading 15 feet. They are mostly winter-flowering in Southern and mild coastal climates, producing oval, glossy green leaves and large waxy flowers in white, pink and red, including bicolors. *Camellia japonica* is the hardiest species and the most widely grown. A smaller-flowered species, *C. sasanqua,* and the larger flowered, *C. reticulata,* are also popular. Thousands of varieties from these three species are available from specialist growers.

How to Grow—Plant from containers. Propagated by seeds and cuttings, though most commercial varieties are the result of grafting onto 2 year-old rootstocks. Plants prefer a moist, fertile, well-drained humus-rich soil, in a sunny or semi-shady location. *C. japonica* can be grown outdoors as far north as Long Island, in a sheltered location, but frost damages the flowers. In Northern states camellias are best grown under glass where frost-exclusion is all that's necessary to ensure superb flowering. Although plants are cold-hardy to Zone 7 (0F-10F), camellias are risky outside of relatively frost-free areas because late frosts frequently damage flowers.

Landscape Use—Widely used for foundation plantings in frost-free areas; also to line driveways. Branches are pliable and plants can be trained flat against a wall to create a beautiful evergreen espalier. Good container plant for atriums and courtyards. Oriental gardeners refer to the camellia as "living jade" and feature it extensively in their gardens.

Camellia japonica 'Victor Emmanuel' flowering at Cypress Gardens, Florida.

CAMPSIS RADICANS
Trumpet Vine

Native to North America, from Pennsylvania to Florida, this fast-growing hardy, deciduous vine is the best plant to grow for attracting hummingbirds. Can make 10 feet of growth in a single season. Grows to 40 feet high, 6 to 8 feet wide. The long, slender stems have tiny clinging roots at every node like ivy, enabling it to scramble up almost any kind of wood or brick support. Flowers are a rich reddish-scarlet, trumpet-shaped and held in clusters of five or six blossoms that all open at one time. Leaves are similar to wisteria, each leaf composed of a series of serrated leaflets splayed out on opposite sides of the mid-rib.

There is a beautiful yellow form 'Flava' and a red form 'Praecox', plus several tender species popular in frost-free areas. Chinese trumpet vine *(C. grandiflora)* has flowers larger than the native species and almost as hardly.

How to Grow—Plant from containers. Propagated easily from softwood cuttings taken in early summer. Also by root division and seeds. Thrives even in poor soils, grows particularly lush in fertile soils, in sun or partial shade. Usually needs heavy pruning in fall to keep the vine in bounds. Grows from Zones 4 to 9; tender species even farther south.

Landscape Use—Good to grow along fence posts, up tall trellises and over arbors. Requires strong, sturdy support.

Campsis grandiflora (trumpet vine) scrambles up a porch at San Juan Bautista, California. Smaller-flowered *Campsis radicans* is native to North America.

CARISSA GRANDIFLORA
Natal Plum

Tender evergreen flowering shrub native to South Africa. Plants have fragrant, white star-shaped flowers followed by bright red plumlike fruits that are edible and sweetly flavored. Leaves are oval, pointed, dark green, shiny and waxlike. Branches are thorny. Though plants will grow to 8 feet high, dwarf, spreading varieties are mostly used in home gardens, kept pruned to 2 to 3 feet high. Flowers and fruit occur year-round in frost-free areas. Grows in Zones 9 and 10.

How to Grow—Plant from containers. Propagated from cuttings. Tolcratcs poor soils—cvcn sandy and stoney soil, in sun or shade. Resists salt spray. Takes heavy pruning year-round.

Landscape Use—Invaluable foundation plant for Southern California, Florida and similar mild climates. Can be sheared to form a dense mound. Excellent as a hedge. In Northern states, natal plums are popular for growing indoors in tubs. Thorny branches make it a good barrier plant.

Carissa grandiflora (natal plum) showing its fragrant star-shaped flowers and edible red fruits that are produced year-round in frost-free areas.

Carpinus betulus 'Fastigata' (upright European hornbeam) planted as a lawn highlight.

Carya laciniosa (shellbark hickory) changing color in fall.

CARPINUS BETULUS
European Hornbeam

Hardy deciduous ornamental tree native to Europe. Grows 25 to 40 feet, spreads 15 to 30 feet. Can reach 50 to 80 feet, but generally kept shorter by shearing. Resembles beech, but form is more slender, branches more upright. Leaves are dark green, oval, pointed and serrated, turning yellow in fall. Flowers are inconspicuous catkins produced in spring, followed by small, ribbed nut cases. Slow growing, shallow rooted and long lived.

Related species include the American hornbeam *(C. caroliniana)* and the Japanese hornbeam *(C. japonica).* The American hornbeam is hardier than the European, its range extending from Zones 2 to 9. It has good fall color, tolerates shade and grows reasonably well in moist soil. The Japanese hornbeam is a small tree that is sometimes used as a lawn highlight. Grows from Zones 4 to 6.

How to Grow — Plant balled-and-burlapped or from containers. Propagated mostly from seeds and grafting. Prefers fertile loam or sandy soil in sun or light shade. Grows from Zones 4 to 9.

Landscape Use — Excellent hedge, screen or windbreak. Good lawn highlight. Hornbeams are favorite trees for *pleaching* to create tunnels and arbors, and also for *pollarding.* These pruning methods are discussed on page 31. A hornbeam *rondel,* or *ellipse,* is a special landscape feature whereby plants are spaced in a circle and the lower limbs pruned. The upper branches are allowed to intermingle their foliage, and the whole canopy is severely pruned to form a squared hedge that appears suspended in mid-air on stilts. This effect can be created using either the European or the American hornbeam.

CARYA
Hickories and Pecans

Hickories and pecans are deciduous, nut-bearing trees native to North America. The pecan *(C. illinoensis)* is native to the Mississipi River Watershed, and though reasonably hardy into Zone 5, nut production is best in Southern and Southwestern states. The shellbark hickory *(C. laciniosa)* and the shagbark hickory *(C. ovata)* produce thick-shelled nuts with sweet kernels. Of these, the shagbark hickory is the hardiest, its natural range extending well into Canada.

The pecan grows 70 to 90 feet high and spreads 40 to 50 feet. Plants have straight trunks, an upright habit and rounded crown. The compound leaves turn golden-yellow in fall when the reddish-brown, thin-shelled nuts ripen inside green, oval nut cases and drop to the ground.

The shagbark and shellbark hickories are similar in habit to the pecan, growing upright with a rounded crown. The shagbark has gray bark that peels in vertical strips along the entire length of the trunk, while the shellbark has smooth, gray bark. In both species the heart-shaped, thick-shelled nuts are borne inside round, green nut cases. Though tasty, the sparse sweet meat is difficult to extract. Beautiful golden yellow fall color occurs early.

How to Grow — Both pecans and hickories develop long taproots and need to be planted when young, from bare-root stock or balled-and-burlapped. They are propagated mostly from seed. Pecan and shellbark hickory are grown from Zone 5 south, shagbark hickory from Zone 4 south. All prefer deep, fertile loam or sandy soils in full sun, but tolerate some shade in their juvenile stages.

Landscape Use — Good lawn specimens where they have room to spread, otherwise best planted in groves. Hickory wood is valued as firewood, especially to add a smoky flavor to hams, bacon and cheeses.

CARYOPTERIS INCANA
Blue Mist Shrub

Native to China, this summer-flowering deciduous shrub has a loose, spreading, fountainlike habit, growing up to 5 feet high, spreading up to 5 feet across. Masses of blue, fragrant flowers are produced in late summer, giving the plant the appearance of a large clump of lavender. Though nurserymen refer to most forms of *Caryopteris* as 'Blue Mist Shrub' the name 'Blue Mist' is actually a varietal name given to a hybrid that resulted from crossing *C. incana* and *C. mongolica*. 'Candida' is a white-flowered form.

How to Grow—Plant from containers. Propagated from softwood cuttings. Tolerates poor soil and prefers full sun. Since flowers are produced on new growth plants can be cut back to within 6 inches of the soil line in winter to keep plantings tidy and compact. Grows from Zone 5 south. If it does suffer winterkill from unusually severe winters it usually springs back from the roots.

Landscape Use — Good for mixing with perennials and other ornamental shrubs in mixed-shrub borders. Especially effective planted in parallel rows to line an avenue, driveway or path.

CASSIA FISTULA
Crown of Gold

An estimated 500 species of *Cassia* are widely distributed throughout the world, ranging from annual herbs to tall trees. *C. fistula* is a spectacular tender, evergreen flowering tree from India, grown in mild-winter climates. Grows to 30 feet, spreads 30 feet, covering itself in golden yellow flower clusters 12 to 18 inches long. Several related species, *C. excelsa*, *C. cremophila* and *C. sturtii* are popular evergreen shrubs, particularly in desert areas because of their drought resistance.

How to Grow—Plant from containers. Propagated from seeds and cuttings. Tolerates poor soil in full sun. Grows in Zones 9 and 10.

Landscape Use—Excellent lawn highlight. Colorful street tree.

Caryopteris incana (blue mist shrub) in full flower during the heat of summer.

Cassia excelsa (shower of gold) flowers in midsummer in frost-free areas.

Castanea mollisima (Chinese chestnut) showing spiny nut cases splitting open to reveal edible nuts.

Catalpa speciosa (Northern catalpa) in full flower.

CASTANEA MOLLISSIMA
Chinese Chestnut

Hardy deciduous nut-bearing tree native to China. Grows 40 to 60 feet, spreads 40 to 60 feet, producing a rounded shape. Dark green leaves are narrow, oblong and tapered, with sharp, serrated edges and prominent veins. Flowers are highly ornamental, appearing in summer. Creamy-white catkins up to 5 inches long are borne in clusters and give off a heavy fragrance that some people consider unpleasant. Prickly nut cases ripen in fall and expel two or three shiny brown, soft-shelled nuts that are edible raw or cooked. Slow growing and long-lived.

Two important related species are the American chestnut *(C. dentata)* and Spanish chestnut *(C. sativa)*. The American chestnut is almost extinct, due to a devastating disease called *chestnut blight,* although a few specimens still survive in isolated places. Both species grow tall and produce extra-large, sweet-flavored nuts.

How to Grow—Plant balled-and-burlapped or from bare-root stock. Propagated mostly from seeds. Prefers fertile, acid loam soil in full sun. Grows from Zones 4 to 8.

Landscape Use—Widely planted as a lawn highlight and orchard tree.

CASUARINA CUNNINGHAMIANA
Australian Pine

Tender evergreen shade tree native to Australia. Resembles a pine tree with its wispy pinelike needles—but it is not a conifer. Fast growing to 60 feet, spreading 50 feet. Graceful, upright feathery branches sway languidly in the slightest breeze. Produces 1/2-inch, hard, round seed cases that resemble a small pine cone. A similar species, *C. equisetifolia*, is also widely grown in mild-winter areas, particularly Florida and Southern California.

How to Grow—Plant from containers. Propagated from seeds. Tolerates a wide range of soils in full sun or partial shade. Takes salt spray, grows in almost pure sand. Highly drought resistant. Thrives on neglect. Grows only in Zone 10.

Landscape Use—Good street tree, though it sheds leaves and seed cases continuously. Excellent windbreak. Can be severely pruned to force low branching for making a dense formal or informal hedge.

CATALPA SPECIOSA
Northern Catalpa

Hardy deciduous shade tree native to North America from Pennsylvania to Arkansas. Catalpas are admired for their large, tropical-looking heart-shaped leaves, showy white flowers in spring and buttercup-yellow foliage in fall. Slender, decorative, foot-long seed pods hang from the tree in fall. Grows 40 to 60 feet high, spreads to 40 feet with an upright, billowing habit. Young trees grow fast. A related species, the Southern catalpa *(C. bignonioides,)* has showier flowers—white with yellow spots—popular in the South, from Zones 6 to 9.

How to Grow—Plant balled-and-burlapped. Mostly grown from seeds. Tolerates poor soil, though it prefers deep, moist, fertile loam in full sun. Northern catalpa is grown from Zones 4 to 8.

Landscape Use—Lawn highlight and street tree. There is a particularly beautiful weeping form that is sensational when pollarded.

CEANOTHUS COERULEUS
California Lilac

Tender broadleaf evergreen shrub native to Mexico. So named because the powdery-blue flowers resemble lilac blooms. There are over 40 related species native to California. Plants grow to 20 feet, spread 10 feet and more, have a mounded habit, flowering in spring.

How to Grow—Plant from containers. Propagated mostly from cuttings. Prefers sandy soil in full sun. Grows from Zones 8 to 10.

Landscape Use—Mostly used in mixed-shrub borders and trained against a wall. Related species have a spreading habit and are used as ground covers. *C. thyrsiflorus* is a particularly fine native California species.

CEDRUS
Cedars

Many evergreen conifers are called cedars because of their aromatic wood—including the Eastern red cedar, which is actually a juniper. Three kinds of true cedars are popular hardy landscape plants—the Atlas cedar, deodar cedar and cedar of Lebanon. They are all noble trees mostly used for skyline effects.

ATLAS CEDAR *(Cedrus atlantica)*

Native to the Atlas Mountains of Morocco, West Africa. Grows to 90 feet and more, spreads 60 feet. Beautiful spirelike habit, blue needles and sharp outline. Two very fine, generally available varieties are 'Glauca', with silvery blue needles and spreading branches that extend all the way to the ground, and 'Glauca Pendula', a weeping form with long, sinuous, rubbery branches that extend horizontally for great distances, dangling vertical branchlets that hang to the ground like a curtain. Trained against a wall, the leader can extend horizontally for up to 100 feet.

How to Grow—Plant balled-and-burlapped or from containers. Propagated from seeds and cuttings. Prefers deep loam or humus-rich sandy soil in full sun. Can suffer severe browning of foliage in cold winters. Grows from Zones 6 to 9 and parts of Zone 10.

CEDAR OF LEBANON *(Cedrus libani)*

Native to Lebanon and Turkey. Magnificent "prestige" tree because of its massive form. Grows to 120 feet, spreads 100 feet. In an open situation the shape is broadly symmetrical. Plants usually form multiple upright main trunks to produce a domed or squared outline. Needles are dark green, appearing almost black from a distance.

Ceanothus coeruleus (California lilac) prefers a coastal, nearly frost-free climate to flower like this.

Cedrus atlantica (Atlas cedar) has silvery blue evergreen needles and sharply defined spire-shaped habit.

Cedrus deodara (deodar cedar) growing as a grove at Hearst Castle, San Simeon, California.

Celastrus orbiculatus (Chinese bittersweet) decorates a wrought-iron fence with colorful berries in fall.

How to Grow—Similar to Atlas cedar, but needs heavier soil, such as clay loam. Grows from Zones 5 to 9.
Landscape Use—This tree improves with age. Impressive lawn highlight for estates, parks and campuses. Excellent skyline tree.

DEODAR CEDAR *(Cedrus deodara)*

Native to the Himalayas. Classic spirelike habit with branches that sweep to the ground and a softness that makes you want to reach out and stroke it. Grows to 100 feet or higher and spreads 45 feet. Needles are bright green in spring, darkening during summer. 'Aurea' is a very fine golden form.
How to Grow—Similar to Atlas cedar. Although its range of hardiness is approximately the same (Zones 6 to 10), it is not quite as hardy as Atlas cedar.

CERCIDIPHYLLUM JAPONICUM
Katsura Tree

Hardy deciduous shade tree native to Japan. Trees are either male or female. Grows 40 to 60 feet high, spreads 30 to 50 feet. Strong, stately trees with a spreading rounded outline. Attractive dark green, heart-shaped leaves and beautiful yellow fall coloring. Leaves have a pleasant cotton-candy fragrance that becomes most pronounced in fall. A rare weeping form, 'Pendula', grows to 25 feet high.
How to Grow—Plant balled-and-burlapped. Propagated from seeds and softwood cuttings. Prefers deep, fertile, well-drained loam soil. Grows from Zones 4 to 8.
Landscape Use—Excellent lawn highlight for large gardens.

CELASTRUS SCANDENS

American Bittersweet

Hardy deciduous vine native to eastern North America. Grows to 25 feet or higher, can become invasive and even strangle small trees if not kept within bounds. Inconspicuous white flowers are followed by pea-size orange-red berries that persist on the vine into winter after the leaves have fallen. The berries are valued as Thanksgiving and Christmas decorations, *but they are poisonous* and should not be eaten. Male and female flowers occur on different plants, though Chinese bittersweet *(C. orbiculatus)*—an equally decorative plant— has males and females together and is more reliably productive.
How to Grow—Plant from containers or bare-root stock. Cuttings root reliably in moist sand. Not fussy about soil. Prefers full sun. Grows from Zones 3 to 8.
Landscape Use—Mostly used to decorate fence rails, poles and arbors. The Chinese bittersweet is considered by many experts as a noxious weed, but the eye-catching berries do have enormous appeal.

CERCIS CANADENSIS
Eastern Redbud

Hardy deciduous flowering shade tree native to the eastern United States. Though relatively short lived, Eastern redbud is valued for its early spring-flowering display, composed of purplish-pink, pealike blossoms that crowd the branches well before the leaves appear. Grows to 35 feet, spreads 25 feet. Has rounded, heart-shaped leaves. Habit is open and irregular.

'Alba' is a beautiful white variety, 'Rosea' a popular pink. 'Forest Pansy' has bronze foliage. Western redbud (*C. occidentalis*) grows as a shrubby tree, forming multiple main branches with magenta-red flowers.

How to Grow—Plant from containers or bare-root stock. Propagated by seeds and layering, also grafting. Prefers fertile, sandy loam soil in full sun or partial shade. Grows from Zones 4 to 9. A fungus disease called *dieback* is a serious problem with redbuds. Branches form cankers, defoliate, crack and dry out. Spraying with a copper fungicide such as copper sulfate is a good preventative measure.

Landscape Use—Good lawn highlight. Also effective to brighten mixed-shrub borders and wooded lots.

Cercidiphyllum japonicum (katsura tree) has fragrant leaves that smell like cotton candy.

CHAENOMELES SPECIOSA
Flowering Quince

Hardy deciduous flowering shrub native to China. Forms a mounded thicket of twiggy branches covered early spring with white, pink, orange and red blossoms, even before the leaves are fully open. Grows 6 to 8 feet high, with an equal spread. Generally kept below 6 feet by heavy pruning in early summer. In fall the leaves have no coloring and drop early, but sometimes the attractive, yellow, astringent fruits persist on the branches into winter.

A related species, Japanese quince (*C. japonica*) is a low, spreading thorny plant, growing 4 to 5 feet high. It is mostly used in rock gardens and dry walls.

How to Grow—Plant from containers. Propagated mostly from cuttings. Not fussy about soil. Needs a sunny location. Can be pruned close to the ground to renew vigor and promote flowering. Grows from Zones 4 to 9.

Landscape Use—Mostly used as a highlight in mixed-shrub borders. Useful as an informal hedge.

Cercis canadensis (Eastern redbud) displays beautiful purple pealike blossoms in early spring even before its leaves appear.

CHAMAECYPARIS
False Cypresses

Mostly hardy evergreen conifers native to the Pacific coasts of North America and Asia. Though the various species are generally tall, upright, columnar trees, there is tremendous variation of habit, color and texture among garden varieties. Foliage is usually soft and scaly or feathery and stringlike. Cones are small and inconspicuous. Leaf colors include blue, light and dark green, yellow, gold and silvery green. A hybrid between the tender Monterey cypress and the hardy Nootka false cypress, Leyland

Chaenomeles japonica (Japanese quince) sometimes produces astringent, yellow fruits after flowering.

Chamaecyparis lawsoniana 'Aurea' lights up the landscape with yellow, lacy foliage.

Chionanthus virginicus (fringe tree) in full flower during spring.

cypress (*Cupressocyparis* ×*leylandii*) is a fine, hardy, upright evergreen. It is one of the fastest growing of all conifers at 3 to 4 feet a year. Following are the most widely planted false cypresses for home gardens:

HINOKI FALSE CYPRESS (Chamaecyparis obtusa)

Native to Japan, these plants have an unusual spiral, pyramidal habit, formed by soft, flat, spreading branchlets arranged in layers. This gives the tree a distinctly Oriental appearance. Grows slowly to 50 feet and spreads 20 feet.

How to Grow — Plant from containers or balled-and-burlapped. Propagated mostly from cuttings taken in fall. Prefers fertile, humus- rich acid soil in full sun. Grows from Zones 4 to 8.

Landscape Use — One of the most attractive conifers for foundation plantings and rock gardens. Excellent for growing in large tubs.

LAWSON FALSE CYPRESS (*C. lawsoniana*)

Native to Oregon, these plants are dark green, conical, grow to 60 feet high and 15 feet wide. Graceful, upright habit though many varieties have been developed that don't match this habit. Dark red male flowers cluster along the branches in early spring.

How to Grow — Plant from containers. Propagated from seeds and cuttings. Prefers high humidity and moist, well-drained soil in sun or partial shade. Languishes in high heat. Grows from Zones 5 to 9.

Landscape Use — Foundation plant, lawn highlight and windbreak.

SAWARA CYPRESS (*C. pisifera*)

Native to Japan, these plants are usually dark green or bright yellow, depending on variety, and conical in shape. Densely covered with fernlike sprays. The large number of varieties offer considerable variation in color and habit. Two examples are 'Filifera' with stringlike leaves and 'Aurea' with a striking golden-yellow color.

How to Grow — Plant from containers. Propagated from cuttings. Prefers moist, acid loam soil in full sun. Takes high humidity. Grows from Zones 3 to 8.

Landscape Use — Beautiful highlight for foundation plantings, lawns and rock gardens. Excellent hedge, screen and windbreak.

CHIONANTHUS VIRGINICUS
Fringe Tree

Native to the eastern United States, this hardy deciduous flowering tree resembles an upright willow. In spring it produces a mass of beautiful, fragrant, white blossoms that hang in thick clusters, followed by blue berries that attract birds. Male and female flowers grow on separate trees, with the males producing the better flowering display. Grows to 25 feet high and spreads 15 feet. Some trees are multi-stemmed. The leaves are an attractive light green, changing to yellow in fall.

How to Grow—Plant from containers. Propagated from

seeds and cuttings. Prefers fertile loam or sandy soil in full
sun. Grows from Zones 4 to 9.
Landscape Use—Good lawn highlight.

CHORISIA SPECIOSA
Floss Silk Tree

Tender deciduous flowering tree native to Brazil. Also
known as kapok tree. Popular in frost-free areas such as
southern Florida and Southern California. Grows to 50
feet high, spreads to 30 feet, though much larger specimens are known. Exotic rose-pink orchidlike blooms
cover the tree in fall during a brief leafless period. The
gray colored trunks of mature trees are often bottle-shaped
and covered with sharp spines. The beautiful 4 to 6 inch
flowers are followed by pear-shaped pods containing silky
threads attached to seeds. Resembling floss, the threads
are used commercially as *kapok* to stuff pillows.
How to Grow—Plant from containers. Propagated from
seeds. Prefers fertile loam soil in full sun. The more heat it
gets in summer, the better. Seed grown trees take up to 10
years to bloom, but grafted varieties such as 'Majestic
Beauty' will bloom within 5 years in 5 gallon cans. Grows
in Zone 10.
Landscape Use—Good lawn highlight and street tree.

Chorisa speciosa (floss silk tree) flowers in autumn in frost-free
areas.

CITRUS
Citrus sinensis and Other Species

The most widely grown citrus is the sweet orange *(C.
sinensis),* a broadleaf evergreen tree native to China. It
can be grown in mild-winter areas of Florida, Texas,
California and Arizona. Closely related to the orange are
lemons, limes, grapefruit, tangerines, pummelos and
kumquats. Fragrant white flowers occur mostly in spring,
followed by fruit which normally starts to ripen in fall,
continuing through winter into the following spring. Trees
grow to 30 feet, with a similar spread, though many dwarf
varieties are available. Branches are thorny and sweep to
the ground if left unpruned.

The most popular orange is the 'Valencia' for its sweet
flavor and juiciness. There is a hardy, extremely thorny,
aromatic, astringent species *(Poncirus trifoliata)* grown as
an ornamental shrub in Northern states. The dwarf citrus
(C. mitis)—also known as Calamondin orange—makes a
highly decorative container plant.
How to Grow—Plant from containers. Propagated from
seeds, layering and cuttings, though most garden-worthy
varieties are grafts. Prefers a deep, fertile, well-drained
soil—particularly a sandy soil enriched with organic matter. Needs full sun. Grows only in Zones 9 and 10.
Landscape Use—Good orchard tree and an excellent
ornamental for foundation plantings, lining driveways and
lawn highlights. For more complete information on growing citrus trees, refer to the book *Citrus, How to Select,
Grow & Enjoy* by Richard Ray and Lance Walheim,
published by HPBooks, Inc.

Citrus mitis (Calamondin orange) is popular for containers and
small spaces. Fruits are sour but edible as preserves.

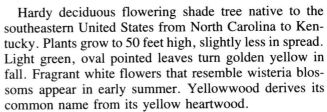

CLADRASTIS LUTEA
Yellowwood

Hardy deciduous flowering shade tree native to the southeastern United States from North Carolina to Kentucky. Plants grow to 50 feet high, slightly less in spread. Light green, oval pointed leaves turn golden yellow in fall. Fragrant white flowers that resemble wisteria blossoms appear in early summer. Yellowwood derives its common name from its yellow heartwood.

How to Grow—Plant balled-and-burlapped. Propagated mostly from seeds. Prefers deep, fertile loam soil in full sun. Drought resistant. Grows from Zones 3 to 8.

Landscape Use—Good lawn highlight.

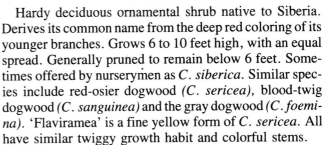

CORNUS ALBA
Red-twig Dogwood

Hardy deciduous ornamental shrub native to Siberia. Derives its common name from the deep red coloring of its younger branches. Grows 6 to 10 feet high, with an equal spread. Generally pruned to remain below 6 feet. Sometimes offered by nurserymen as *C. siberica*. Similar species include red-osier dogwood *(C. sericea)*, blood-twig dogwood *(C. sanguinea)* and the gray dogwood *(C. foemina)*. 'Flaviramea' is a fine yellow form of *C. sericea*. All have similar twiggy growth habit and colorful stems.

How to Grow—Plants are so easy to grow that any softwood or hardwood cutting stuck into moist soil will root reliably. Sold either bare-root or in containers. Tolerates all kinds of soil conditions, but does best in moist loam in full sun. Needs heavy pruning in spring to maintain compact growth and to encourage new wood which has the most intense red coloring.

Landscape Use—Brings color to gardens in winter. Mostly planted where its leafless red branches can be seen against a background of snow, a white picket fence or stucco wall.

Cladrastis lutea (yellowwood) makes a fast-growing shade tree.

CORNUS FLORIDA
Flowering Dogwood

Hardy deciduous flowering tree native to the eastern United States. Famous for its spectacular spring flowering display in white, pink or red. Though mostly single-flowered, there is a scarce double-flowering variety. Grows 20 feet high, spreads 15 feet. The flowers are actually composed of four bracts, resembling petals, with the true flowers clustered in the center like a pompon. The leaves are oval, pointed, turn bronze in fall, the fall coloring enhanced by clusters of bright red berries attractive to songbirds. The flowering display is particularly beautiful because it occurs before the leaves fully unfold.

'Cherokee Chief' has deep red flowers and 'Fragrant Cloud' has fragrant white flowers. A related species, Pacific dogwood *(C. nuttallii)*, grows wild from the Pacific Northwest to Southern California. Flowers are larger than the Eastern species—up to 4 inches across, com-

Cornus alba 'Sibirica' (red-twig dogwood) highlighted against snow.

pared to 2 inches—but it does not do well east of the Rockies.

How to Grow—Plant balled-and-burlapped. Propagated by seed and softwood cuttings taken after flowering. Prefers acid, humus-rich loam soil in full sun or partial shade. Grows from Zones 4 to 9.

In recent years dogwoods on the Eastern seaboard have begun to die off at an alarming rate, infected by a virulent form of *anthracnose* fungus disease, commonly called *lower branch dieback.* It first attacks the lower branches, killing them, and eventually spreads to the entire tree. Dogwoods in shaded locations are more prone than those in open, sunny situations. Though sprays of Captan and Benomyl administered by a professional tree service can help in protecting undamaged or slightly infected trees, once the disease has a firm hold it is almost impossible to eradicate. The Korean dogwood is immune to this disease.

Landscape Use—A favorite ornamental tree for suburban yards, used mostly as a lawn highlight. Also suitable for containers. Magnificent in woodland gardens where the flowers look like flocks of butterflies rising through the trees.

CORNUS KOUSA
Korean Dogwood

Hardy deciduous flowering tree native to Korea and China. Grows to 30 feet high, spreads 35 feet. Similar in appearance to the common dogwood, except the flower bracts are sharply pointed. They also appear up to a month later in spring and compete with the leaves for attention. In fall the tree bears attractive, edible, sweetly flavored orange fruits. Good winter appearance on account of its mottled bark and stout radiating branches. 'Milky Way' is a profuse flowering variety that almost hides its leaves with snow-white flowers.

How to Grow—Plant balled-and-burlapped. Propagated from seeds and cuttings. Prefers acid, humus-rich, sandy soil in full sun. Unlike common dogwood, flowering is severely reduced by shade. Grows from Zones 5 to 8.

Landscape Use—Many experts recommend the Korean dogwood as a substitute for the disease-prone flowering dogwood, but this is like comparing apples to coconuts, since the flowering display occurs much later and the plant performs poorly in shade where the flowering dogwood excels. Nevertheless, the Korean dogwood is an excellent choice for foundation plantings and as a lawn highlight.

Cornus florida rubra (pink dogwood) shows perfect pyramidal form on a front lawn.

Cornus kousa (Korean dogwood) flowers several weeks after the native dogwoods.

Corylus avellana 'Contorta' (contorted hazel) features curiously twisted weeping branches.

Corylopsis spicata (winter hazel) is one of the first flowering shrubs to bloom in spring.

CORYLUS AVELLANA
European Hazelnut

The European hazelnut and the American hazelnut (*C. americana*) are both hardy, deciduous, nut-bearing, shrublike trees. They are similar in appearance, growing multiple trunks and a rounded habit, up to 20 feet high and 20 feet wide. An exceptionally good ornamental form is the European contorted hazel, also called corkscrew hazel. It is highly decorative when planted against a wall or fence where its winter silhouette of coiled branches can be highlighted. Though these plants will grow to 10 feet high, they are best pruned to keep them below 6 feet. In addition to the lovely 'Contorta' there is a beautiful weeping variety, 'Pendula'.

How to Grow—Plant from containers. Propagated from seed and softwood cuttings taken in spring. Prefers a fertile, loam soil in full sun or partial shade. Heavy pruning in fall or winter is needed to keep the contorted and weeping forms decorative. Grows from Zones 4 to 7.

Landscape Use—The species are good for hedgerows and nut production. 'Contorta' is best used as a foundation plant and 'Pendula' as a lawn highlight.

CORYLOPSIS SPICATA

Winterhazel

Hardy deciduous flowering shrub native to Japan. Grows to 10 feet high and slightly less in spread. Valued for its extremely early pendant lemon-yellow flowers that are pleasantly fragrant. They hang in profusion from naked branches before the leaves unfurl.

How to Grow—Plant balled-and-burlapped or from containers. Propagated from seeds and softwood cuttings taken in summer. Best planted in sheltered, sunny location in acid, humus-rich, moist soil. Grows from Zones 5 to 8.

Landscape Use—Mixed-shrub borders and heather gardens.

COTONEASTER HORIZONTALIS

Rockspray Cotoneaster

There are numerous species of cotoneaster used in garden plantings. The hardy, semi-evergreen rockspray cotoneaster, with its ground hugging, spreading habit and bright red berries, is by far the most widely used. Native to China, its dense branches splay out like a fan, spreading 5 to 8 feet wide and 2 to 3 feet high. The leaves are small and oval, and the flowers small, pink and not very conspicuous though the berry display that follows is eye-catching.

How to Grow—Plant from containers. Propagated by seeds and cuttings. Plants tolerate a wide range of soil conditions, including dry soils, but do best in fertile loam in a sunny or partly shaded location. Susceptible to fireblight which blackens twigs and discolors fruits (see page 58). Grows from Zones 4 to 7.

Landscape Use—Excellent ground cover. Good winter highlight in rock gardens and along dry walls.

Cotoneaster horizontalis (rockspray cotoneaster) lays out a mantle of bright red berries in fall. It makes a good large-scale ground cover.

COTINUS COGGYGRIA
Smoke Tree

Hardy deciduous shrub or small tree native to Asia. Plants grow to 15 feet high, producing a cluster of main branches from a short trunk. Attractive small, oval leaves. Flowering occurs in midsummer with an extraordinary display of billowing, fluffy blooms that resemble cotton candy, colored pink or smoky white. Fall color is usually spectacular.

'Royal Purple' has dark purple foliage and deep purple-pink flowers. A native North American species—the American smoke tree *(C. obovatus)*—is a tall, open plant growing to 25 feet high with especially good fall color, but best used in naturalized plantings.

How to Grow—Plant from containers. Propagated from seeds and cuttings taken in late spring. Plants tolerate a wide range of soil conditions, including poor soils, but prefer fertile loam and a sheltered, sunny location. The wood is brittle, can be split apart in windstorms. Grows from Zones 4 to 9.

Landscape Use—Good lawn highlight in a sheltered position. Best used in mixed-shrub borders and as a foundation plant.

CRATAEGUS
Hawthorn

Though there are more than 1,000 species of hawthorn native to North America, Europe and Asia, the two most widely grown as ornamentals are English hawthorn *(C. oxyacantha)* producing rosy red flowers, and Washington hawthorn *(C. phaenopyrum)* with white flowers. Both bear clusters of decorative red berries (haws) in fall. These are edible, persist into winter and attract songbirds. Plants flower when young (2 years), growing to small trees 20 feet high. Sometimes the trees are multiple stemmed, forming a dense hedgerow with sharp thorns. Leaf shapes vary among species but in the English hawthorn have three to five lobes, sharply toothed, turning bronze in fall.

How to Grow—Plant balled-and-burlapped. Propagated by seeds, which take two years to germinate. Named varieties are usually grafted. Plants prefer loam soils enriched with organic material, in a sunny location. Tolerates limestone soil. Grows from Zones 4 to 8. Susceptible to mildew in humid climates, also fireblight, leaf blight and cedar-apple rust. (See page 58).

Landscape Use—Good lawn highlight. Popular for mixed-shrub borders. Creates a beautiful hedgerow.

CRYPTOMERIA JAPONICA
Japanese Cedar

Hardy evergreen conifer native to Japan. Grows to 100 feet high, spreads 30 feet. Beautiful spirelike form when young. The straight trunk has decorative reddish-brown, peeling bark. Bright green needles turn bronze in fall. The needles are long, formed in clusters, giving the tree an

Cotinus coggygria (smoke tree) is a billowing mass of fluffy pink flower clusters during midsummer in the author's garden.

Crataegus phaenopyrum (Washington hawthorn) displays showy red berry clusters in fall.

Cryptomeria japonica (Japanese cedar) is a spire-shaped evergreen that tolerates partial shade.

Cupressus sempervirens (Italian cypress) punctuates the skyline at Hearst Castle in San Simeon, California.

unusual softness not common among needleleaf evergreens.

How to Grow—Easily grown from bare-root stock or containers. Best propagated from cuttings taken in late summer because seed germination is generally poor. Prefers deep, fertile, moist, acid soil in a sunny or lightly shaded location. Grows from Zones 5 to 9.

Landscape Use—Good as a lawn highlight and to form avenues or groves. Good sentinel tree to use in rock gardens and Oriental gardens.

CUPRESSUS
Cypresses

Many true cypresses are native to the mild coastal regions of California and the Pacific Northwest. Exceptions are Italian cypress and Arizona cypress, which prefer drier climates. Both are surprisingly drought tolerant. They have soft branch tips covered with scalelike leaves and bear small rounded cones. The two most widely planted species are the massive, spreading Monterey cypress and the elegant, narrow spirelike Italian cypress.

ITALIAN CYPRESS *(C. sempervivens)*

Native to the Mediterranean. Though the species is variable in habit, the variety 'Stricta' is popular for its narrow, slow-growing, dark green columnar habit. Some of the finest specimens can be seen at Hearst Castle, San Simeon, California.

How to Grow—Plant balled-and-burlapped. Propagated mostly from cuttings. Prefers a mild, dry climate and well-drained loam soil. Grows from Zones 8 to 10.

Landscape Use—Good accent plant to use in a formal landscape, as exclamation points. Useful in foundation plantings, especially as matching pairs at entryways. Outstanding as a tall hedge. Popular for screening swimming pools.

MONTEREY CYPRESS *(C. macrocarpa)*

Native to the Monterey Peninsula of Northern California. In the wild, there is nothing quite so beautiful as these trees hugging the sheerest cliffs and shrouded in mist. Even in death, the naked trunks and bleached limbs have a sculptural beauty. Plants grow to 50 feet high, spread 40 feet and more, have a spreading pyramidal habit when young, mature into a mounded dark green crown with strong radiating branches. Grows moderately fast. Highly resistant to salt spray and fierce winds.

How to Grow—Plant balled-and-burlapped or from containers. Propagated mostly from seeds. Prefers a moist atmosphere and well-drained sandy or humus rich soil in full sun. Grows from Zones 7 to 10.

Landscape Use—Invaluable in mild coastal gardens as a windbreak on account of its salt-tolerance. Also good as a lawn specimen, though it needs room to spread.

CYCAS REVOLUTA
Sago Palm

Tender evergreen palmlike tree native to southern Japan. Dark green, glossy arching fronds cascade like a fountain from the crown on top of a thick, fibrous dark brown or black trunk. Plants are extremely slow growing, reaching 10 feet high and are often seen growing in clumps. Male and female flowers, resembling cones, appear on separate plants.

How to Grow—Plant from containers. Propagated from seeds and offsets that are produced around the base of parent plants and removed when plants are dormant. Prefers fertile, organic-rich sandy or loam soil in sun or partial shade. Grows in Zones 9 and 10. In Japan these plants are so highly valued as ornamentals, gardeners grow them outdoors in frost-prone areas by pruning away fronds before winter and swathing the trunk and crown in burlap or straw *overcoats*.

Landscape Use—Unsurpassed for foundation plantings and atriums. Good to grow in containers. Widely grown under glass in Northern states.

Cycas revoluta (Sago palm) makes a beautiful grove in the Japanese Garden at Huntington Botanical Gardens, near Los Angeles, California.

CYTISUS SCOPARIUS
Scotch Broom

Native to Europe, brooms are hardy deciduous shrubs that have never been as popular in North America as they are in European gardens, where numerous species and hybrid varieties are cultivated for their billowing, dense spreading habit and masses of pealike flowers that appear in spring. There is one exception—the lemon-yellow Warminster broom (*C. ×praecox*), which is a hybrid cross between yellow-flowered *C. purgans* and white-flowered *C. multiflorus*. Plants grow 6 to 10 feet high.

How to Grow — Plant from containers. Propagated by seeds and cuttings. Cuttings taken in summer root readily in moist sand. Prefers sandy soil and a sunny location. Usually not long-lived in the United States. Tired specimens may need pruning back to the soil line after 5 years, to rejuvenate them. Severe winters can cause serious winterkill. Grows from Zones 5 to 8.

Landscape Use — Good for foundation plantings and mixed-shrub borders. Widely used on golf courses.

Cytisus ×praecox (Warminster broom) makes a handsome lawn highlight.

Daphne 'Carol Mackei' is an eye-catching, fragrant flowering shrub for mixed-shrub borders.

DAPHNE ×BURKWOODII
Burkwood Daphne

Hardy broadleaf evergreen flowering shrub native to Europe. Several species are grown in North America— rose daphne *(D. cneorum)*, winter daphne *(D. odora)* and Burkwood daphne *(D. ×Burkwoodii)*. Most plants sold under these names have fragrant, pink flowers that appear in spring. Depending on variety, plants grow from 6 inches to 4 feet high. *D. ×Burkwoodii* is a cross using *D. cneorum* as one of the parents, and grows to 4 feet high with a dense, rounded habit. The variety 'Carol Mackei' is particularly beautiful. It has white leaf margins and fragrant, pale pink flowers.

Davidia involucrata (dove tree) displays curious, white flowers that flutter in the breeze.

How to Grow — Plant from containers. Tolerates acid and slightly alkaline soils in full sun or partial shade. Benefits from mulching to conserve soil moisture. Grows from Zones 4 to 7.

Landscape Use — Dwarf forms like *D. cneorum* make excellent mass plantings and flowering ground covers, growing just 6 inches high, spreading 2 feet. Taller plants such as 'Carol Mackei' make good specimen plants for rock gardens and mixed-shrub borders.

DAVIDIA INVOLUCRATA
Dove Tree

Hardy deciduous flowering shade tree native to China. Also called ghost tree and pocket-handkerchief tree because of its strange white flowers that cover the tree for about two weeks in spring. The flower is surrounded by two large petal-shaped bracts. The lower bract extends about 6 inches down, fluttering in the breeze like a handkerchief. The flowers are followed by bitter green fruits. Grows to 40 feet high, spreads 30 feet with spreading branches and a rounded crown. Leaves are heart-shaped with toothed edges.

How to Grow—Plant balled-and-burlapped. Propagated by seed or cuttings taken in summer. Likes a sheltered location and a moist, well-drained soil high in organic matter. Grows from Zones 5 to 8.

Landscape Use—Handsome lawn highlight.

DELONIX REGIA
Royal Poinceana

Tender deciduous flowering tree native to Madagascar. Plants are fast growing to 40 feet high, spread 40 feet wide, usually with a flattened out-stretched crown. Leaves are similar to those of mimosa, casting light shade. Flowers are magnificent, orange or red in color, borne in clusters and in well-grown specimens completely cover the tree. These are followed by brown, beanlike pods.

How to Grow—Plant from containers. Propagated mostly from seeds, though cuttings root easily. Tolerates poor soil, especially sandy soil. Grows only in frost-free areas, Zone 10.

Landscape Use—Spectacular lawn highlight. Outstanding street tree. Often described as "the world's most beautiful flowering tree."

Delonix regia (royal poinceana) has brilliant orange-red blossoms during summer in frost-free areas.

DEUTZIA GRACILIS
Slender Deutzia

Hardy deciduous flowering shrub native to Japan. Popular for its mound of pure white flowers that appear in spring. Plants grow to 4 feet high, spread 4 feet. There are several pink and rosy red hybrids, including 'Carminea'.
How to Grow—Plant from containers. Propagated by softwood cuttings taken during summer. Tolerates a wide range of soil conditions, including poor soil. Prefers full sun or partial shade. Prune soon after flowering to maintain a dwarf habit. Grows from Zones 4 to 8.
Landscape Use—Sometimes used as a short hedge, but mostly used singly in mixed-shrub borders to prolong the spring-time flowering display after azaleas and dogwoods are finished.

DIOSPYROS KAKI
Japanese Persimmon

Tender deciduous fruiting tree native to Japan. Plants grow to 20 feet high, sometimes more, spread slightly less. Large light green oval leaves and slightly weeping branches form a rounded crown. After the leaves drop in fall the female trees are covered with edible round or egg-shaped fruits that are juicy and sweet when fully ripe. A hardier species *D. americana* (common persimmon) has a natural range extending from Zones 4 to 9. Plants grow upright to 60 feet, bearing golf-ball size, astringent fruits.
How to Grow—Plant from containers. Propagated from seeds or grafts. Prefers fertile, moist loam soil. Grows from Zones 7 to 10.
Landscape Use—Foundation plantings, orchards, containers.

ELAEAGNUS ANGUSTIFOLIA
Russian Olive

Hardy deciduous shade tree or large shrub native to Europe and Asia. Grows 15 to 20 feet high, with an equal spread. Foliage is narrow, oblong willowlike, silvery blue or silvery gray in color. Rounded habit, often multistemmed. The branches have small spines. Yellow flowers are small, scented, inconspicuous, produced in spring; followed by small, oval yellowish fruit. A sweet sherbet is made from the fruit in the Orient. Medium fast growing, long lived. A related species, *C. umbellata*, also known as 'Autumn olive', has edible red fruit that ripens in fall and attractive orange fall color.
How to Grow—Mostly planted from containers or bareroot stock. Propagated from seed, layering and cuttings. Prefers sandy, loam soil but thrives almost anywhere. Drought resistant. Tolerates salt spray. Takes heavy pruning. Can even be sheared to make a formal hedge. Grows from Zones 2 to 7.
Landscape Use—Good lawn highlight, hedge and windbreak. Very tough, popular in coastal gardens and cities because of pollution tolerance.

Diospyros kaki (Japanese persimmon) drops its leaves in fall, leaving decorative orange fruits on bare branches. Edible fruits are crisper in texture than American persimmon.

Elaeagnus angustifolia (Russian olive) has unusual silvery, willowy leaves.

Erythrina caffra (coral tree) needs a frost-free location to produce its spectacular floral display.

Escallonia exoniensis seems to smother itself in dainty pink blossoms, though it needs a fairly frost-free location.

ENKIANTHUS CAMPANULATUS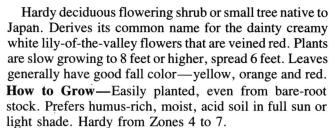
Red-vein Enkianthus

Hardy deciduous flowering shrub or small tree native to Japan. Derives its common name for the dainty creamy white lily-of-the-valley flowers that are veined red. Plants are slow growing to 8 feet or higher, spread 6 feet. Leaves generally have good fall color—yellow, orange and red.

How to Grow—Easily planted, even from bare-root stock. Prefers humus-rich, moist, acid soil in full sun or light shade. Hardy from Zones 4 to 7.

Landscape Use—Good companion plants for rhododendrons and azaleas. The flowering display is not spectacular from a distance, but attractive when seen close up, as a foundation plant.

ERYTHRINA CAFFRA
Coral Tree

Tender evergreen flowering shade tree native to South Africa, mostly grown in frost-free areas of Southern California and Florida. Also known as 'Kaffirbloom' for the exotic crimson tubular-red blossoms that appear in summer, *E. caffra* grows to 25 feet and spreads 25 feet. A related dwarf species, *E. humeana,* grows shrublike, flowers at an early age.

How to Grow—Plant from containers. Tolerates a wide range of soil conditions, including dry soil. Prefers full sun. Grows only in Zone 10.

Landscape Use—Excellent lawn specimen and street tree. Dwarf, shrubby types make dense, informal hedges.

ESCALLONIA EXONIENSIS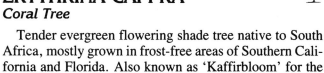
Escallonia

Tender broadleaf evergreen flowering shrub native to South America. Popular ornamental in frost-free areas such as Southern California and Florida. Plants grow to 10 feet high, spread 10 feet, and are dense, mounded and bushy. Masses of small red flowers occur in early summer. *E. exoniensis* is a related species. The variety 'Pink Princess' has rich, rose-pink flowers.

How to Grow—Plant from containers. Prefers moist, acid soil and a coastal location. Grows from Zones 7 to 10.

Landscape Use—Excellent lawn highlight and informal hedge. Good to plant close to low walls and fences so the topmost arching branches cascade over them.

EUCALYPTUS CINEREA
Silver Dollar Tree

The genus *Eucalyptus* is a vast family of trees and shrubs—representing more than 500 species native to Australia. They are popular throughout California, Florida and other mild-climate areas. Many are extremely fast-growing tall trees used as windbreaks and too big for the average suburban garden.

One of the most widely planted for ornamental effect is the silver dollar tree *(E. cinerea)*. Mostly grown as a shrub or small tree by pruning, it has arching branches and round, leathery, silvery blue leaves that are delightfully fragrant and arranged on the branches like a spiral. Ultimately growing 20 to 50 feet high, spreading 30 feet wide, it has attractive cream-colored flowers, but the leaves are its most decorative feature. The highly fragrant branches are used extensively to create long-lasting fresh or dried indoor arrangements.

There are many other eucalyptus grown for decorative value, either for their exotic flowers, unusual leaves or ornamental bark coloring. For sheer flowering value the scarlet-flowered gum *(E. ficifolia)* is especially beautiful. Planted extensively as a street tree throughout California, it has fuzzy red flower clusters that appear in midsummer, competing with oleanders and crape myrtle for flowering effect.

How to Grow—Plant from containers. Propagated from seeds and cuttings. Plants tolerate a wide range of soil conditions—even poor, sandy soil. They are effective in coastal locations and prefer full sun. Silver dollar grows from Zones 8 to 10. Scarlet-flowering gum is more tender, confined to Zones 9 and 10.

Landscape Use—Both the silver dollar and scarlet-flowering gum are particularly fine street trees and lawn highlights.

Eucalyptus cinerea (silver dollar tree) has rounded, pleasantly fragrant leaves that appear to form spirals.

EUONYMUS ALATUS
Burning Bush

Hardy, deciduous shrub native to China also called winged euonymus because of slender, brittle protrusions along the branches. Though seen mostly as a mound-shaped shrub or hedge 4 to 6 feet high, plants will develop into an impressive small tree up to 20 feet high. A most appealing ornamental quality is its brilliant red fall coloring.

How to Grow—Plant from containers. Propagated mostly by cuttings taken in spring or summer. Tolerates poor soil. Turns deeper fall color in full sun, but also effective in partial shade. Susceptible to scale infestation; see page 56 for control. Grows from Zones 3 to 8.

Landscape Use—Excellent hedge. Good lawn highlight and foundation shrub. Especially attractive when planted in a mass beside a reflecting pool or lake.

Euonymus alatus (burning bush) in full fall color.

Euonymus fortunei 'Longwood' (wintercreeper) creates an attractive, hard-wearing ground cover.

Euonymus japonicus 'Aureus' (Japanese euonymus) has bright yellow leaves with green centers.

EUONYMUS FORTUNEI
Wintercreeper

Hardy broadleaf evergreen shrub native to China. Plants grow 6 inches high when left to sprawl along the ground, or 30 to 40 feet high when given a support on which to climb. Small, oval, pointed dark green leaves have silvery veins. Growth is fast. Some good green-and-gold and green-and-silver variegated forms are available.

How to Grow—Plant from containers, although bare-root stock is generally used for mass plantings. Propagated mostly from cuttings which root easily in spring and summer. Plants tolerate poor soils, but prefer acid loam, in full sun or deep shade. Susceptible to scale infestation; see page 57 for control. Grows from Zones 4 to 9.

Landscape Use—Excellent hard-wearing ground cover. Vigorous creeper to cover walls, like ivy—but because of its daintier leaves, it is more attractive than ivy.

EUONYMUS JAPONICUS
Japanese Euonymus

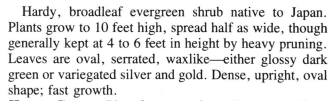

Hardy, broadleaf evergreen shrub native to Japan. Plants grow to 10 feet high, spread half as wide, though generally kept at 4 to 6 feet in height by heavy pruning. Leaves are oval, serrated, waxlike—either glossy dark green or variegated silver and gold. Dense, upright, oval shape; fast growth.

How to Grow—Plant from containers. Propagated from cuttings that root easily during spring and summer. Plants tolerate heavy clay soil, salt spray; thrive in full sun and heavy shade. Takes severe pruning any time of year. Susceptible to scale infestation; see page 57 for control. Grows from Zones 6 to 9.

Landscape Use—Good accent plant for foundation plantings and mixed-shrub borders. Useful as a low hedge.

EXOCHORDA RACEMOSA
Pearlbush

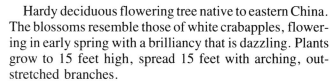

Hardy deciduous flowering tree native to eastern China. The blossoms resemble those of white crabapples, flowering in early spring with a brilliancy that is dazzling. Plants grow to 15 feet high, spread 15 feet with arching, outstretched branches.

E. × macrantha is a hybrid cross between *E. racemosa* and a related species, *E. korolkowii*. A dwarf form of this, 'The Bride', grows just 4 feet high, bushy and compact.

How to Grow—Plant from containers. Mostly grown from cuttings taken in summer because started plants are not readily available from local nurseries. Prefers fertile loam soil in a sunny location. To maintain a compact habit prune plants after flowering. Grows from Zones 4 to 8.

Landscape Use—Deserves to be much more widely grown as an accent plant. Good for mixed-shrub borders and to cascade over stone walls or split rail fences. Dwarf forms are superb planted in a rock garden.

FAGUS
Beech

Though there are about 10 species of beech native to Europe, Asia and North America, the two species most often grown in suburban gardens are the American beech and the European beech. They are both magnificent hardy deciduous shade trees, creating an immense rounded form and casting dense shade with long, spreading branches that sweep to the ground. The American beech is more widely adaptable than the European, though many more distinct varieties have been developed from the European beech.

AMERICAN BEECH *(Fagus grandiflora)*

Hardy, deciduous shade tree native to eastern North America. Plants grow 60 to 80 feet high, spread 50 to 60 feet. Leaves are oval, pointed and coarsely toothed. Attractive gray bark. Horizontal and upright spreading branches create a mounded shape, the lower branches sweeping the ground in exposed locations. The insignificant flowers are followed by small, prickly nut cases enclosing a triangular nut. Slow growing, shallow rooted and long lived.

How to Grow—Plant balled-and-burlapped. Propagated mostly by seed, named varieties by grafting. Prefers well-drained, porous, slightly acid loam soil in a sunny or lightly shaded location. Grows from Zones 3 to 9.

Landscape Use—Good specimen tree where it has room to spread, mostly used as a lawn highlight. Reasonably good fall color—bronze or gold.

EUROPEAN BEECH *(Fagus sylvatica)*

Hardy deciduous shade tree native to Europe. Grows 60 to 90 feet high, spreads 50 to 80 feet. Leaves are attractive bright green in spring, oval and slightly pointed, turning bronze in fall. Some varieties are purple-leafed. Habit of the species is rounded with upright, spreading branches, but fastigate, contorted and weeping forms are available. The insignificant flowers produce triangular nuts enclosed in a hard, spiny case. Slow growing, shallow rooted, long lived.

How to Grow—Plant balled-and-burlapped. Propagated by seed and by grafts. Prefers deep, well-drained, fertile soil, either acid or slightly alkaline, in sun or partial shade. Grows from Zones 4 to 7.

Landscape Use—Lawn highlight, screen or windbreak. Needs room to spread. Often planted in the middle of open meadows. Withstands heavy pruning and makes a spectacular hedge.

FATSIA JAPONICA
Japanese Aralia

Tender, broadleaf evergreen shrub native to Japan. Mostly grown in mild-climate areas of the South and California. Tolerates frost, but not freezing. Deeply cut, pointed leaves, up to 16 inches wide and glossy dark green, have a tropical appearance. Plants grow to 10 feet

Exochorda macrantha 'The Bride' (pearlbush) features snow-white flowers in spring on a dwarf, mounded plant.

Fagus sylvatica 'Pendula' (European weeping beech) creates spectacular lawn highlight.

Fatsia japonica (Japanese aralia) makes beautiful foundation plant for mild-climate areas.

Ficus carica (fruiting fig) has ornamental leaves as well as edible fruit.

high, spread 10 feet, create a bold accent. A hybrid, ×*Fatshedera lizei*, is a cross between *F. japonica* and English ivy *(Hedera helix)*. It has the ability to climb up a trellis.

How to Grow — Plant from containers. Propagated from cuttings. Prefers moist, humus-rich sandy soil in a shaded location. Grows from Zones 8 to 10.

Landscape Use — Excellent for containers and foundation plantings. Good for atriums, courtyards and entryways. Because of its low light requirements it is used extensively as a house plant throughout North America.

FICUS
Figs

Related to rubber trees, there are more than 800 species of figs, chiefly native to Asia. Though some of these can be grown as ornamentals in frost-free (or nearly frost-free) areas of North America, only the deciduous common fig, or edible fig, is relatively hardy. Other popular figs that are grown chiefly in the Gulf states, Southwestern states and California, include the incredible "believe-it-or-not" banyan tree, fiddleleaf fig, the Indian laurel, Moreton Bay fig, rubber tree and the weeping fig. These plants share a common trait of oozing a milky sap (a source of rubber) when cut. All make good ornamentals for the house or conservatory, grown in tubs and as bonsai subjects.

BANYAN TREE *(F. benghalense)*

Held sacred in India, the largest banyan tree in the United States, outside of Hawaii, is located in Ft. Myers, Florida, on the grounds of Thomas Edison's winter home. A gift of Harvey Firestone, the rubber tire magnate, it was a 4-foot sapling in 1925 when Edison accepted it for his botanical collection as a gift. Today, its enormous side branches extend more than 100 feet. The horizontal branches are held firm by a thicket of *brace roots*. These initially hang down from the tree as thin, brown threads, then thicken on contact with soil, into massive buttresses. Growing up to 100 feet high, this behemoth of the plant world makes a wonderful shade tree for large subtropical estates and public parks. Grows only in Zone 10.

COMMON FIG *(F. carica)*

Grows to 30 feet high, spreads 30 feet. Mostly grown as a multi-branching shrub against a wall to create a decorative foundation plant. Also can be trained as a tree or espalier. The leaves are large, decorative, deeply lobed. Delicious, juicy edible fruits ripen in late summer. In some varieties, pollination is possible only by a small insect called the *gall wasp*. Propagated by cuttings. Fruit production occurs after 2 to 4 years. Where temperatures fall below 10F (-12C), trees can be wrapped in tarpaper or burlap. Alternatively, the plants can be pruned of excessive growth and the main trunks bent low to the ground for covering with loose earth or shredded leaves. Sometimes the roots along one side must be chopped with a spade to allow the tree to bend low enough. Three of the most popular varieties are 'Mission', 'Brown Turkey' and 'Kadota', none of which require the gall wasp for pollination. With protection, 'Brown Turkey' will survive outdoors to Zone 5.

CREEPING FIG *(F. pumila)*

This plant is valued as a clinging vine in southern states, surviving outdoors south of Charleston, South Carolina. The leaves are small, oval and dense, growing well against brick walls by means of fibrous roots, like ivy. Grows from Zones 8 to 10.

INDIAN LAUREL FIG *(F. retusa)*

Similar to the rubber tree, with smaller leaves and a more dense, rounded crown. Good shade tree for dry, frost-free climates. Grows to 30 feet high, used mostly for patio shade, lawn highlight and lining streets. Popular choice for tree topiaries. Grows aerial roots that can form buttresses if allowed to root in soil. Grows in Zones 9 and 10 only.

MORETON BAY FIG *(F. macrophylla)*

Also called the serpentine tree because of its sinuous, snakelike above-ground roots, which can extend more than 200 feet. Plants are native to eastern Australia. The largest in the continental United States is located in downtown Santa Barbara, California. The tree grows a massive smooth, gray single trunk that flares out at the base giving it good protection from wind storms. The high, spreading, dense canopy of foliage offers substantial shade, and though specimens in North America grow to 60 feet in height, wild specimens are known to reach 200 feet. Grows in Zone 10 only.

RUBBER TREE *(F. elastica)*

Though widely grown as a foliage house plant in homes and offices throughout North America, the rubber tree grows well outdoors in frost-free areas, especially Southern California and tropical Florida, where it forms a dense, spreading crown. Valued as a medium-size evergreen shade tree, it grows to 25 feet or more, spreads 30 feet. Lower branches can be pruned away to provide room for seating. Pointed, broad leaves are up to 12 inches long. Good lawn highlight. Variety 'Decora' has bright red growth tips. Grows in Zones 9 and 10.

WEEPING FIG *(F. benjamina)*

Because of its handsome weeping habit and small, glossy, leathery green leaves and its tolerance of low light conditions, weeping fig is popular as a house plant. It grows outdoors in frost-free climates where it makes a decorative lawn highlight. Normally grows to 30 feet. Grows in Zone 10 only.

Ficus elastica (rubber tree) thrives in frost-free areas, such as Southern California and Southern Florida.

Ficus retusa (Indian laurel fig) pruned to a 'poodle' shape on a street in Los Angeles.

Forsythia × intermedia makes a beautiful lawn highlight, flowering in early spring.

Fothergilla major features lovely pompon flowers in spring.

FORSYTHIA × INTERMEDIA
Forsythia

Native to Europe and Asia, this popular hardy, deciduous shrub is valued for its bright yellow flowering display in early spring, long arching branches crowded with flowers even before the leaves appear. Plants grow 8 feet high, spread 10 to 12 feet wide, suckering freely to create a thicket of arching branches. Many forms are available, including upright and weeping. Flower color varies from lemon-yellow to deep golden yellow.

'Lynwood Gold' is a spectacular upright form—a branch sport from 'Spectabilis'—discovered in an Irish garden. 'Densiflora' is a spreading plant with weeping branches and lemon-yellow flowers, similar in appearance to *F. suspensa* 'Sieboldii'—the weeping forsythia. The dwarf form 'Bronxensis' is useful for small spaces

How to Grow—Planted easily even from bare-root stock. Easily rooted from softwood or hardwood cuttings. Tolerates a wide range of soil conditions, but flowering is improved if plenty of organic material is added to the soil and the plant is heavily pruned soon after flowering. Plants that have become old and rangy can be cut to the ground, fertilized and brought back to flowering glory. Grows from Zones 5 to 8. However, some varieties extend the range from Zones 4 to 9.

Landscape Use—Often planted as a lawn highlight and in foundation plantings. Also makes a fine flowering hedge. A particularly spectacular forsythia planting is the Forsythia Hill at Dumbarton Oaks, Washington, D.C., where weeping forms cover an entire hillside criss-crossed with paths.

FOTHERGILLA GARDENII
Fothergilla

Hardy deciduous flowering shrub native to North America, from Virginia to Georgia. Fothergillas are valued for their fragrant white flowers that resemble giant pussy willows. Appearing in early spring, there are basically two kinds to choose from—dwarf fothergilla *(F. gardenii)* growing to 4 feet high and large fothergilla *(F. major)* growing 6 to 10 feet high, with an equal spread. The small oval leaves have good scarlet-red fall coloring.

How to Grow—Plant from containers. Propagated by seed and softwood cuttings taken in summer. Prefers acid, organic-rich, sandy soil in full sun. Grows from Zones 4 to 8.

Landscape Use—Top-rated foundation plant for even small suburban gardens. Exquisite planted beside reflecting pools and ponds. Combines well with spring flowering bulbs. In mixed-shrub borders it complements forsythia, flowering almond, magnolias, Korean azaleas and redbuds because it flowers about the same time.

FRANKLINIA ALATAMAHA
Franklin Tree

Named for Benjamin Franklin by botanist John Bartram, who discovered the tree growing wild along the sandy shores of the Alatamaha River in Georgia. The tree is now extinct in the wild, but there are cultivated specimens readily available to gardeners. Plants are sensitive to root rot and demand good drainage. When Southerners began planting cotton, the cotton introduced a devastating root disease which wiped out the wild species.

Franklin tree is hardy, deciduous and rarely reaches more than 20 feet high, with a spread of 15 feet. It resembles a camellia in appearance, with numerous trunks clustered around the base, and smooth, sinuous branches. Leaves are similar to those of dogwood and turn red in fall. The beautiful, 3-inch-wide white flowers resemble a single-flowered camellia, appearing in late summer when other trees have finished flowering.

How to Grow—Plant balled-and-burlapped. Propagated from seeds and cuttings. Demands a loose, fertile, well-drained soil, preferably sandy and in an open, sunny location. Grows from Zones 5 to 10.

Landscape Use—Mostly grown as a lawn highlight.

Franklinia alatamaha (Franklin tree) has fall flowers that resemble camellias.

FRAXINUS AMERICANA
White Ash

Hardy, deciduous shade tree native to North America. Plants grow 50 to 80 feet high with an equal spread. Compound dark green leaves and upright spreading branches form a rounded crown. Inconspicuous flowers are followed by winged seeds that persist into winter, borne in clusters like maple seeds. Medium fast growth, deep-rooted, long-lived trees.

Two other species of ash are popular landscape plants: green ash *(F. pennsylvanica)* and European ash *(F. excelsior)*. Both grow from Zones 3 to 9.

How to Grow — Plant balled-and-burlapped or from bare-root stock. Propagated mostly from seeds and grafts. Prefers deep, fertile loam soil. Tolerates alkaline soil. Needs full sun. Grows from Zones 3 to 9. Susceptible to borers.

Landscape Use — Good lawn highlight. Attractive yellow fall color. The European ash variety, 'Aurea' has particularly good golden yellow fall coloring.

Fraxinus excelsior 'Aurea' (golden ash) displays spectacular golden yellow fall color.

Fuchsia hybrid trained to a single stem grows from a gallon tub in the main conservatory at Longwood Gardens, Pennsylvania.

Gardenia jasminoides produces fragrant waxy white flowers in early spring in frost-free areas or under glass in the North.

FUCHSIA HYBRIDA
Lady's Ear Drops

Tender, deciduous flowering shrubs native to Central and South America, also New Zealand. There are about 50 species worldwide, and over 3,000 hybrids. The flowers are pendant, borne in profusion during summer on slender, arching branches. Leaves are smooth and spear-shaped. Flower colors include white and shades of pink, red and purple, as well as many bicolors. Popular as outdoor plants in coastal California, particularly in the San Francisco Bay Area. Over the rest of the country they are grown mostly indoors in containers to decorate decks and patios during frost-free months. Habit varies from mounded shrubs to trailing types that are popular for hanging baskets. Shrub types grow to 8 feet or higher with an equal spread and can be pruned to make a small tree.

F. magellanica is a special hardy species that can be grown to Zone 6. Flowers are bright red with purple inner petals.

How to Grow—Plant from containers. Propagated mostly from softwood cuttings taken any time of year. Fuchsias prefer fertile, organically-rich soil that retains moisture, yet drains well. Give sun or partial shade. In fall, plants are best pruned back to the ground to keep them rejuvenated. Generally can be grown outdoors only in Zones 9 and 10 on the Pacific Coast.

Landscape Use—Shrub forms good for mixed-shrub borders, foundation plantings and containers. Trailing kinds are excellent for hanging baskets. Widely grown indoors or under glass in Northern climates.

GARDENIA JASMINOIDES
Gardenia

Native to China, gardenia is a dense, tender evergreen shrub valued for its highly fragrant, waxy white, flowers up to 4 inches across. Flowers resemble those of camellias. Outdoors, blooms continue over a period of several months from spring to mid-summer. Grown indoors in tubs, they flower during winter months. Grows to 6 feet high with an equal spread and has shiny, dark green leaves. The variety 'Fortuniana' has the largest flowers, which are exceedingly fragrant. The spreading form 'Prostrata' is good for hanging baskets and mass plantings on slopes.

How to Grow—Plant from containers. Propagated from softwood cuttings that root easily. Prefers moist, acid, humus-rich soil and protection from cold winds. Tolerates light frost but severely injured by freezing weather. Takes full sun or partial shade. Grows from Zones 8 to 10.

Plants are susceptible to powdery mildew and canker diseases; also common insect pests such as aphids, scale, mites, mealybugs, nematodes and thrips. Needs timely pruning, spraying and annual addition of organic matter to maintain healthy growth.

Landscape Use—Even in the South gardenias are most often grown in tubs so plants can be moved indoors in the event of unexpected frosts or freezing weather. The flowers are popular for boutonnieres and corsages. Plants are best situated near a patio or deck so their heady fragrance can be fully appreciated.

GINKGO BILOBA
Maidenhair Tree

Hardy deciduous shade tree native to China. Huge forests of ginkgo trees once covered North America. They are among the oldest surviving trees on earth, with fossil evidence dating back 150 million years. They have a unique appearance with main, upright branches positioned low on the trunk and secondary branches spreading outward, usually weeping at the tips. Trees grow 50 to 80 feet high with a spread of 25 to 40 feet. Medium-green leaves are an unusual fan shape, with a cleft in the center of the outer edge. In fall, leaves turn a golden yellow. Irregular outline, medium fast growth, deep rooted, long lived. Male and female flowers are produced on separate trees, though sex cannot be determined until flowering, which occurs after the tree is about 20 years old. Female trees produce yellow plumlike fruits with an unpleasant odor reminiscent of rotten eggs.

How to Grow—Plant balled-and-burlapped. Propagated by seeds and grafts. Plants grown from seed may be male or female. Grafted stock is usually male. Prefers deep, sandy soil or loam, either alkaline or acid. Dislikes moist soil. Tolerates salt spray and industrial pollution. Grows from Zones 3 to 10.

Landscape Use—'Fastigata' is a beautiful upright form favored as a lawn highlight and street tree. 'Autumn Gold' is a spreading form with exceptional fall color.

GLEDITSIA TRIACANTHOS INERMIS
Thornless Honeylocust

Gleditsia triacanthos inermis (honeylocust) grows into an attractive shade tree.

Honeylocust is a hardy deciduous shade tree native to North America, from Pennsylvania to Texas. The thornless variety 'Inermis' is best for landscape use because the original species, *G. triacanthos,* is armed with vicious spines all along its trunk and branches. Plants grow to 75 feet high with a spread of 50 feet. The graceful, airy foliage admits sufficient light for grass to grow up to the trunk. The white, wisterialike blossoms appear in summer. They are followed by long, brown, spiraling seed pods that contain bean-size seeds. The pods exude a sweet, syrupy gum for which the tree gets its common name. Leaves turn yellow in fall. There are many varieties of *G.t. inermis,* including 'Sunburst', which displays golden yellow leaves that turn lime green in summer.

How to Grow—Plant balled-and-burlapped or from bare-root stock. Propagated from seeds and grafts. Prefers deep, moist, loam soil. Survives moderate salt spray. Needs full sun. Widely adapted range (Zones 3 to 9).

Landscape Use—Good lawn highlight or stree tree.

Ginkgo biloba (maidenhair tree) on the verge of changing color in fall.

Halesia monticola (Mountain silverbell) dangles clusters of charming spring flowers that resemble lily-of-the-valley.

Hedera helix (English ivy) trained to a single stem, growing in 1-gallon tub.

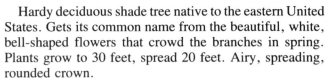

HALESIA CAROLINA
Carolina Silverbell

Hardy deciduous shade tree native to the eastern United States. Gets its common name from the beautiful, white, bell-shaped flowers that crowd the branches in spring. Plants grow to 30 feet, spread 20 feet. Airy, spreading, rounded crown.

The variety 'Rosea' is a pale pink form. Moutain silverbell (*H. monticola*) is a tall-growing native species growing to 90 feet high.

How to Grow—Plant from containers. Propagated by seeds and softwood cuttings. Prefers fertile, humus-rich, acid soil, in sun or partial shade. Grows from Zones 4 to 8.

Landscape Use—Good foundation plant and lawn highlight.

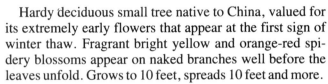

HAMAMELIS MOLLIS
Chinese Witchhazel

Hardy deciduous small tree native to China, valued for its extremely early flowers that appear at the first sign of winter thaw. Fragrant bright yellow and orange-red spidery blossoms appear on naked branches well before the leaves unfold. Grows to 10 feet, spreads 10 feet and more.

There is a native American species—the common witchhazel (*H. virginiana*), but it is not as ornamental as hybrids of the Chinese witchhazel, such as 'Ruby Glow' (orange-red flowers) and 'Brevipetala' (golden yellow flowers).

How to Grow—Plant from containers. Propagated from seed and cuttings. Thrives in organically-rich, acid soil in sun or shade. Grows from Zones 5 to 8.

Landscape Use—Foundation plantings and mixed-shrub borders.

HEDERA HELIX
English Ivy

Hardy broadleaf evergreen vine native to Europe. As a ground cover, plants grow just 6 to 8 inches high. Allowed to climb, plants will reach up to 90 feet, clinging to wood or stone by means of penetrating roots that sprout all along the stems. The dark green leaves are pointed when young, change to a smooth diamond shape when old. Established plants are fast growing. There are numerous related species and varieties, including variegated kinds. Algerian ivy (*H. canariensis*) is more popular for Zones 9 and 10, where it is widely used for slope covers.

How to Grow—Plants easily from bare-root stock. Propagated mostly from cuttings. Needs plenty of moisture until well established. Prefers humus-rich, acid or alkaline soil in full sun or shade. Grows from Zones 4 to 9.

Landscape Use—Popular for covering unsightly walls—particularly cinder block—and as a slope cover.

HIBISCUS SYRIACUS
Rose of Sharon

Hardy deciduous flowering shrubs native to China. Also known as *Althaea* from an earlier botanical name. Produces white, rose-red and violet-blue flowers in late summer, flowering continuously until frost. Grows 8 to 10 feet, spreads 6 to 8 feet. The 4-inch flowers can be double or single, usually with a contrasting 'eye'. 'Blue Bird' is a popular violet-blue variety. 'Red Heart' is an appealing white with a red eye.

Chinese or Hawaiian hibiscus *(Hibiscus rosea-sinensis)* is a popular flowering shrub in frost-free areas of coastal California, Florida, the Gulf Coast and Southwest desert. Grows in Zone 10 and frost-protected locations in Zone 9. Upright, spreading shrub that grows 6 to 8 feet, but may reach 10 to 15 feet under ideal conditions. Many varieties available with flowers up to 10 inches across in white and shades of yellow, pink, orange and red. Extensively grown under glass in Northern states.

How to Grow—Plant from containers. Easily grown from seeds that germinate reliably if scarified. Cuttings taken in summer also root readily. Flowers best in moist, humus-rich soil in full sun. Benefits from heavy pruning after flowering. Grows from Zones 5 to 9.

Landscape Use—Good lawn highlight. Also makes an attractive hedge and windbreak.

Hibiscus syriacus 'Red Heart' covers itself in beautiful flowers in late summer.

HYDRANGEA MACROPHYLLA
Hydrangea

Hardy deciduous flowering shrub native to Japan. Fast growing to 8 feet with an equal spread. Cultivated varieties are grouped into two kinds—*hortensias* and *lacecaps*. The hortensias have mostly globular flowers, up to 10 inches in diameter, in white, pink, red and blue. The lacecaps have flat flower heads that splay out like a fan—a center of small flowers surrounded by larger ones. Though the lacecaps are less spectacular, they have a sophisticated appeal and are especially attractive in lightly shaded locations.

Two other hydrangea species are extremely popular for their late summer flowers—the peegee hydrangea *(H. paniculata* 'Grandiflora') and the oak leaf hydrangea *(H. quercifolia)*. Both are white-flowered with unusually large flower heads. The peegee hydrangea is easily trained into a tree form, pruned of lower side branches.

How to Grow—Plant from containers. Propagated mostly from softwood cuttings easily rooted in moist sand. Prefers acid soil, rich in leaf mold for blue flowers. In neutral and alkaline soil flowers turn pink and red. Likes sun or partial shade. Hardiness depends on variety—lacecaps, peegee and oak leaf hydrangeas grow from Zones 6 to 9; hortensias from 7 to 10.

Landscape Use—Foundation plantings, mixed-shrub borders, hedges and containers.

Hydrangea macrophylla planted to form an avenue at Filoli Garden, near San Francisco, California.

Hypericum calycinum flowers continuously all summer. The large, golden yellow blooms are enhanced by a yellow *crest*.

Ilex opaca (American holly) displays beautiful, spire-shaped habit on a section of lawn.

HYPERICUM CALYCINUM
Hypericum

Hardy deciduous flowering shrub native to Europe, though a number of species are native to North America. Plants grow to 4 feet with equal spread, forming a dense mound of foliage covered in spring with numerous yellow flowers up to 3 inches across, accented by a prominent golden yellow *crest* of stamens. After the initial spring flush, flowers occur sporadically all summer.

How to Grow—Plant from containers. Not fussy about soil, takes sun or partial shade. Grows from Zones 5 to 10.

Landscape Use—Mostly mixed-shrub borders, rock gardens and dry walls.

ILEX
Hollies

A diverse group of both evergreen and deciduous plants, some with prickly leaves, others with smooth ones. Five distinct species are popular ornamental plants in North American gardens — American holly, Chinese holly, English holly, Japanese holly and winterberry. Also superb are the Meserve hybrids, or blue hollies, described here under English holly, which is one of its parents.

AMERICAN HOLLY (*Ilex opaca*)

Hardy broadleaf evergreen tree native to the eastern United States. Grows 15 to 30 feet high, spreads 10 to 20 feet, is variable in habit but usually forms a pyramid shape. Spiny leaves are dull green on top, yellow-green on the underside. Flowers are white and inconspicuous, with male and female flowers borne on separate trees in spring. Only the female trees bear berries. These turn bright red in fall and persist through winter. Plants are long lived, and slow growing once past the initial juvenile stage. Dwarf and yellow-berried varieties are available. Not as good looking as the English holly, but hardier.

How to Grow — Plant from containers or balled-and-burlapped. Mostly propagated from seeds and by layering. Prefers acid, well-drained (preferably sandy) moist soil in sun or partial shade. Subject to leaf scorch in windy or dry locations. For good berry production plant one male for every six females. Grows from Zones 5 to 9.

Landscape Use — Lawn highlight and foundation plantings. Good hedge, screen and windbreak.

CHINESE HOLLY (*Ilex cornuta*)

Tender broadleaf evergreen shrub native to China. Grows to 10 feet, spreads 10 feet, but usually kept more compact by heavy pruning. Glossy, dark green leaves are armed with sharp spines, though some smooth-leafed varieties have been developed. Habit is bushy, dense and mounded. Small white flowers appear in spring, followed by beautiful bright red berries that persist through winter.

How to Grow — Plant from containers. Propagated mostly from cuttings. Prefers humus-rich, acid soil but adaptable to poor soil. Grows from Zones 6 to 9.

Landscape Use — Especially popular in Southern gardens. Good for foundation plantings, containers and hedges.

ENGLISH HOLLY *(Ilex aquifolium)*

Reasonably hardy broadleaf evergreen shrub native to Europe. Grows 30 to 50 feet, spreads 10 to 30 feet. Dense, pyramidal shape with glossy, gark green prickly leaves and clusters of blood-red berries. English holly is one of the parents of the now famous Meserve hybrids, or blue hollies *(I. ×meserveae)*. 'Blue Prince' (male) and 'Blue Princess' (female) are particularly good varieties.

How to Grow — Though English holly is not reliably hardy north of Zone 6, the Meserve hybrids grow from Zones 4 to 8. Best planted from containers. Propagated from cuttings. Prefers acid sandy or loam soil.

Landscape Use — Excellent as lawn highlight, foundation plant or formal hedge.

Ilex crenata 'Green Lustre' (Japanese holly) makes an easy-care foundation plant and hedge.

JAPANESE HOLLY *(Ilex crenata)*

Hardy broadleaf evergreen shrub native to Japan. Grows 4 to 9 feet, with an equal spread, generally kept low and compact by heavy pruning. Multi-stemmed plants have a rounded habit and tight growth. Leaves vary according to variety—there are about 200 named varieties available—usually small, shiny and jade green, either oblong or rounded. Inconspicuous white flowers are male or female, produced on separate plants. Females develop small, black berries of little ornamental value.

How to Grow—Plant from containers. Propagated mostly from layering. Prefers acid soil, either sandy or loam, in sun or partial shade. Excessive heat encourages spider mites. Grows from Zones 5 to 8.

Landscape Use—Excellent for formal hedges and topiary. Good foundation plant. Helps establish solidity to mixed-shrub borders.

Ilex verticillata (winterberry) is a deciduous holly that drops its leaves in fall, but keeps exotic berry displays well into winter.

WINTERBERRY *(Ilex verticillata)*

Hardy deciduous ornamental shrub native to the eastern United States and Canada. Prolific numbers of bright red berries ripen in fall and persist on leafless branches well into winter. Grows to 10 feet, spreads 10 feet and more. Dark green leaves are small, oblong and pointed. Habit is mounded, dense and twiggy. A very fine variety, 'Christmas Cheer', is an especially heavy berry bearer.

How to Grow — Plant from containers or bare-root stock. Propagated from cuttings taken in summer. Prefers acid, moist soil, either sandy or heavy loam. Tolerates soil subjected to periodic flooding. Grows from Zones 3 to 9.

Landscape Use — Good lawn highlight, foundation plant or informal hedge. Especially beautiful planted along stream banks and lake margins.

JACARANDA ACUTIFOLIA
Jacaranda

Tender, briefly deciduous flowering shade tree native to Brazil. Also known as *J. mimosifolia*. Covers itself in

In frost-free areas, *Jacaranda acutifolia* covers itself in spring with large clusters of blue flowers that resemble foxglove.

Gelsemium sempervirens (Carolina yellow jasmine) covers a chain-link fence in Atlanta, Georgia.

Juglans nigra (black walnut) offers cool shade in summer, edible nuts in fall.

clusters of violet-blue flowers in early spring, even before leaves unfurl. Multi-stemmed with an open, spreading, rounded habit. Mimosalike leaves cast light shade. Branches are brittle. Grows to 50 feet, spreads 35 feet.

How to Grow—Plant balled-and-burlapped. Propagated from seeds and softwood cuttings. Prefers acid, humus-rich, sandy soil in full sun. Grows in Zones 9 and 10.

Landscape Use—Good lawn highlight and street tree.

JASMINUM NUDIFLORUM
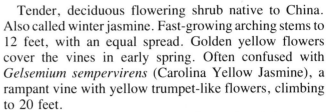
Winter Jasmine

Tender, deciduous flowering shrub native to China. Also called winter jasmine. Fast-growing arching stems to 12 feet, with an equal spread. Golden yellow flowers cover the vines in early spring. Often confused with *Gelsemium sempervirens* (Carolina Yellow Jasmine), a rampant vine with yellow trumpet-like flowers, climbing to 20 feet.

How to Grow—Plant from containers, though bare-root stock is available. Easily propagated from cuttings taken in summer. Not fussy about soil. Grows well in sun or partial shade. Can be heavily pruned to keep it within bounds. Grows from Zones 6 to 10.

Landscape Use—Best planted against a chain link fence, trellis or wall. Also used as a ground cover.

JUGLANS
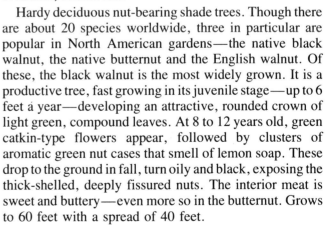
Walnuts, Butternut

Hardy deciduous nut-bearing shade trees. Though there are about 20 species worldwide, three in particular are popular in North American gardens—the native black walnut, the native butternut and the English walnut. Of these, the black walnut is the most widely grown. It is a productive tree, fast growing in its juvenile stage—up to 6 feet a year—developing an attractive, rounded crown of light green, compound leaves. At 8 to 12 years old, green catkin-type flowers appear, followed by clusters of aromatic green nut cases that smell of lemon soap. These drop to the ground in fall, turn oily and black, exposing the thick-shelled, deeply fissured nuts. The interior meat is sweet and buttery—even more so in the butternut. Grows to 60 feet with a spread of 40 feet.

The butternut *(J. cinerea)* is similar in appearance, except the English walnut *(J. regia)* is much more spreading in habit. Many varieties of English walnut are available and it is used commercially because its nuts are easier to crack. The Carpathian strain is hardy into Canada.

How to Grow—Plant balled-and-burlapped or from bare-root stock. Prefers deep, fertile, well-drained soil in full sun. Butternut is hardy from Zones 3 to 7; black walnut and Carpathian strain of English walnut from Zones 4 to 8.

Landscape Use—Black walnuts are long-lived shade trees valued for investment because the rich, brown wood is used in making fine furniture. Take care in planting black walnuts in the landscape because the roots exude a chemical (juglone) that inhibits the growth of many plants, including azaleas and rhododendrons.

JUNIPERS

Junipers

About 70 species of junipers are widely distributed throughout the world. Many are concentrated in the Northern Hemisphere, some extending into the Arctic Circle. Junipers are extremely diverse in habit, from ground-hugging plants that resemble heather, covering vast areas of steppes in Siberia, to tall, slender spires punctuating the skylines of mountain peaks. They are generally tough, dependable, long-lived plants that thrive even in poor soil. Because of their versatility, they are without doubt the most widely used evergreen conifers in North American gardens.

Foliage color varies from dark green through blue and yellow. The cones are small, resembling blueberries in shape. Though junipers are valuable landscape plants, some of the upright forms have an unfortunate trait—they are host to a disease called *cedar-apple rust,* which can defoliate crabapples, hawthorns and other ornamental trees. The disease over-winters on junipers—particularly the native *J. virginiana,* developing slimy octopuslike yellow growths in spring and releasing wind-borne spores that infect species of apples and pears in summer. Another disease problem that limits their usefulness is *juniper-tip blight.* Susceptibility differs greatly among different varieties.

Following is a sampling of the more important juniper species:

CHINESE JUNIPER *(J. chinensis)*

The original species grows 50 to 60 feet high and spreads 20 feet, but numerous varieties have been developed for special landscape effects. 'Obelisk' is a rapid-growing, narrow, upright, blue-gray form growing to 10 feet high. It is frequently displayed in rock gardens and as door sentinels. Grows from Zones 4 to 10. The variety 'Kaizuka', also known as Hollywood juniper, has curious spiral dark green leaders and fast growth. It grows from Zones 5 to 10, favored for foundation plantings in southern climates, particularly coastal areas of Southern California. Plants grow up to 15 feet high. 'Phitzerana' is a low, spreading type admired for its feathery arching branches, used to cover slopes. The golden form 'Aurea' is especially attractive, growing 5 to 6 feet high and spreading 12 feet. 'San Jose' is another good low-growing variety. Its bright, blue-gray needles and sinuous, spreading branches make it a favorite choice for artistic pruning—particularly *poodle* forms—and training as a bonsai subject.

CREEPING JUNIPER *(J. horizontalis)*

Ground-hugging shrub that grows only 1 to 2 feet high and spreads up to 8 feet wide. Used mostly as a ground cover. The most popular variety is 'Wiltonii', also known as 'Blue Rug'. Grows from Zones 4 to 10. It has silvery blue foliage and grows only 6 inches high, spreading up to 8 feet.

Juniperus chinensis 'Kaizuka' is a favorite lawn highlight in Southern states and California.

Juniperus horizontalis 'Blue Rug' makes one of the finest ground covers available.

Kalmia latifolia (mountain laurel) is an eye-catching foundation plant for acid soils.

Kerria japonica (Japanese kerria) tolerates shade. Both single- and double-flowered kinds are available.

EASTERN RED CEDAR (J. virginiana)

Plants are native to North America, grow to 50 feet high, spread 20 feet, thrive in the poorest soils and grow from Zones 3 to 9. The wild species has green leaves, but some forms are gray-green and silvery blue. Popular for creating windbreaks and lining driveways. 'Skyrocket' is a narrow, upright form used for foundation plantings and for planting as pairs on either side of a doorway.

How to Grow—Most junipers are planted from containers, though bare-root stock is widely available, and extra large specimens are offered balled-and-burlapped. Propagation is by seeds or cuttings. Plants tolerate a wide range of soils, even stoney soil and poor, sandy soil, though acid loam suits them best. However, all require full sun. Grows from Zones 3 to 10, depending on variety.

Landscape Use—Horizontal kinds are used mostly as ground covers, especially on slopes. Upright forms make good screens, windbreaks and sentinels, and are also popular to line long driveways. Junipers are favorite subjects for bonsai and potted topiaries.

KALMIA LATIFOLIA
Mountain Laurel

Hardy evergreen flowering shrub native to North America from Canada to Florida. Grows 8 to 10 feet high, spreads 10 feet. Mound-shaped plants covered with clusters of white or pink flowers in late spring. The floral display is extraordinary—in the bud stage, the flower clusters resemble clumps of exotic sea coral, then open out into five-sided, cup-shaped flowers. Often described as America's most beautiful native shrub, it is the state flower of both Pennsylvania and Connecticut. 'Ostbo Red' is a fine rose-red developed by the Connecticut Agricultural Experiment Station.

How to Grow—Propagated mostly by seed, layering and grafts. Plants prefer partial shade and a cool, moist, well-drained, organically rich acid soil. Worth preparing a special bed of leaf mold to encourage the masses of blooms that well-grown specimens can produce. Grows from Zones 4 to 9.

Landscape Use—Good foundation plant. Also effective planted along rustic paths for a naturalized effect.

KERRIA JAPONICA
Japanese Kerria

Bushy evergreen flowering shrub native to China. Grown mostly for its arching stems covered in spring with yellow flowers, either single or double, though the double-flowered form is more common. Plants grow to 6 feet high, spread 8 feet. 'Pleniflora', a double-flowered variety, has the largest flowers—up to 2 inches across.

How to Grow—Plant from containers. Propagated easily from cuttings. Prefers fertile loam or humus-rich soil. Performs well in sun, but better in light shade because the flowers last longer and develop a richer yellow coloring. Grows from Zones 4 to 9.

Landscape Use—Popular for semi-shaded locations, especially foundation plantings and mixed-shrub borders.

KOELREUTERIA PANICULATA
Golden Rain Tree

Hardy, deciduous flowering tree native to China and Japan. Beautiful rounded, spreading habit. Grows to 30 feet, spreads 20 feet. Starting in mid-summer, it covers itself with clusters of fragrant, golden yellow flowers, followed by decorative, lantern-shaped seed cases that turn from lime-green to golden brown. Mid-green leaves are compound, composed of many serrated leaflets, turning yellow in fall. A related species, the Chinese flame tree *(K. elegans)* is less hardy (Zone 9). It produces orange-red seed pods like Chinese lanterns.

How to Grow—Best planted balled-and-burlapped. Propagated by seed and cuttings. Tolerates heat and drought, and a wide range of soils, including alkaline soil, as long as soil drains well. Needs full sun. Grows from Zones 5 to 10.

Landscape Use—Excellent lawn highlight and flowering shade tree. Good street tree because of pollution tolerance.

Koelreuteria paniculata (golden rain tree) in full flower. Flowers are followed by decorative seed cases resembling Chinese lanterns.

KOLKWITZIA AMABILIS
Beauty Bush

Hardy deciduous flowering shrub native to China. Plants are fast growing to 10 feet high, spreading 8 feet. Long, arching stems are covered with pink, yellow-throated, trumpet-shaped flowers in early summer. 'Pink Cloud' and 'Rosea' are two popular varieties. Spectacular floral display.

How to Grow—Best planted from containers. Propagated by seed and softwood cuttings. Plants grow in acid or alkaline soil in full sun. Heavy pruning helps keep the plants rejuvenated. Grows from Zones 5 to 8.

Landscape Use—Mostly used as foundation plantings and in mixed-shrub borders, also as a short informal hedge. It is an "old fashioned" shrub that adds character to old houses, especially when planted near entryways.

LABURNUM ×VOSSII
Golden Chain Tree

Hardy deciduous flowering tree hybridized from species native to Europe. For 2 weeks in late spring, this small-to-medium size tree puts on a fine flowering display with masses of long, pealike flower clusters up to 20 inches long, hanging down like golden chains. Grows to 20 feet, spreads 15 feet. Branches are spreading and pliable. The clover-shaped leaves are composed of three leaflets. *Caution: All parts of this tree are poisonous.*

Care should be taken in the choice of varieties. The common laburnum, *L. anagyroides,* has small flower clusters compared to *L. ×vossii,* which is a hybrid between the common laburnum and Scotch laburnum *(L. alpinum).*

How to Grow—Plant from containers or balled-and-burlapped. Can be propagated by seeds and layering, but modern varieties are produced by grafting and budding

Laburnum ×vossii (golden chain tree) in author's garden fills its leafy canopy with glorious yellow flower clusters.

Lagerstroemia indica (crape myrtle) makes a dramatic lawn high-light in midsummer.

In frost-free areas, *Lantana camara* (shrub verbena) almost smothers itself in lovely orange-pink blossoms.

onto seedling stocks. Prefers full sun but tolerates light shade. Grows best in moist, fertile well-drained soils in a sheltered location. Grows from Zones 5 to 7.

Landscape Use—Good to plant up against a sunny wall of the house, and as a lawn highlight. One of the most sophisticated uses is a *laburnum tunnel* whereby parallel lines of laburnums are planted on either side of strong metal arches, their branches trained over the metal framework to form a tunnel so that the flowers hang down like grapes trained over an arbor.

LAGERSTROEMIA INDICA
Crape Myrtle

Native to China, but first discovered growing in India, the crape myrtle is a tender, deciduous flowering tree popular throughout the Southern states. In its juvenile stage it is most often seen as a shrubby, upright tree with long, whiplike branches topped by heavy clusters of lilac-like flowers, mostly in pink, white, red and lavender. With age, several main trunks will dominate, devoid of lower branches. These older trunks become curiously twisted and highly decorative as the smooth, shining bark flakes away in long strips to reveal lighter colored bark beneath. Mature size is 25 feet high, with a spread of 20 feet.

'Indian Tribes' is a new hybrid collection developed by the National Arboretum. They possess extraordinary vigor, hardiness and resistance to mildew and other diseases. The 'Petites' are dwarf varieties suitable for container culture and for creating low hedges.

How to Grow—Best planted balled-and-burlapped. Propagated by seeds and cuttings. Demands full sun, but tolerates poor soils. Hardiness varies according to exposure to cold winds. Grows from Zones 7 to 10.

Landscape Use—Most often used along property lines and as foundation plantings. At Colonial Williamsburg, Virginia, crape myrtles are widely used in the small formal Colonial-style gardens, the base of the tree generally circled with a ground cover and the smooth, shiny trunks contrasting against a dark boxwood hedge or brick wall. Dwarf kinds are good in tubs to decorate decks and patios.

LANTANA CAMARA
Shrub Verbena

Tropical evergreen flowering shrub native to South and Central America, mostly grown outdoors in frost-free areas. The bushy plants cover themselves in white, pink, yellow or orange flowers resembling annual verbenas. Plants flower continuously through summer, grow to 4 feet high and spread up to 6 feet. Can be trained to a single woody stem. There is a very similar related species, *C. montevidensis* (trailing lantana) with rose-purple flowers. It is used as a ground cover or as a hanging plant.

How to Grow — Easily grown from bare-root cuttings and seeds. Tolerates a wide range of soil conditions including alkaline soil. Good plant for coastal gardens because of its tolerance to salt spray. Takes high heat and drought. Prefers a sunny location. Plant 3 to 4 feet apart for dense ground cover. Plants can be sheared back to the soil line in winter to maintain compact, dense growth. Grows in Zones 9 and 10.

Landscape Use — Excellent flowering ground cover, especially for slopes. In cold climates, shrub verbenas are popular as flowering house plants, especially in hanging baskets.

LARIX KAEMPFERI
Japanese Larch

Three kinds of larch are common in North American gardens—the European larch *(L. decidua)*, Japanese larch *(L. kaempferi)* and American larch *(L. laricina)*, all of which are named for their places of origin. Of these, the most popular for ornamental value is the Japanese larch.

This hardy deciduous conifer grows to 90 feet, spreading to 40 feet. Open, pyramidal shape and strong, spreading pendulous branches. Leaves are arranged along the branches in spikey clusters. They are bright green in summer, turn golden in autumn and drop as the tree enters winter dormancy. Egg-shaped cones are borne upright. A weeping form, 'Pendula', is especially attractive in the landscape.

How to Grow—Best planted balled-and-burlapped when dormant, either in autumn or early spring. Propagated mostly from seeds. Prefers deep, acid loam soil in full sun. Grows from Zones 4 to 7.

Landscape Use — Mostly used in groves and as skyline trees. Also used in open spaces such as parks, golf courses and estates.

LEUCOTHOE FONTANESIANA
Drooping Leucothoe

Hardy broadleaf evergreen shrubs native to the Appalachian Mountains of North America. Plants have graceful, arching branches and long, pointed leaves. New leaves are sometimes tipped with red coloring. Slow-growing to 4 feet high. White flowers resembling lily-of-the-valley appear in spring, hanging in dense clusters from the branch tips. A related species, *L. racemosa* (silverbells), is an attractive dwarf plant. A number of outstanding hybrids are available. 'Scarletta' has rich burgundy leaf color through winter, changing to scarlet in spring.

How to Grow—Best planted from containers. Propagated from seed and cuttings taken in spring. Prefers humus-rich, acid soil in full sun or dense shade. Grows from Zones 4 to 6.

Landscape Use—Good for underplanting among trees and as a cover for shaded slopes.

Larix kaempferi (Japanese larch) appears to be evergreen, but actually turns brown and loses its needles in winter.

Leucothoe fontanesiana (drooping leucothoe) dangles attractive flowers in spring from arching branches.

Ligustrum japonicum (Japanese privet) makes a dense, evergreen hedge.

Liquidamber styraciflua is a superb tree for foundation plantings. Leaves turn red in fall.

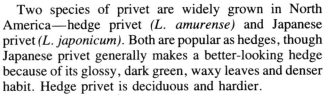

LIGUSTRUM
Privet

Two species of privet are widely grown in North America—hedge privet (*L. amurense*) and Japanese privet (*L. japonicum*). Both are popular as hedges, though Japanese privet generally makes a better-looking hedge because of its glossy, dark green, waxy leaves and denser habit. Hedge privet is deciduous and hardier.

There are many other widely used hedge privets. California privet (*L. ovalifolium*) is semi-evergreen and native to Japan. Hardy to Zone 5. European privet (*L. vulgare*) is subject to severe dieback from fungus disease and is used much less than it used to be. It grows from Zones 4 to 7. Golden privet (*L.* × *vicaryi*) is a slow-growing hybrid of *L. vulgare*. It has bright golden yellow foliage and is best planted in full sun. Popular for foundation plantings and entryways, it is hardy to Zone 5 and is evergreen in mild climates.

HEDGE PRIVET (*L. amurense*)

Also known as Amur privet for the area of Northern China where it grows wild. Plants are fast growing, upright, multi-stemmed. Grows to 15 feet high, spreads 10 feet, has small oval leaves and white flower clusters which rarely have a chance to show on hedges because of shearing.

How to Grow — Hedge privet is easily planted from bare-root stock. Tolerates poor soil and heavy pollution in sun or light shade. Reliable even close to busy highways. Demands heavy pruning with shears. Grows from Zones 3 to 7.

Landscape Use — Tall or medium-size hedge.

JAPANESE PRIVET (*L. japonicum*)

Plants are extremely dense — like a large-leaf version of boxwood. Evergreen, upright, fast growth to 12 feet, spreads 6 to 8 feet. Flowers are white and reasonably ornamental, but are usually absent because of heavy pruning.

How to Grow — Plant from containers. Thrives in a wide range of soils, except overly moist soil. Prefers sun, tolerates shade. Enjoys heavy pruning, repeated shearing. Grows from Zones 6 to 10.

Landscape Use — Mostly formal hedges, topiary and trained forms such as pompons. Can be pruned of lower branches to make a small tree. Popular foundation plant, especially for entryways.

LIQUIDAMBAR STYRACIFLUA
Sweetgum

Hardy deciduous shade tree native to the eastern United States. Produces a fragrant resin known as *sweet gum*. Grows 60 to 80 feet, spreads 40 to 60 feet. Maple-shaped leaves are dark green, turning deep crimson in fall. Flowers are inconspicuous. Produces pendant, globular seed cases that persist through winter and are considered an ornamental feature. Branches develop prominent corky wings after several years of growth. Medium-fast rate of growth, long lived.

How to Grow—Plant balled-and-burlapped. Propagated from seeds, named varieties by layering. Prefers deep, fertile, moist, acid soil in full sun. Tolerates wet or boggy soils. Grows from Zones 5 to 10.

Landscape Use—Good lawn highlight and windbreak. Fall color can be variable. One of few sources of fall color in mild-winter climates.

LIRIODENDRON TULIPIFERA
Tulip Tree

Also known as tulip poplar and yellow poplar, the tulip tree is a hardy deciduous flowering shade tree native to eastern North America. Related to magnolias, it is tall, fast growing to 90 feet and more, spreading 40 feet. Fastest growth occurs during the tree's juvenile years—growth rates of up to 6 feet a year have been recorded. The trunk grows as straight as a telephone pole. At 10 to 15 years of age, beautiful golden yellow flowers appear in spring. These are shaped like tulips and are the size of small teacups. The flowers are followed by slender cone-shaped seed capsules that persist through winter and are scattered by the wind in spring. Its large leaves are light green in summer, and distinct in shape with prominent lobes at the base and an almost square top. Fall coloring is spectacular—bright golden yellow.

How to Grow — Plant balled-and-burlapped or from bare-root stock. Mostly propagated from seed, though germination is erratic, owing to a high percentage of infertile seeds. Prefers deep, moist, well-drained soil in a sunny location. Grows from Zones 3 to 9.

Landscape Use — Excellent lawn highlight. Popular choice for creating a wooded lot.

LONICERA
Honeysuckle

More than 150 species of honeysuckle are widely distributed throughout the Western Hemisphere, mostly hardy deciduous shrubs and vines. Some are evergreen or semi-evergreen. The garden-worthy types are mostly admired for their decorative, trumpet-shaped, sweetly scented flowers that attract hummingbirds. By far the most popular species for home gardens are Japanese honeysuckle *(L. japonica)* and red trumpet honeysuckle *(L. sempervirens)*.

JAPANESE HONEYSUCKLE *(Lonicera japonica)*

Hardy, semi-evergreen flowering vine native to Japan and China. Plants grow to 30 feet, twining up supports or spreading over the ground. Trumpet-shaped flowers are white and yellow, with a sweet fragrance that carries a long distance. A heavy flush of bloom occurs in early summer, but blooms continue sparsely into fall. Plants have escaped into the wild over most of North America and can be a serious pest, killing small trees with their

Liriodendron tulipifera (tulip poplar) towers above a grove of maples.

Lonicera japonica 'Halliana' (Hall's Japanese honeysuckle) has fragrant yellow flowers that appear in early summer.

Magnolia × soulangiana (saucer magnolias) underplanted with daffodils at Longwood Gardens, Pennsylvania.

Magnolia grandiflora (Southern magnolia) displays massive white flowers and glorious glossy green leaves.

suffocating, strangling growth. 'Hall's' is the most widely used variety.

How to Grow — Easily planted from bare-root stock. Propagated mostly by root division and cuttings taken in summer. Not fussy about soil. Takes heavy pruning. Plants can be cut back to the soil line every year to keep them compact. Grows from Zones 4 to 9.

Landscape Use — Mostly used to cover chain link fences, trellis and arbors. Makes a decorative hedge if given wires for support. Also useful as a ground cover on difficult, exposed sites.

RED TRUMPET HONEYSUCKLE (L. sempervirens)

Similar in many respects to *L. japonica* except the flowers are scarlet-red with yellow throats and not fragrant. Native to North America, from New England to Florida, plants are especially popular in the South. 'Magnifica' is a free-flowering red; 'Sulphureus' is yellow flowering.

MAGNOLIA
Magnolias

There are 80 species of magnolias, mostly native to China and North America. The deciduous Chinese species include the billowing saucer magnolia (*M. soulangiana*) and the more diminutive star magnolia (*M. stellata.*) The North American species include the Southern magnolia (*M. grandiflora*), which produces large, shiny, evergreen leaves and enormous white flowers up to 12 inches across.

Other native magnolias such as the cucumber magnolia (*M. acuminata*) and the big leaf magnolia (*M. macrophylla*) have spectacular flowers, but are more often confined to large estates and parks.

SAUCER MAGNOLIA (M. × soulangiana)

Grows to 30 feet high, spreads 20 feet and covers itself in early spring with magnificent, waxlike flowers resembling exotic waterlilies. Color ranges from pure white in the variety 'Alba' through pink—the most popular color—to deep purple in some of the hybrids such as 'Lennei'. Usually a cluster of multiple trunks emanate from the base, the bark colored dark gray and smooth in texture. Tree flowers when young. Individual flowers can be up to 10 inches across when fully open. Though it grows from Zones 4 to 10, the saucer magnolia's flowers are sensitive to frost damage. In exposed locations there is a tendency for the tree to burst into full flower during an early warming spell, only to have the whole glorious display blasted by a sudden return of frost, rendering the blossoms limp and brown.

SOUTHERN MAGNOLIA (M. grandiflora)

This grows to be a towering tree up to 90 feet high, with enormous leaves resembling those of laurel. Flowering in summer, the huge, bowl-shaped, fragrant flowers are followed by large, ornamental feltlike seed pods filled with brilliant red, bean-size seeds. Because of its sensitivity to cold, the Southern magnolia is often grown against walls.

Two of the best varieties are 'Majestic Beauty', offering a beautiful pyramid shape, and 'Little Gem', a dwarf slow-growing form. 'Edith Boque' is a particularly hardy form. Grows from Zones 6 to 10.

STAR MAGNOLIA (M. stellata)

This shrublike tree grows to 15 feet high with an equal spread. It almost smothers itself in star-shaped flowers made up of many slender, strap-shaped petals. Flowering a little ahead of their larger-flowered cousins, the saucer magnolias, most star magnolias have white flowers, though there is a good pale pink hybrid form, 'Leonard Messel'. Grows from Zones 3 to 8.

How to Grow—Plant balled-and-burlapped. Saucer magnolias and star magnolias are propagated mostly from cuttings, the Southern magnolias mostly from seeds. Magnolias prefer open, sunny locations and a fertile, organically rich, acid soil. Southern magnolias tolerate shade.

Landscape Use—Saucer magnolias make the best lawn highlights for suburban gardens. Star magnolias can be grown in smaller spaces, including tubs for decorating decks and patios. An underplanting of daffodils is an exquisite combination with saucer and star magnolias because flowering occurs simultaneously. Southern magnolias are more often used to line driveways or to delineate a vista on large estates. Also, they can be effectively espaliered against the side of a house to make a much more appealing green wall cover than ivy or other vines.

MAHONIA AQUIFOLIUM
Oregon Grape, Holly Grape

Hardy evergreen shrub native to the Pacific Northwest. Grows 3 to 6 feet high, spreads 4 to 5 feet. The prickly, dark green, glossy leaves resemble holly leaves, arranged in regimented rows on either side of each stem. Flowers are bright yellow, appear in early spring and hang down from the plant in long clusters. These are followed by berries resembling small, black grapes that persist into winter months. New leaves show bronze coloring. Winter leaf color is purplish.

LEATHERLEAF MAHONIA (M. bealei)

This is a related species. The leaves are more prickly, even more hollylike and blue-green in color. The fragrant flowers are light yellow and are followed by sky-blue berries that hang down the plants in a curtain. Grows from Zones 5 to 8.

How to Grow—Plant from containers. Propagated mostly from seed and softwood cuttings. Prefers humus-rich, acid soil in partial shade. Leaves are highly susceptible to sun scald and wind burn in exposed locations. Grows from Zones 5 to 8.

Landscape Use—Good for foundation plantings and mixed-shrub borders in partial shade.

Magnolia stellata (star magnolia) covers itself in brilliant white flowers, even before leaves appear.

Mahonia bealei (leatherleaf mahonia) exhibits grapelike clusters of berries that persist through winter.

Malus 'Candy Apple' is a lovely weeping crabapple with deep pink flowers.

Malus 'Radiant' is a rosy red, spreading crabapple favored by suburban homeowners.

MALUS SPECIES
Crabapples

These hardy deciduous flowering trees are widely dispersed throughout the temperate regions of North America, Europe and Asia, numbering about 30 distinct species, plus hundreds of hybrids. Along with flowering cherries and dogwoods, crabapples are among the most widely planted flowering trees in North America. In many varieties, the blizzard of white, pink or carmine-red flowers is often followed by yellow, orange or red ornamental fruits that persist on the trees after the leaves have fallen. In addition to the rounded, spreading forms so popular as lawn highlights, there are also upright and weeping varieties. When selecting varieties, consideration should be given to disease resistance, particularly to *scab, cedar-apple rust, mildew* and *fireblight*—the four major disease problems. The following species and varieties of crabapple are especially recommended for small suburban gardens:

MALUS 'ADAMS'

Dense, rounded, pink-flowering variety with red fruit that persists into winter. Grows to 20 feet, spreads 20 feet. Excellent resistance to disease, notably scab, cedar-apple rust and fireblight. Mildew resistance is rated good.

MALUS 'CANDIED APPLE'

Magnificent weeping habit. Flowers are deep pink—considered better than weeping 'Red Jade', which opens pale pink and fades to white. Bright red fruits persist after leaves fall. Grows 15 feet, spreads 15 feet. Excellent overall disease resistance.

MALUS 'DOROTHEA'

Dense, rounded, pink-flowering variety with yellow fruit that persists after the leaves drop. Grows to 25 feet, spreads 25 feet. Poor disease resistance.

MALUS FLORIBUNDA

Spreading, irregular shape. Pink flowers fade to white, followed by yellow or red fruits. Grows to 20 feet, spreads 25 feet. Excellent resistance to cedar-apple rust, moderate resistance to scab, fireblight and mildew.

MALUS 'RADIANT'

Attractive rounded shape, with deep red flowers followed by bright red fruits. Grows to 30 feet, spreads 25 feet. Moderate disease resistance, though susceptible to scab.

MALUS SARGENTII

Low, spreading habit. White flowers, red fruit persisting after leaves fall. Height 8 feet, spread 12 feet. Excellent resistance to scab, cedar-apple rust and mildew; good resistance to fireblight.

MALUS 'SNOWDRIFT'

Upright, spreading, rounded shape. White flowers followed by orange fruits. Height 20 feet, spread 20 feet.

Good resistance to scab; no resistance to fireblight.

How to Grow—Crabapples do well in North America wherever there is snow cover in winter. Easily planted, even from bare-root stock. Cultivated varieties are almost always self-sterile and must be propagated by grafting. Though crabapples are not fussy about soil, a humus-rich acid soil is preferred. Conditioning the soil with compost or animal manures—such as cow and horse manure—works wonders. Crabapples demand a sunny location and good air circulation. Hardiness range generally extends from Zones 4 to 8.

Landscape Use—Superb lawn highlight. A valuable use for ornamental crabapples is in apple orchards where growers are finding that ornamental varieties planted among regular apples are increasing pollination and fruit production.

METASEQUOIA GLYPTOSTROBOIDES
Dawn Redwood

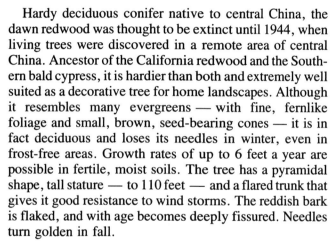

Hardy deciduous conifer native to central China, the dawn redwood was thought to be extinct until 1944, when living trees were discovered in a remote area of central China. Ancestor of the California redwood and the Southern bald cypress, it is hardier than both and extremely well suited as a decorative tree for home landscapes. Although it resembles many evergreens — with fine, fernlike foliage and small, brown, seed-bearing cones — it is in fact deciduous and loses its needles in winter, even in frost-free areas. Growth rates of up to 6 feet a year are possible in fertile, moist soils. The tree has a pyramidal shape, tall stature — to 110 feet — and a flared trunk that gives it good resistance to wind storms. The reddish bark is flaked, and with age becomes deeply fissured. Needles turn golden in fall.

How to Grow — Plant from containers and bare-root stock. Mostly propagated from seeds. Prefers moist, humus-rich acid soil — especially beside lakes and along stream banks in a sunny location. Grows from Zones 4 to 9, and even in parts of Zone 10. There is a fine specimen in the Huntington Botanical Gardens, near Los Angeles.

Landscape Use — Excellent lawn highlight. Good street tree because of pollution resistance. Excellent tree for establishing a wooded lot because shedding of needles in winter creates a thick, springy, natural mulch that suffocates weed growth.

MYRICA CERIFERA
Southern Wax Myrtle

Tender evergreen shrub native to the southeastern United States, from Maryland to Florida. Widely grown in Southern gardens. Grows to 15 feet high and spreads to 12 feet. Forms a dense canopy of small, light green, pointed leaves that have a fragrance similar to bayberry. Closely related to the hardy Northern bayberry *(M. pensylvanica)*, which is widely used in Northern gardens as a hedge and slope cover.

Metasequoia glyptostroboides (dawn redwood) can grow up to 6 feet a year. Though it appears to be evergreen, it turns bronze in fall and loses its leaves.

Myrica cerifera (Southern wax myrtle) is pruned of lower side branches and clipped to form matching domes.

How to Grow—Best planted from containers. Propagated from seeds and cuttings. Prefers fertile, sandy soil in sun or partial shade. Grows from Zones 7 to 9.

Landscape Use—Takes heavy pruning. Makes a beautiful formal hedge. Also popular in containers. The lower branches can be pruned away and the top sheared to create a tight, rounded dome for placing at entryways.

NANDINA DOMESTICA
Heavenly Bamboo

Tender evergreen shrub producing ornamental red berries that persist through winter. Native to China. Grows to 8 feet, spreads 5 feet. Erect habit, forming a thicket of slender, canelike stems vaguely resembling bamboo. 'Harbor Dwarf' is a good low-growing variety used as a ground cover. Popular in the South, Southwest and Southern California.

How to Grow—Best planted from containers. Propagated mostly by cuttings taken in fall. Not fussy about soil though it does best in moist, acid, sandy or humus soil, in full sun or light shade. Grows from Zones 6 to 10. Plants are best left unpruned because pruning exposes bare canes and generally ruins the natural form.

Landscape Use—Mixed-shrub borders and foundation plantings. Tall types can be used as an informal hedge, dwarf kinds for covering narrow, hard-to-plant places.

Nandina domestica (heavenly bamboo) decorates its evergreen branches with clusters of bright red berries that persist through winter in the South.

NERIUM OLEANDER
Oleander

Tender evergreen flowering shrub native to Asia. Can be grown to a single trunk, or as a thicket of branches with a rounded habit. Oleanders are popular flowering plants in areas that escape winter freezes, covering themselves in clusters of fragrant, 1-inch flowers in white, pink, salmon and red, blooming non-stop all summer. Plants grow to 12 feet high, spread 12 feet. *Caution: All parts of plant are poisonous.*

'Calypso' has beautiful cherry-red flowers and is one of the hardiest kinds. 'Hawaii' has lovely salmon-pink flowers with yellow throats. 'Petite Salmon' is a compact, dwarf salmon-pink.

How to Grow—Plant from containers. Propagated from seeds and softwood cuttings taken in midsummer. Plants can also be divided. Thrives in a wide range of soils including poor, sandy soil. Tolerates salt spray and is widely used in coastal gardens. Grows from Zones 8 to 10.

Landscape Use—Attractive hedge and windbreak. Also good lawn highlight when pruned to a single stem. Popular for growing in tubs to decorate decks and patios, and as a container plant under glass in Northern states.

Nerium oleander is an excellent lawn highlight for frost-free areas.

NYSSA SYLVATICA
Tupelo, Black

Hardy deciduous shade tree native to North America, from Quebec to Florida. Also known as black gum, this is one of America's most beautiful trees for fall color. Grows to 50 feet, spreads 30 feet. Has a majestic spreading outline, the dark green, oval, pointed leaves changing to crimson in fall, contrasting beautifully with its charcoal gray branches and trunk.

How to Grow—Best planted balled-and-burlapped, though bare-root stock is also reliable. Propagated from seeds. Tolerates a wide range of soil conditions, but grows best in deep, acid, loam soils, in full sun or partial shade. Grows from Zones 3 to 9.

Landscape Use—Makes a good, long-lived lawn highlight. Good for lining driveways.

OLEA EUROPAEA
European Olive

Tender broadleaf evergreen tree native to the Mediterranean. Slow growing to 30 feet high, spreading 30 feet. Billowing shape, gnarled trunk and attractive silvery foliage help to make it a popular medium-size shade tree for dry climates. Plants can be multi-stemmed. Insignificant yellow flowers in spring are followed by black, oval fruits that ripen in fall. Olives are edible only when pickled and are a source of olive oil. Many special landscape varieties have been developed, including varieties that do not bear fruit, to avoid flower and fruit litter. 'Manzanillo' is a favorite landscape variety. It develops an artistic cluster of main stems and a compact round-headed crown. Lower branches on the multiple trunks are usually pruned away.

How to Grow—Plant from containers. Propagated mostly from cuttings. Tolerates a wide range of soils, including dry stony soil, but does best in deep fertile loam or sandy soil. Grows from Zones 8 to 10.

Landscape Use—Excellent lawn specimen. Popular for planting in rows to line a street or driveway. Good for growing in containers. Superb for planting in groves. Popular tree for shading patios, decks and parking lots.

OSMANTHUS HETEROPHYLLUS
Holly Osmanthus

Tender broadleaf evergreen shrub native to Japan. Also known as false holly because of its striking resemblance to holly. Grows to 10 feet, spreads 8 feet, but mostly kept low and compact by heavy pruning and shearing. There are numerous varieties, such as 'Aureus' with yellow-edged leaves, and 'Variegatus' with leaves margined white. Also, several related species and hybrids are used as landscape plants, including Fortune's osmanthus *(O. ×fortunei)*, which is similar in appearance to holly osmanthus, but hardier and more vigorous.

Nyssa sylvatica (black tupelo) lights up the sky with magnificent red foliage in fall.

Olea europaea (European olive) makes a handsome shade tree for frost-free areas.

Pachysandra terminalis (Japanese spurge) is a superb ground cover for shady areas.

Washingtonia filifera (California fan palm) is native to Arizona and Southern California.

How to Grow—Plant from containers. Mostly propagated from cuttings. Prefers humus-rich, moist, acid soil in full sun or partial shade. Takes heavy pruning. Grows from Zones 7 to 9.

Landscape Use — Good low hedge, screen or windbreak. Tolerates salt spray.

OXYDENDRUM ARBOREUM
Sourwood

Hardy deciduous shade tree native to North America, from Pennsylvania to Florida. Also called sorrel tree and lily-of-the-valley tree. Oval, lancelike leaves turn from dark green to scarlet or purple-red in fall. Clusters of white flowers that resemble lily-of-the-valley cascade down the tree in midsummer. Grows to 35 feet high, spreads 20 feet, with drooping branches and an attractive pyramid habit. Slow growing.

How to Grow—Plant balled-and-burlapped. Propagated by seed and softwood cuttings taken in midsummer. Prefers moist, acid, well-drained soil and full sun. Grows from Zones 5 to 9.

Landscape Use—Excellent lawn highlight. Popular tree for parks and golf courses. Because fall color can be variable it pays to observe young trees for good color before buying to plant the following spring.

PACHYSANDRA TERMINALIS
Japanese Spurge

Hardy broadleaf evergreen ground cover native to Japan. Grows to 12 inches high, spreads horizontally by means of underground stolons. Forms whorls of toothed leaves on top of slender, woody stems. A fine variegated form 'Variegata', has silver leaf margins.

How to Grow—Plant from bare-root stock. Propagated from cuttings. Prefers moist, humus-rich, acid soil in light shade, though plants will tolerate fairly heavy shade. Grows from Zones 3 to 8.

Landscape Use—Top-notch ground cover, especially for slopes.

PALMS
Palms

Tender evergreen shade trees associated with the tropics, mostly grown for skyline effects. Palms add such a distinctive touch to the landscape, dwarf kinds are frequently grown in tubs so that in Northern states they can be moved indoors during cold winter months. A surprising number of palms are in fact native to North America. Perhaps the most noteworthy is the cabbage palm *(Sabal palmetto)* that grows outdoors as far north as Myrtle Beach, North Carolina (Zone 8). On the West Coast there is the magnificent California fan palm *(Washingtonia filifera)*. Though palms generally thrive in sandy soils they actually do best in soils high in organic matter.

Following are some of the best varieties for North America:

CABBAGE PALM (Sabal palmetto)
Native to the southeastern United States. Dark green, fan-shaped leaves. Trunk has a criss-cross basketweave pattern. Grows to 20 feet high. Yellow flowers appear in summer. Dwarf palmetto (S. minor), grows to 3 feet and is trunkless.

How to Grow—Best planted balled-and-burlapped or from containers. Propagated from seeds. Tolerates salt spray and moist soil, in full sun or light shade. Grows from Zones 8 to 10.

Landscape Use—Lawn highlight or street tree. Good in clumps.

CALIFORNIA FAN PALM (Washingtonia filifera)
Native to Southern California and Arizona. Dark green, fan-shaped leaves, broad fibrous trunk to 40 feet tall, occasionally higher. Old leaves droop around the trunk to make a *skirt* or *petticoat*. Female trees produce long streamerlike blossoms in summer followed by navy-blue fruits.

How to Grow—Plant balled-and-burlapped. Propagated from seeds. Tolerates poor soil, prefers full sun. Needs dry climate. Grows in Zones 9 and 10.

Landscape Use—Good skyline tree. Mostly used to line streets and wide driveways.

CANARY ISLAND DATE PALM (Phoenix canariensis)
Native to Canary Islands. Slow growing to 60 feet. Large, cascading crown of dark green, feathery fronds. Broad trunk has a diamond pattern formed by stubs of fallen leaf stems. Plants produce broomlike flowers in summer, followed by decorative, rosy red, inedible dates. A closely related species, Arabian date palm (P. dactilyfera) is not so luxurious but produces edible, orange dates.

How to Grow—Plant from containers. Propagated from seeds. Tolerates poor soil, but fertile, organic-rich soil produces best specimens. Needs full sun. Grows in Zones 9 and 10 on both Atlantic and Pacific coasts.

Landscape Use—Good lawn accent. Popular for decorating swimming pools and lining long driveways.

CHINESE FAN PALM (Livistonia chinensis)
Native to China. Bright green leaves are splayed out like a Chinese fan, with prominent ribs. Slow growing to 40 feet. Takes many years to develop a trunk.

How to Grow—Best planted from containers. Propagated from seed. Tolerates poor soil, considerable shade. Grows in Zones 9 and 10.

Landscape Use—Good lawn highlight. Popular for containers to decorate atriums, decks and patios.

Phoenix canariensis (Canary Island date palm) showing clusters of inedible but highly decorative fruits.

Cocos nucifera (coconut palms) thrive in Southern Florida south of Vero Beach.

Livistonia chinensis (Chinese fan palm) growing in Sarasota, Florida.

Parthenocissus tricuspidata (Boston Ivy) decorates a wall with brilliant red leaves in fall.

COCONUT PALM *(Cocos nucifera)*

Widely dispersed throughout the tropics, the coconut palm is known as "the tree of life" for its source of building materials and nutritious nuts, produced year round. Plants grow to 80 feet high, with a curved trunk that is usually flared at the base. Leaves are large, arching fronds, used for thatching roofs.

How to Grow—Easily grown from seed (the coconut). The nut often germinates on deserted beaches, rooting in clumps of seaweed. Tolerates salt spray. Prefers full sun and high humidity. Grows only in Zone 10, from Vero Beach, Florida and south.

Landscape Use—Best planted in groves. Popular lawn specimen and accent plant for decorating outdoor swimming pools.

MEXICAN FAN PALM *(Washingtonia robusta)*

Native to Mexico. Fast growing to 100 feet. The slender trunk rarely exceeds 14 inches diameter. Old leaves make a straw-colored frill under the crown similar to California fan palm.

How to Grow—Plant balled-and-burlapped. Propagated from seeds. Prefers good garden soil in full sun with ample moisture. Grows in Zones 9 and 10.

Landscape Use—Skyline tree. Mostly used as a street tree and as an accent plant towering above malls, mansions, motels and tall buildings.

ROYAL PALM *(Roystonea regia)*

Native to Cuba, plants grow to 60 feet high. The slender trunk has dark and light green rings and usually swells out in the middle, tapering to a green point from which large, feathery fronds arch out. Boat-shaped sheaths produce cream-colored flowers followed by red fruit clusters that change to purple when fully ripe.

How to Grow—Best planted from containers. Propagated from seeds. Tolerates poor soil. Prefers full sun and abundant moisture. Grows only in Florida Zone 10.

Landscape Use—Excellent street tree. One of the finest plantings in North America is at Fort Myers, Florida. Started by Thomas A. Edison the inventor, one street planting extends for several miles along the coastal highway.

PARTHENOCISSUS QUINQUEFOLIA
Virginia Creeper

Hardy deciduous vine native to North America, from New England to Florida. Fast growing to 30 feet or more, often growing 10 feet in a single season. Pointed, ivy-shaped leaves have a rich green color in summer that changes to brilliant red in fall. A related species, Boston ivy *(P. tricuspidata)* is native to China. Grows from Zones 4 to 8.

How to Grow—Plant from containers. Propagated from cuttings. Not fussy about soil. Takes full sun or partial shade. Grows from Zones 3 to 9.

Landscape Use—Good to cover walls, fences and trellises.

PAULOWNIA TOMENTOSA
Empress Tree

Reasonably hardy, deciduous flowering shade tree native to China. Also called princess tree. Fast growing in its juvenile stage—up to 8 feet a year. Has magnificent, tropical-looking, heart-shaped leaves up to 12 inches long. Grows to 65 feet, spreads 30 feet. Produces masses of lavender-blue flowers in spring, resembling foxgloves, even before the tree is in full leaf. Flowering begins when plant is 4 to 5 years old.

How to Grow—Plant from bare-root stock. Propagated from seeds. Not fussy about soil. Needs full sun. Grows from Zone 5 to 10, though plants are root-hardy farther north. This means that the tops will die down but a shrubby cluster of long, whiplike branches and decorative leaves will appear from the root system each spring.

Landscape Use—Good lawn highlight. Popular for lining wide driveways.

PHILADELPHUS CORONARIUS
Mock Orange

Hardy deciduous flowering shrub native to Europe and Asia. Grows 10 feet, spreads 10 feet. Makes a dense mound of weeping branches covered in early summer with fragrant, white flowers, either single or double-flowered. 'Minnesota Snowflake' is an excellent dwarf variety, which grows only 4 feet high.

How to Grow—Plant from containers. Propagated from cuttings and layers. Not fussy about soil. Needs full sun. Grows from Zones 4 to 9.

Landscape Use—Good lawn highlight and foundation plant. Useful informal hedge. Old-fashioned favorite for mixed-shrub borders.

PHOTINIA SERRULATA
Chinese Photinia

Tender evergreen flowering tree native to China, popular in Southern gardens. Grows to 25 feet, spreads 18 feet. White flowers have an unpleasant fragrance, but they are showy, borne in clusters in spring—a beautiful contrast with the dark green, lance-shaped leaves. A popular hybrid for the South, Southwest and California is Fraser's photinia *(P. ×fraseri),* also commonly called red tips photinia. It has a dense, shrubby habit and is highly ornamental because of the intense red coloring of its new leaves. Plants grow 10 to 15 feet high and are often used as a distinctive formal hedge.

How to Grow—Easily planted from containers. Propagated from cuttings. Prefers fertile, sandy soil in sun or partial shade. Grows from Zones 7 to 9.

Landscape Use—Takes heavy pruning. Forms a good hedge or small tree. Especially decorative when pruned of lower branches.

Paulownia tomentosa (empress tree) in full flower at Longwood Gardens, Pennsylvania.

Philadelphus coronarius (mock orange) covers itself with fragrant, double or single white flowers in spring.

Picea pungens glauca (Colorado blue spruce) contrasts beautifully with a background of deciduous white ash trees.

Picea abies (Norway spruce) is a favorite evergreen conifer to plant as a lawn highlight and windbreak.

PICEA
Spruce

More than 40 species of spruce are widely distributed throughout the Northern Hemisphere — many of the best are native to North America. They are hardy evergreen conifers with sharp, short needles and a spirelike habit. The cones of most types are hanging and egg shaped. The Norway spruce and the Colorado spruce are popular as Christmas trees.

COLORADO SPRUCE (Picea pungens)

Native to Colorado. Grows to 60 feet, spreads 25 feet. Though the species is dark green, the most popular variety is 'Glauca', which has blue needles. Forms a dense, narrow pyramid with stiff, spreading branches reaching to the ground.

How to Grow—Plant balled-and-burlapped or from bare-root stock. Propagated from seeds and cuttings. Not fussy about soil provided it drains well. Needs full sun. Susceptible to spider mite infestations (see Pests, page 56). Grows from Zones 2 to 7.

Landscape Use — Lawn highlight, windbreak.

NORWAY SPRUCE (Picea abies)

Native to Europe. Grows to 60 feet, spreads 30 feet. Makes a broad, dense, dark green pyramid. The extremely beautiful weeping form, 'Pendula', is prized as a lawn highlight.

How to Grow — Plant balled-and-burlapped, from containers or from bare-root stock. Not fussy about soil, provided drainage is good. Needs full sun. Grows from Zones 2 to 6.

Landscape Use — Excellent windbreak. Good for lining driveways.

WHITE SPRUCE (Picea glauca)

Native to Canada and Alaska. Grows to 60 feet, spreads 20 feet. Dense, spirelike habit and dark green leaves. A particularly fine form is the variety 'Conica', known as dwarf Alberta spruce. It is extremely slow growing—just 2 to 4 inches a year—quickly becoming the most widely planted of dwarf conifers for foundations. Popular for its extremely dense, symmetrical cone-shaped outline.

How to Grow—Plant balled-and-burlapped. Propagated from seeds and cuttings. Not fussy about soil. Needs full sun. Susceptible to spider mites (see page 56.) Grows Zones 2 to 6.

Landscape Use—The species makes a good windbreak and a decent lawn highlight. 'Conica'—dwarf Alberta spruce—is excellent for rock gardens, dry walls, foundations and entryways.

PIERIS JAPONICA
Japanese Andromeda

Hardy broadleaf evergreen shrub native to China and Japan. Valued for its early spring flowers. Grows 10 feet, spreads 10 feet. Leaves are oval, pointed, dark green and arranged in whorls. Flowers are mostly white, hang in long clusters, resemble lily-of-the-valley. There are some beautiful pink-flowering kinds, such as the variety 'Red Bud'.

How to Grow—Plant from containers. Propagated from seed and cuttings. Prefers moist, acid, humus-rich soil in sun or partial shade. Grows from Zones 4 to 8.

Landscape Use—Foundation plantings and mixed-shrub borders. Blends particularly well with rhododendrons, azaleas and camellias.

PINUS
Pines

More than 110 species of pines are widely distributed throughout the Northern Hemisphere from the Arctic Circle to the tropics. About 40 are native to North America. They are mostly hardy evergreens bearing woody cones and long, slender green needles. Though variable in habit, pines are admired for their rugged good looks, scaly resinous bark and wispy needles. Pines are favorite bonsai subjects because of their ability to be trained into "weathered" forms. In addition to the especially fine landscape plants described here, there are many pines that enjoy localized popularity, such as the Loblolly pine (*P. taeda*) popular in the South.

EASTERN WHITE PINE *(Pinus strobus)*

Native to North America from Canada to Georgia. Fast growing to 80 feet high, spreading 40 feet. Up to 2 feet of growth a year. Pyramid shape, soft feathery appearance. Dwarf and weeping forms available.

How to Grow—Plant balled-and-burlapped or bare-root stock. Propagated mostly from seed. Prefers sandy, acid soil in full sun. The bark disease *white pine blister rust* can kill a tree. This disease is prevalent in areas where currants and gooseberries are grown. Grows from Zones 3 to 8.

JAPANESE BLACK PINE *(Pinus thunbergii)*

Native to Japan. Medium-fast growing to 90 feet high, spreads 40 feet. Though juvenile plants have a pyramid shape, they soon develop an open, flat-topped habit with a rugged mountainous look. The dark—almost black—rough bark enhances its craggy appearance.

How to Grow—Plant balled-and-burlapped. Propagated from seeds. Prefers sandy, acid soil in full sun. Salt tolerant. Grows from Zones 5 to 10.

Landscape Use—Good windbreak, especially for coastal gardens. Beautiful planted as a grove. Popular in Oriental gardens, rock gardens and as a subject for bonsai training.

Pieris japonica (Japanese andromeda) drapes itself with panicles of white flowers in early spring.

Pinus strobus (white pine) is fast growing and easily trimmed to maintain a rounded shape.

Pinus mugo (mugo pine) is a ground-hugging plant with a mounded evergreen habit.

Pittosporum tobira tolerates salt spray and has lovely fragrant yellow flowers.

MUGO PINE *(Pinus mugo)*

Native to the Alps, plants are low-growing, forming a mound, usually less than 6 feet high and up to 12 feet wide. Extremely slow growing—just a few inches a year. Light green to medium green leaf color.

How to Grow—Plant from containers or bare-root stock. Propagated mostly from seeds. Prefers deep loam soil in full sun, but tolerates stony and alkaline soil. Subject to scale infections that can be controlled by spraying with a scalecide. Grows from Zones 2 to 7.

PISTACIA CHINENSIS
Chinese Pistachio

Tender deciduous medium-size shade tree native to China. It is not the source of pistachio nuts, which come from another species, *P. vera*. Grows to 30 feet high, spreads 25 feet. Upright, spreading oval habit. The dark green leaves turn orange in fall, even in Southern California where fall color is rare.

How to Grow—Plant from containers. Propagated from seeds. Not fussy about soil, alkaline tolerant. Prefers full sun. Grows from Zones 7 to 10.

Landscape Use—Good lawn highlight and street tree.

PITTOSPORUM TOBIRA
Pittosporum

Tender evergreen broadleaf shrub native to Japan and China. Popular in mild climate areas of the South and Southwest. Grows to 10 feet, spreads 20 feet. Dense, compact habit, glossy dark green slender leaves. Fragrant yellow flowers are small but eye-catching.

How to Grow—Plant from containers. Propagated from cuttings. Thrives in poor soils, including sandy, alkaline soil. High tolerance to salt spray, drought resistant. Thrives in sun or shade, takes heavy pruning. Grows from Zones 8 to 10.

Landscape Use—Excellent hedge and windbreak, especially for coastal gardens. Good for erosion control. A silver-leaf variegated form is especially beautiful for containers and foundation plantings.

PLATANUS OCCIDENTALIS
American Buttonwood

Hardy deciduous shade tree native to North America from Canada to Florida. Also known as sycamore and American plane tree. Grows to 100 feet high, spreads 75 feet. The maple-shaped leaves can exceed 10 inches across and turn parchment-brown in fall. Mature trees develop colorful bark patterns—a mosaic of olive-green, gray and white patches caused by peeling bark. Round, spiny seed cases hang from the tree in fall and persist long after the leaves have fallen. A related hybrid, the London plane tree *(P. × acerifolia)* is used extensively as a street tree for its pollution tolerance.

How to Grow — Plant balled-and-burlapped or bare-root stock. Propagated from seeds. Prefers deep, humus-rich, moist soil in full sun to attain massive stature, but not fussy about soil. Grows from Zones 4 to 9.

Landscape Use — Good lawn highlight for large gardens. Has an appealing winter silhouette for skyline plantings. Popular for parks and golf courses.

PODOCARPUS MACROPHYLLUS
Yew Podocarpus

Tender evergreen upright tree native to Japan, grown mostly in mild-climate areas of the South and West Coast. Resembles a conifer. Gets its common name for the yew-like appearance of its dark green needlelike leaves. Slow growing to 50 feet high, spreading 20 feet. Red berries ripen in summer and are edible as preserves. The variety 'Maki' is more shrublike. A related species, fern podocarpus *(P. gracilior)* has more-graceful, blue-green foliage, but is restricted to Zone 10.

How to Grow—Plant from containers. Propagated from cuttings. Prefers fertile, sandy soil in full sun or partial shade. Tolerates salt spray. Susceptible to root rot in wet soil. Grows from Zones 8 to 10.

Landscape Use—Good hedge and tall windbreak. Mostly seen heavily sheared to a columnar form for use in foundation plantings. Popular container plant can be artistically pruned to form a large bonsai subject. Pliable branches are easy to espalier.

Podocarpus macrophyllus (yew podocarpus) takes severe shearing to create a smooth, rounded outline.

POLYGONUM AUBERTII
Silver Lace Vine

Hardy deciduous flowering vine native to China. Extremely fast growing, aggressive plants. Grows to 30 feet and more—often more than 15 feet in one season. Plentiful, white flowers occur in late summer. Light green, heart-shaped leaves are highly decorative. A related species, *P. reynoutria*, has pink flowers.

How to Grow—Planted easily from bare-root stock. Mostly propagated from root division because plants spread by underground stolons. Even a small piece will produce a new plant. Grows almost anywhere in Zones 4 to 7.

Landscape Use—Good to cover chain link fences and arbors. Can suffocate a small tree. The twining vines and masses of small stems can cover a barn. Has escaped into the wild in many Northeastern states.

Polygonum aubertii (silver lace vine) is a vigorous summer-flowering vine that can cover a barn.

Poncirus trifoliata (hardy orange) bears sharp spines and decorative yellow fruit that is aromatic and astringent, and persists after the leaves drop.

Populus nigra 'Italica' (Lombardy poplar) has a narrow, upright outline.

PONCIRUS TRIFOLIATA
Hardy Orange

Hardy deciduous multi-stemmed shrub native to China. Unusual yellow golf-ball-size fruits resemble oranges, are delightfully fragrant. Grows to 20 feet, spreads 15 feet, but normally kept at 6 feet by heavy pruning. Branches are armed with vicious spines, like nails. Grown mostly for the extraordinary abundance of eyecatching fruit that covers the tree in fall and persists long after the leaves have fallen. Though highly astringent, the fruit is supposedly edible as preserves. Flowers are white, inconspicuous, not fragrant.

How to Grow—Plant from containers. Not fussy about soil. Needs full sun. Grows from Zones 5 to 10.

Landscape Use—Excellent barrier plant. Makes a good, impenetrable informal hedge. Excellent lawn and foundation highlight. Plants have a beautiful wintry silhouette, especially when selectively pruned to remove smaller stems and open up the center.

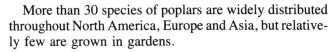

POPULUS
Poplars

More than 30 species of poplars are widely distributed throughout North America, Europe and Asia, but relatively few are grown in gardens.

EASTERN COTTONWOOD (P. deltoides)

Native to eastern North America, fast growing to 60 feet or higher, with pyramidal habit. Gets its name from the cottony hairs attached to its seeds. Good windbreak, but losing favor to hybrids developed from crossing it with European poplars. Grows from Zones 2 to 9.

LOMBARDY POPLAR (P. nigra 'Italica')

This is the upright European poplar immortalized by French Impressionist painters like Monet, used extensively to line driveways, avenues and country roads. Male and female flowers grow on separate trees, and it is the females that have the striking columnar habit. Unfortunately, this species is losing its popularity because of susceptibility to a canker disease that causes rapid dieback and death. Grows from Zones 3 to 9.

QUAKING ASPEN (P. tremuloides)

This is probably North America's hardiest deciduous tree, and certainly the most widely distributed in the wild. The leaves shimmer in the slightest breeze, hence its common name. Trunk is straight, white and spotted with black bands like a white birch. Fall color is spectacular—glowing golden yellow and orange. Good for naturalizing in groves. Grows from Zones 1 to 6.

WHITE POPLAR *(P. alba)*

Native to Europe and Asia, this poplar has small, maple-shaped leaves with silvery white undersides that shimmer in the wind. Tall, spreading habit makes white poplar useful as a windbreak. Unfortunately, it has an invasive root system that sends up numerous suckers and must be kept clear of drains. Rapidly losing favor to the new hybrid poplars discussed next.

HYBRID POPLARS *(Populus hybrida)*

This group of hybrids was developed over a period of 30 years from an intensive breeding program involving the U.S. Forest Service and the New York Botanical Garden. Growth rates of up to 8 feet a year have been reported. Involving crosses between American poplars (mostly *P. deltoides)* and European kinds, they are extremely hardy and widely adaptable. Habit varies according to variety, but one of the best, the 'Imperial Carolina' strain, has a spreading, pyramidal, upright growth habit. After an initial surge of fast growth, plants slow down and spread out to a mature size of 50 feet high and 20 feet wide. Life span is about 40 years.

How to Grow—Growth is so vigorous, plants can be started from unrooted cuttings, which will develop roots and sprout leaves within weeks of inserting them into moist soil. Bare-root and balled-and-burlapped plants are also available. There appears to be no limit to the ability of these trees to thrive in any type of soil. They are used to cover raw-strip mines, waste-disposal sites and desert soils. Grows from Zones 2 to 10.

Landscape Use—Lawn highlight, screen, windbreak. Good for lining driveways, erosion control and as a street tree.

Populus hybrid 'Imperial Carolina' grows up to 8 feet a year. This specimen is only in its third year.

POTENTILLA FRUTICOSA
Bush Cinquefoil

Hardy deciduous flowering shrub widely dispersed throughout the Northern Hemisphere. Plants are slow growing to 4 feet, spread 4 feet. Ornamental flowers that resemble buttercups appear in spring and continue sporadically until fall frost. Numerous varieties have been developed, including 'Red Ace' (scarlet-red) and 'Royal Flush' (pink). However, they were bred by European plantsmen and have not proven garden worthy for the more severe North American climate, except for mild coastal regions of California and the Pacific Northwest.

How to Grow—Best planted from containers. Propagated mostly from softwood cuttings. Tolerates poor soils, including dry, sandy soil. Flowers best under moist, cool conditions. Prune in fall to maintain a compact shape. Grows from Zones 2 to 7.

Landscape Use—Edging and low hedges. Good specimen plant for rock gardens and foundation plantings.

Potentilla fruticosa 'Gold Drop' is a bushy shrub that bears yellow, buttercup flowers.

Prunus glandulosa (flowering almond) brightens a mixed-shrub border in early spring.

Prunus subhirtella 'Pendula' (weeping Higan cherry) produces a cascading fountain of flowers in early spring.

PRUNUS
Almonds, Apricots, Cherries, Peaches and Plums

The genus *Prunus* includes over 400 species of almonds, apricots, cherries, peaches and plums, mostly native to China and Japan, plus hundreds more hybrids developed by Oriental, European and American plant breeders. They are generally hardy deciduous flowering trees valued for their early spring blossoms. Many of them provide spectacular fall color. This genus also includes some fine evergreen species useful as hedges, notably *P. caroliniana* and *P. laurocerasus*.

In most cases, the flowering display occurs slightly ahead of the leaves in early spring. Though many ornamental *Prunus* varieties are sterile and do not produce fruit, some produce decorative small fruits as an added bonus. Most trees are small, making them ideal for suburban lots. Some are large, with a beautiful, domed, spreading habit that makes them a perfect lawn centerpiece that can serve double-duty as a shade tree. Others are upright or weeping. Following is a sample of the most beautiful kinds for ornamental effect:

ALMOND, FLOWERING *(Prunus glandulosa)*
Beautiful pink or white powderpuff flowers crowd the upright stems in early spring. Plants are shrublike, multistemmed and not fruitful. Popular for foundations and mixed-shrub borders, though not long-lived. 'Alba Plena' has double white flowers; 'Rosea Plena' is a double pink. Plant bare-root stock or from containers. Propagated from cuttings. Grows from Zones 4 to 8.

APRICOT, MANCHURIAN *(Prunus mandshurica)*
Rounded shrub or small tree with delicate white blossoms, tinted pink, followed in summer by golden yellow fruits. Though nurseries generally offer seedling stock that can vary in fruit size and flavor, fruit quality is generally excellent—sweet and juicy. Mostly sold bare-root. Grows from Zones 3 to 8.

CHERRY, HIGAN *(Prunus subhirtella)*
The weeping variety 'Pendula' is the most widely grown. Plants grow to 40 feet high and spread 40 feet. They have graceful, arching branches that present a curtain of delicate pink double blossoms that bloom at same time as forsythia and daffodils. Best planted balled-and-burlapped. Propagated from cuttings. Grows from Zones 4 to 10.

CHERRY, NANKING *(Prunus tomentosa)*
Sometimes called bush cherry or hedge cherry. Plants grow bushy, multi-stemmed to 10 feet, spread 15 feet. Masses of small, pale pink flowers are followed in early summer by loads of sweet red fruits, hundreds on a single branch. Two-year-old plants can produce fruit. Mostly sold bare-root for growing as a short hedge. Propagated from seeds and cuttings. Can be sheared after fruiting to a formal hedge shape. Grows from Zones 2 to 8.

CHERRY, SARGENT'S (*Prunus sargentii*)

One of the longest-lived flowering cherries and the best choice for shade. Plants grow to 50 feet high, spread 50 feet and produce a cloud of pale pink, single flowers. Bark is decorative — shining, reddish-brown. Grows from Zones 4 to 7.

CHERRY, SERRULA (*Prunus serrula*)

Chiefly grown for its extremely beautiful smooth bark, which is reddish-brown and polished, with rings around the trunk and main branches, caused by peeling strips of outer bark. Clusters of white flowers are hidden by the leaves in spring. Reaches 25 feet in height. Grows from Zones 5 to 7.

CHERRY, YOSHINO (*Prunus* × *yedoensis*)

A complex hybrid involving *P. serrulata* and *P. sub-hirtella*. This is the cherry that is most widely planted around Washington, D.C. Plants grow to 40 feet high, spread a little less, producing a billowing mass of pale, pink-and-white, semi-double flowers, which are followed by small, black, inedible fruits. Best planted balled-and-burlapped. Propagated mostly from cuttings. Grows from Zones 5 to 8.

PEACH, FLOWERING (*Prunus persica*)

Though many home gardeners prefer to plant fruiting peaches as ornamentals — particularly the special *genetic dwarf* varieties developed in recent years — nurserymen do offer a few special ornamental selections that are mostly double-flowered and poor fruit producers. Flowers range from pink with dark centers on fruiting peaches to deep red on ornamental selections. Plants grow to 25 feet, spread 25 feet. Bare-root stock and containerized plants are widely available. Peach borer is a serious insect pest — see Pests, page 55 for controls. Grows from Zones 5 to 8.

PLUM, FLOWERING (*Prunus cerasifera*)

A very fine attribute of flowering plums is the number of varieties with bronze or purple foliage. 'Atropurpurea' (also called Pissard plum) and 'Thundercloud' are two particularly fine ornamental types, producing a handsome upright oval crown covered in fragrant, white flowers. A hybrid form, *P.* × *blireana* (Blireana plum) produces double pink flowers and bronze foliage. Plants grow to 25 feet, spread 15 to 20 feet. Mostly planted as bare-root stock or balled-and-burlapped. Propagated from cuttings. Grows from Zones 3 to 8.

How to Grow — Hardiness ratings and propagation details are given with each description. In general, types of *Prunus* prefer fertile loam or sandy soils in full sun. Pruning should be done immediately after flowering unless fruits are desired, in which case you prune after fruiting when the tree has gone dormant.

Most species of *Prunus* are highly susceptible to attack from borers — tough little larvae that burrow into the trunk, leaving a telltale dribble of gummy sap oozing from

Prunus persica (fruiting peach) displays ornamental flowers followed by juicy peaches in summer.

Prunus cerasifera 'Atropurpurea' (Pissard plum) develops purple leaves after flowering.

Pseudolarix amabilis (golden larch) is a deciduous conifer, changing color in fall from dark green to golden, then dropping its needles.

Pseudotsuga menziesii (Douglas fir) is a fast-growing evergreen conifer popular as a Christmas tree.

the bark. Also, tent caterpillars like to build large, silky webs or 'tents' among the branches, and these can be unsightly. For control of these insects see Pests, page 55.

Several kinds of leaf spots caused by fungus can defoliate trees. The most common is *shot hole*. The reddish infected shot-size blemishes dry up and fall away leaving a round hole. Spraying with a general purpose fungicide containing Benlate or Captan will help control the disease.

Landscape Use — Ornamental forms of *Prunus* that grow as trees make excellent lawn highlights, particularly the weeping and spreading kinds. These are also excellent for planting in lines to create avenues. Those producing edible fruits are exceptional orchard trees. Nanking cherry makes an attractive flowering, fruiting hedge. For exquisite lake reflections few trees can outshine the weeping varieties, such as the weeping Higan cherry.

PSEUDOLARIX AMABILIS
Golden Larch

Hardy deciduous conifer native to China. Handsome pyramid shape and widely spaced, spreading branches that weep at the tips. Light green needles in summer turn spectacular yellow or gold in fall. Grows to 60 feet and more, spreads 40 to 50 feet.

How to Grow—Plant balled-and-burlapped. Prefers deep, moist, well-drained acid soil in full sun. Grows from Zones 4 to 7.

Landscape Use—Valued for its dramatic fall color. Needs plenty of room. Most often planted as a skyline tree.

PSEUDOTSUGA MENZIESII
Douglas Fir

Tall hardy evergreen conifer native to the Pacific Northwest. Plants are fast growing to 300 feet high in the wild, but most garden plants are a subspecies, variety 'Glauca', from the Rocky Mountains. These plants attain a height of 100 feet, spread 30 feet. 'Glauca' has blue-green needles and is widely offered by garden centers as a Christmas tree. Douglas firs are considered better than the traditional spruce for this purpose because they retain their needles longer indoors. The trunk is straight as a telephone pole and the shape beautifully spirelike. It is a very handsome evergreen.

How to Grow—Plant from containers, balled-and-burlapped or bare-root. Prefers humus-rich, moist, acid soil. Plants are mostly propagated from seeds. Grows from Zones 4 to 9.

Landscape Use—Excellent lawn highlight. Widely planted as a windbreak.

PTEROSTYRAX HISPIDA
Epaulette Tree

Hardy deciduous flowering shade tree native to Japan. Grows to 30 feet, spreads 30 feet. Billowing, rounded habit. Fragrant, white ornamental flowers resemble wisteria blossoms and hang from the tree in early summer when few other trees are in flower.

How to Grow—Plant from containers or balled-and-burlapped. Propagated from seed and softwood cuttings taken in summer. Prefers moist, humus-rich, acid soil in full sun. Grows from Zones 4 to 8.

Landscape Use—Good lawn highlight. Ideal for small suburban gardens.

PYRACANTHA COCCINEA
Firethorn

Semi-evergreen flowering and fruiting shrub native to Europe. Valued for its white flower displays in early summer and magnificent fall berry clusters in scarlet, orange or yellow, depending on variety. The berries are attractive to birds, though fermenting fruit can make them behave intoxicated. Plants are armed with sharp spines. Grows to 15 feet, spreads 6 feet or more. Has an open, upright habit. The long, stiff branches are pliable and can be trained flat against a wall as an espalier. 'Navaho' is a particularly fine hybrid red variety popular in mild-winter regions of the South, for it will not take freezing weather.

How to Grow—Plant from containers. Propagated from cuttings. Not fussy about soil. Needs full sun to set good berry displays. Takes heavy pruning. Grows from Zones 5 to 10, depending on variety.

Plants are highly susceptible to *fireblight*, a bacterial disease that turns the branch tips black and discolors fruit. To control, see page 58—or plant a disease-resistant variety such as 'Lalandi' or 'Mohave'.

Landscape Use—Good foundation plant and informal hedge. A pair can be trained on opposite sides of an arch to create a berried canopy. Plants do well in containers.

PYRUS CALLERYANA
Callery Pear

Hardy deciduous flowering shade tree native to China. Selected varieties of Callery pear—particularly the 'Bradford'—are among the finest ornamental trees for suburban gardens. In early spring the 'Bradford' pear covers itself in a blizzard of snow-white flowers. In summer its serrated, heart-shaped leaves are a lustrous dark green, turning crimson in fall. In winter its small, red fruits attract song birds—a tree for all seasons. Upright, oval shape growing to 60 feet high, 30 feet wide.

How to Grow—Nurserymen offer two kinds of planting stock—rooted cuttings and seedlings. Only rooted cuttings will grow the true and original form of 'Bradford' pear—a single tree found in an experimental block at the National Arboretum, Washington, D.C. Cheap seedling

Pterostyrax hispida (epaulette tree) flaunts beautiful white flower clusters in midsummer.

Pyracantha coccinea (firethorn) is one of the most beautiful of all fruiting bushes.

Pyrus calleryana (Bradford pear) produces a blizzard of snow-white flowers in spring and a beacon of fire from intense red leaves in fall.

Quercus agrifolia (California live oak) stays green even when hillsides are parched and dry from months of drought.

stock is vastly inferior and not normally representative of the genuine 'Bradford' pear.

Though bare-root stock is available through catalogs, trees are best planted balled-and-burlapped or from containers. Tolerates poor soil, but demands full sun. Drought and pollution resistant. Good resistance to fireblight disease. Grows from Zones 4 to 8.
Landscape Use—Excellent lawn highlight and street tree. Does well in containers.

QUERCUS
Oaks

There are about 450 species of oaks widely dispersed throughout north temperate regions of the world and high-elevation tropical areas. A symbol of strength, more than 50 species are native to North America, but some oaks are hard to identify because of many natural hybrids resulting from cross-breeding between the species. Though valued for their hard, durable wood—for both woodworking and firewood—a number of North American species are popular as ornamental shade trees. Mostly slow growing, they have distinctive seeds called *acorns*—some of which are edible after removal of bitter tannins by boiling—and usually a distinctive, scalloped leaf shape.

Perhaps the most serious pest in recent years—especially in the Northeast—has been the *gypsy moth caterpillar,* which is hatched from eggs laid in the deeply fissured bark of oaks. Black and hairy, ranging in size from 1 to 2 inches, the gypsy moth caterpillar has a voracious appetite and will quickly defoliate a forest. Fortunately, the degree of destruction appears to run in cycles, and most oaks have a chance to recover the following season. Sprays of Sevin or *Bacillus thuringiensis* are effective as the caterpillars begin to hatch in spring.

Many kinds of forest fungi (toadstools) favor oaks, entering through wounds in the bark and causing rot. These generally occur near the soil line and cause hollow trees. Once a tree has been invaded by forest fungi, control is extremely difficult, except to rout out the infected area and fill with cement. Galls on branches are caused by tiny insects and generally do no harm. A soil-borne infection called oak-root fungus is a problem of some native California oaks and can also infect some kinds of fruit trees in areas where oaks grow.

Following is a sampling of America's most beautiful native oaks:

CALIFORNIA LIVE OAK *(Quercus agrifolia)*
Tender evergreen shade tree native to California. When the golden hills of California's coastal valleys are parched and dry from months of drought, the dark green, spreading domes of California live oaks punctuate the landscape in bold defiance of the harsh environment. Grows 30 to 50 feet, spreads up to 70 feet. Shiny, leathery, hollylike leaves persist on sinuous branches. Small inconspicuous flowers (catkins) are followed by pointed, narrow acorns that usually separate from the shallow cups when they fall

to the ground. Tree is deep rooted, slow growing and long lived.

How to Grow—Plant balled-and-burlapped or from containers. Propagated from seeds. Tolerates poor soils, even stony soil, and is highly drought resistant—a true survivor. Prefers full sun but tolerates light shade. Grows from Zones 9 to 10.

Landscape Use—Many California estates feature live oaks to line wide driveways, also as a highlight around which the entire garden is designed. Its spreading, sinuous branches cast cooling shade over a large area.

PIN OAK *(Quercus palustris)*

Hardy deciduous shade tree native to the eastern United States. Grows 60 to 70 feet high, spreads 30 to 35 feet. Elegant pyramidal shape, lower branches sweeping the ground. Dark green leaves are deeply lobed with sharp, pointed tips, changing to parchment-brown in fall and persisting on the tree all winter. Small, inconspicuous flowers produce shallow-cupped acorns. Fastest growing native oak (2 feet a year), shallow rooted, long lived.

How to Grow—Plant balled-and-burlapped or from bare-root stock. Propagated from seeds and grafts. Prefers fertile, moist, acid loam soil though it will take clay soil and occasional flooding. Grows from Zones 4 to 8.

Landscape Use—Excellent lawn highlight. Good street and driveway tree or windbreak.

RED OAK *(Quercus rubra)*

Hardy deciduous shade tree native to Eastern North America. Grows 60 to 80 feet high, spreads 40 to 60 feet. Handsome rounded shape. Dark green leaves are deeply lobed with pointed tips, turn russet-red in fall. Flowers are small and inconspicuous, followed by shallow-cupped acorns that take 2 years to mature. Fairly fast growing, deep rooted and long lived.

How to Grow—Plant balled-and-burlapped or bare-root stock. Propagated mostly from seeds. Prefers light, well-drained, slightly acid loam in full sun. Grows from Zones 4 to 8.

Landscape Use—Good lawn highlight where it has sufficient space to spread. Good windbreak. Popular choice for creating a wooded lot.

SCARLET OAK *(Quercus coccinea)*

Hardy deciduous shade tree native to eastern North America. Grows 70 to 80 feet high, spreads 40 to 60 feet. Dark green leaves have narrow, deeply cut lobes with sharply pointed tips, turning brilliant red in fall. Spire shape is similar to pin oak to which it is closely related. Small, inconspicuous flowers are followed by acorns with deep cups. Medium-fast growth, deep rooted and long lived.

How to Grow—Plant balled-and-burlapped or bare-root stock. Propagated mostly from seeds. Prefers sandy loam soil in sun or shade. Grows from Zones 4 to 7.

Landscape Use—One of the best trees for fall color. Excellent lawn highlight and windbreak. Popular choice for creating wooded lot.

Quercus palustris (pin oak) has parchment-brown leaves in fall, which persist through winter.

Quercus rubra (red oak) displays beautiful red leaf coloring in fall.

Quercus virginiana (Southern live oak) decorates lawn of a Florida home.

Quercus phellos (willow oak) presents a beautiful rounded outline on a farm in Virginia.

SOUTHERN LIVE OAK *(Quercus virginiana)*

Tender evergreen shade tree native to the southeastern United States from Virginia to Florida and West to Mexico. Considered the most beautiful of American evergreen oaks. Grows 40 to 70 feet, spreading 60 to 110 feet. Broad, rounded shape. Dark green leaves are narrow, oblong and leathery. Small, inconspicuous flowers are followed by acorns that ripen the same year. Branches are frequently covered with Spanish moss and epiphytic ferns. Fairly fast growing, deep rooted, long lived.

How to Grow—Best planted balled-and-burlapped or bare-root stock. Propagated from seed. Prefers well-drained, sandy soil, but really not fussy because it thrives even in stony and moist soils. Grows from Zones 7 to 10.

Landscape Use—Street tree, large estates. Popular for lining driveways to Southern plantations. Good windbreak.

WHITE OAK *(Quercus alba)*

Hardy deciduous shade tree native to the eastern United States. Grows 100 feet or higher, spreads up to 80 feet. Beautiful, majestic, rounded shape. Dark green leaves are the typical scalloped oak leaf shape and turn bronze in fall. Small, inconspicuous flowers are followed by acorns. Slow growing, deep rooted, extremely long lived (300 years and more).

How to Grow—Plant balled-and-burlapped or from bare-root stock when young as long taproot makes transplanting of older trees difficult. Propagated mostly from seeds. Prefers deep, acid, moist, loam soil in full sun. Grows from Zones 3 to 8.

Landscape Use—Lawn highlight where it has space to spread. Good windbreak.

WILLOW OAK *(Quercus phellos)*

Hardy deciduous shade tree native to eastern United States. Grows 40 to 60 feet high, spreads 30 to 50 feet. Upright, rounded shape. Pale green leaves are narrow and willowy. Small, inconspicuous flowers followed by small, shallow-cupped acorns. Fairly fast growth, deep rooted and long lived.

How to Grow—Plant balled-and-burlapped or bare-root stock. Propagated from seed. Prefers acid soil and full sun; tolerates wet and heavy clay soils. Grows from Zones 5 to 9.

Landscape Use—Popular street tree in the South. Good lawn highlight where it has room to spread. Effective windbreak.

RAPHIOLEPIS INDICA
Indian Hawthorn

Tender evergreen flowering shrub native to India, grown in frost-free areas of the United States. Grows to 6 feet high, spreads 6 feet. Lustrous, dark green waxy leaves. Flowers are mostly pink or white, appear in spring and resemble hawthorn flowers. The fine hybrid tree form, *R. delacourii*, makes a handsome small tree to 10 feet.

How to Grow—Best planted from containers. Propagated from cuttings. Prefers fertile loam soil in full sun or partial shade. Can be sheared after flowering to maintain compact growth. Grows from Zones 8 to 10.

Landscape Use—Lawn highlight, mixed-shrub borders, foundations, informal or formal hedge. Good for containers. Grows well under glass in Northern states.

RHODODENDRON
Rhododendrons

Rhododendron is such a diverse genus it deserves a book to itself. The genus also includes azaleas which are generally smaller leaved and much easier to grow. Because they are so distinctly different than true rhododendrons they have been treated separately and listed in this book under the heading *Azaleas,* on page 74.

Most garden-worthy rhododendrons are hardy broadleaf evergreen flowering shrubs. The tree rhododendron *(R. arboreum)* is capable of growing to 40 feet high with a trunk 5 feet in diameter, but most garden varieties are slow-growing shrubs that remain below 10 feet in height, spreading 10 feet or less. Multiple trunks form a thicket of branches hidden by the broad, oval, pointed leaves. Flowers are mostly bell-shaped, formed in a truss up to 12 inches across. Colors include white and shades of pink, red, lavender, purple and yellow. Flowering occurs from early spring to midsummer, depending on variety.

There are literally thousands of species and varieties in cultivation. Varieties vary in adaptation, so those popular in the Northeast are not always suitable for the Northwest. By far, the most popular are the 'Ironclads'—of which 'America' (red), 'Roseum Elegans' (pink), 'Boule de Neige' (white) and 'Nova Zembla' (lavender) are the most widely grown. The early-flowering 'PJM' (small lavender flowers), 'Windbeam' (small white flowers) and 'Scintillation' (a large-flowered heat-resistant pink) are also popular American hybrids.

How to Grow—Plant from containers or balled-and-burlapped. Propagated from seeds, cuttings and layering. Prefers a moist, humus-rich, acid soil in partial shade. Needs a cool, humid atmosphere and plenty of moisture during dry spells. The site must drain well. Some of the hardiest North American species, such as *R. maximum* are hardy to Zone 3. Tropical species, native to Indonesia—such as *R. zolleri*—extend the range into Southern Florida and other mild-winter areas.

However, most rhododendrons are fairly limited in adaptation. They cannot withstand hot summers or extremely cold winters. Because of this, rhododendrons are mostly confined to the Northeast, the Appalachias, the Pacific Northwest, the Northern California coast and the southern edges of the Great Lakes in the Midwest.

Dehydration through exposure to cold winds or lack of moisture in summer is the biggest cause of losses.

Landscape Use—Excellent lawn highlight. Superb for foundation plantings and mixed-shrub borders. Popular for lining driveways. Dwarf, free-flowering varieties— such as 'Mist Maiden'—are good for containers.

Raphiolepis indica (Indian hawthorn) is a popular flowering shrub or small tree in frost-free areas.

Rhododendron 'America' is a hardy Ironclad hybrid with large red flower trusses in late spring.

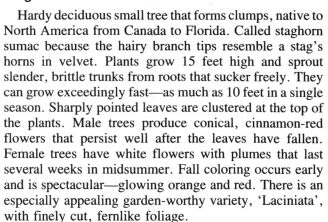

RHUS TYPHINA
Staghorn Sumac

Hardy deciduous small tree that forms clumps, native to North America from Canada to Florida. Called staghorn sumac because the hairy branch tips resemble a stag's horns in velvet. Plants grow 15 feet high and sprout slender, brittle trunks from roots that sucker freely. They can grow exceedingly fast—as much as 10 feet in a single season. Sharply pointed leaves are clustered at the top of the plants. Male trees produce conical, cinnamon-red flowers that persist well after the leaves have fallen. Female trees have white flowers with plumes that last several weeks in midsummer. Fall coloring occurs early and is spectacular—glowing orange and red. There is an especially appealing garden-worthy variety, 'Laciniata', with finely cut, fernlike foliage.

How to Grow—Plant from bare-root stock. Propagated from seed and root division. Plants tolerate a wide range of soils, even dry, stony soil. Grows from Zones 3 to 8.

Landscape Use—Considered by many landscape architects as a *weed tree*—hard to eradicate—but it can look appealing in isolated clumps at the extremities of a garden.

Rhus typhina (staghorn sumac) is one of the first trees to change color in fall.

ROBINIA PSEUDOACACIA
Black Locust

Hardy deciduous shade tree native to North America, from Pennsylvania to Florida. Tall, straight trunk, deeply furrowed dark grey bark with an attractive basket-weave texture. Plants are fairly fast growing—up to 2 feet a year. Grows to 50 feet, spreads 30 feet. Airy leaves resembling those of acacia turn yellow in fall. Fragrant white flowers are showy, hang in dense clusters like wisteria in early summer.

How to Grow—Plant bare-root stock or balled-and-burlapped. Mostly propagated from seeds and cuttings. Impressive natural survival strength. Tolerates a wide range of soils, except waterlogged soil. Takes salty conditions. Needs full sun. Grows from Zones 3 to 7.

Landscape Use—Good lawn highlight. Popular for groves, wooded lots and land reclamation. Excellent street tree. Beautiful skyline tree and winter silhouette.

ROSA
Roses

Though most garden roses sold in North America require considerable care to keep up their appearances—particularly hybrid teas, grandifloras and floribundas—many native and introduced species make handsome, carefree flowering shrubs.

CHEROKEE ROSE *(Rosa laevigata)*

Though native to China, plants have naturalized successfully throughout the South from South Carolina to Texas and Florida. The large, single, gleaming-white, 4-inch flowers appear in spring, closely arranged on long,

Robinia pseudoacacia (black locust) stands tall and green in mid-summer.

arching canes. Grows to 10 feet, spreads 15 feet and more. The state flower of Georgia.

How to Grow—Easily planted from bare-root stock. Propagated by cuttings. Prefers moist, fertile, acid soil—does well at the edge of streams, rivers and lakes. Grows from Zones 7 to 9.

Landscape Use—Best used as a climber, trained along fences, walls and up trellis or tree trunks.

LADY BANKS ROSE *(Rosa banksiae)*

Native to China, this is one of the finest shrub roses for Southern gardens. Grows to 15 feet high. It is mostly seen trained as a climber—the long, pendulous canes covering themselves in clusters of small, yellow, double flowers in spring. There is also a white-flowered form.

How to Grow—Plant from containers. Propagated mostly from layers and cuttings. Not fussy about soil. Takes full sun or partial shade. Grows in Zones 8 and 9.

Landscape Use—Beautiful when allowed to trail along fences and over walls. One of the best possible flowering plants for creating an arbor.

RUGOSA ROSE *(Rosa rugosa)*

Native to China, plants are especially tolerant of salt spray, and are most often seen planted close to the ocean, even among sand dunes. Plants have naturalized all along the Eastern seaboard. Grows to 6 feet, spreads 6 feet and more. The leaves have a lustrous, dark green texture. Reddish-purple, 3 to 4 inch flowers are produced continuously all summer, followed by large, decorative, dark red rose hips.

How to Grow—Plant from containers. Propagated from cuttings. Not fussy about soil. Grows from Zones 2 to 7.

Landscape Use—Low informal hedge and ground cover for difficult sites.

Rosa laevigata (Cherokee rose) from China is now naturalized throughout the South.

Rosa rugosa (Rugosa rose) loves the seashore, produces beautiful, big, orange-red fruits (hips) after flowering all summer.

Salix babylonica (weeping willow) touches the ground with weeping branches. It likes moist soil.

SALIX BABYLONICA
Willow, Weeping

Hardy deciduous shade tree native to Central Asia. Graceful drooping habit and rapid growth rate, up to 5 feet a year in its juvenile stage. Narrow, lance-shaped leaves appear early in spring and fall late in autumn. The long, slender, pliable branches sway in the slightest breeze, flashing the silvery undersides of the leaves. Plants reach a mature height of 50 feet and spread almost as wide. Small, erect, catkinlike flowers, mostly yellowish, appear in early spring after trees are 10 years old. Male and female flowers are borne on different plants. These are soon followed by small, conical seed capsules that split open to release tiny seeds with white, silky hairs distributed by the wind. The bark is dark gray and deeply furrowed.

The golden weeping willow *(S. ×chrysocoma)* is especially popular because of its extreme hardiness and unusually beautiful yellow branches that are a decorative skyline highlight in winter.

How to Grow — Plant balled-and-burlapped or bare-root stock. Cuttings root easily when pressed into moist soil. Prefers moist loam soil in full sun. Grows from Zones 2 to 9, and parts of Zone 10 if given enough water.

Landscape Use — Best planted beside a lake or stream where the weeping effect can be reflected by water. Excessive shedding of branches occurs during winter but in spite of this, it is popular as a lawn highlight.

SALIX DISCOLOR
Pussy Willow

Hardy, deciduous flowering shrub or small tree native to North America, from Canada to Missouri. Famous for its whiplike, upright stems that are studded with furry, silvery flowers called *catkins*. These appear very early in spring. Grows to 20 feet, but generally kept below 10 feet by heavy pruning.

Several related species are also grown as "pussy willows," including *S. gracilistyla* and *S. caprea*.

How to Grow—Can be planted from unrooted cuttings inserted into moist soil, or from bare-root stock and containers. Tolerates moist soils, prefers an open, sunny location. Demands heavy pruning in spring after flowering to keep it from becoming overgrown. Grows from Zones 4 to 10.

Landscape Use—Lawn highlight. Young branches can be cut when flowers are in bud for taking indoors to flower extra early and produce beautiful indoor floral arrangements.

Salix discolor (pussy willow) is admired for its soft, furry flowers that appear in early spring.

SAMBUCUS CANADENSIS
American Elder

Hardy deciduous multi-stemmed bush or small, shrubby tree native to Canada and eastern United States. Grows 12 feet high and spreads 12 feet or more by means of suckers. Irregular habit. Compound leaves average seven toothed, tapered leaflets. Small, white flowers are formed in large, flat clusters 5 to 10 inches across, freely borne in early summer. These are followed by heavy clusters of shiny, purple-black berries that are used in wine and preserves. Fast growing, shallow rooted and long lived.

How to Grow—Plant from containers or bare-root stock. Propagated by seeds and cuttings. Tolerates wide range of soils, including poor and wet soil. Grows from Zones 3 to 9.

Landscape Use—The wild species is mostly considered a weed tree. The variety 'Adams' is valued for its decorative, edible fruit and makes a good informal hedge. The variety 'Aurea' has bright yellow leaves and is used as a highlight in mixed-shrub borders.

SAPIUM SEBIFERUM
Chinese Tallow Tree

Tender, deciduous flowering shade tree native to China, extensively naturalized in Florida and coastal Louisiana. Plants grow rapidly to 40 feet and more, spreading 30 feet. Bright green leaves are oval and pointed. Yellow flowers are borne profusely in long catkinlike clusters during summer. Branches are brittle and exude a milky sap that is poisonous. A waxy coating on the pea-size seeds is used by the Chinese to make candles, hence its common name.

How to Grow—Plant from containers. Propagated mostly from seeds. Tolerates a wide range of soils, including sandy and alkaline soil, in full sun. Grows from Zones 8 to 10.

Landscape Use—Lawn highlight and windbreak.

SASSAFRAS ALBIDUM
Sassafras

Hardy deciduous small tree native to North America, from New England to South Carolina. Plants grow to 30 feet high, spread 30 feet, and are often milti-stemmed. Leaves have three distinct shapes—smooth and oval, smooth on one side and indented on the other like a mitten, or indented on both sides—all occurring on the same plant. Sassafras forms thickets, especially along hedgerows. Fantastic fall color—orange, red and purple tones often occurring on the same plant.

How to Grow—Plant balled-and-burlapped. Difficult to transplant after juvenile stage because of long taproot. Propagated mostly from root cuttings collected in fall. Plants prefer loam, or humus-rich acid soil in full sun. Grows from Zones 4 to 8.

Sambucus canadensis 'Aurea' (golden elder) makes an interesting highlight in a mixed-shrub border at Hershey Gardens, Pennsylvania.

Sassafras albidum is capable of spectacular fall coloring, as seen here in a hedgerow.

Sciadopitys verticillata (Japanese umbrella pine) is a beautiful evergreen conifer popular in mixed-shrub borders.

Skimmia japonica (Japanese skimmia) features beautiful red berry clusters in fall.

Landscape Use—Good to use in a naturalized landscape. Sassafras tea and root beer are made from the fragrant bark of the roots.

SCIADOPITYS VERTICILLATA
Japanese Umbrella Pine

Hardy evergreen conifer native to Japan. Plants are spire-shaped, slow growing to 30 feet, spreading 15 feet. Long, bright green needles are arranged in whorls.
How to Grow—Plant bare-root stock or balled-and-burlapped. Prefers humus-rich, acid soil in sun. Grows from Zones 4 to 8.
Landscape Use—Excellent foundation plant, lawn highlight and bonsai subject. Considered by many landscape architects as the very best conifer for specimen use. Popular in Oriental gardens.

SEQUOIADENDRON GIGANTEUM
Big Tree, Giant Sequoia

Hardy, evergreen conifer native to the western slopes of the Sierra Nevada mountains in central California. Grows to 250 feet and more, with a massive, straight, smooth trunk up to 35 feet thick. Forms an oval, rounded canopy of dark green needles.

A related species, the coast redwood (*Sequoia sempervirens*), is much more tender, confined to the foggy coastal ranges of Northern California, but more widely planted as a landscape tree on the West Coast. These trees have a spire-shaped habit and thick, reddish-brown bark that is deeply fissured. They are the tallest trees in the world, growing 300 feet or more.
How to Grow—Best planted from containers. Propagated mostly from seeds. Prefers deep, moist, loam or sandy soil in full sun. Grows from Zones 5 to 9.
Landscape Use—Mostly grown as a novelty, lawn highlight, or to crown a hill. On the East Coast a particularly beautiful grove can be seen at Longwood Gardens, Pennsylvania.

SKIMMIA JAPONICA
Japanese Skimmia

Reasonably hardy evergreen shrub native to Japan. Plants grow to 3 feet high, spread 4 feet. Makes a dense, compact mound of oval, medium-green leaves. Decorative white flower clusters are followed by bright, ornamental red fruit resembling holly berries. However, berries are produced only on female plants.
How to Grow—Plant from containers. Propagated mostly from cuttings taken in fall. Prefers moist, humus-rich acid soil in full sun or partial shade. To get good berry displays, one male plant should be planted for every six females. Grows from Zones 6 to 7.
Landscape Use—Handsome, low-growing, spreading habit for edging mixed-shrub borders and rock gardens.

SOPHORA JAPONICA
Japanese Pagoda Tree

Hardy deciduous flowering shade tree native to China. The common species grows medium-fast to 50 feet and more, with an almost equal spread. Leaves are dark green and compound. White flowers appear in midsummer, borne in long clusters. A fine weeping form, 'Pendula', makes a handsome lawn highlight.

How to Grow—Plant balled-and-burlapped or from containers. Propagated mostly from seeds. Prefers loam soil in full sun. Drought resistant. Grows from Zones 4 to 9.

Landscape Use—Good street tree. Also used for lawns, golf courses and parks.

SORBUS AUCUPARIA
Mountain Ash

Hardy deciduous ornamental shade tree native to Europe. Plants grow 30 to 40 feet high, spread 20 to 30 feet. Attractive, white flower clusters in spring are followed by decorative clusters of orange or red berries that attract songbirds. Dark green, compound leaves have downy undersides when young. Upright, spreading branches form an oval crown. Rate of growth is medium fast. Generally short lived if it does not like the soil or planting site.

How to Grow—Plant balled-and-burlapped. Species propagated mostly from seed, named varieties by budding or grafting. Prefers moist, cool conditions. Dislikes alkaline soil. Plants will scorch if soil is too dry or too well drained. Highly susceptible to fireblight—for control, see page 58. Grows from Zones 3 to 6, Zone 7 in high-elevation areas only.

Landscape Use—Excellent lawn highlight. Although the leaves have no fall color and drop early, the beautiful berries persist on the tree long after the leaves have fallen.

SPIRAEA PRUNIFOLIA
Bridal-wreath

Hardy deciduous shrub native to China. Grows to 8 feet, spreads 8 feet, but generally kept below 6 feet by heavy pruning. Forms a thicket of slender, arching stems covered with small, white aspirin-size flowers in early spring.

Two other kinds of spirea are popular in home gardens: the Japanese spirea *(S. japonica)*—a low-growing mound-shaped shrub with usually pink flowers—and Vanhoutte spirea *(S. ×vanhoutei)*. This is basically a more robust, larger flowered version of bridal-wreath that is especially popular as a hedge. *Note:* The genus name of these plants is correctly spelled *Spiraea*, but the common name is spelled *spirea*. When offered for sale in nurseries and mail-order catalogs, it is often labeled *spirea*.

How to Grow — Plant from containers or bare-root stock. Propagated from cuttings. Prefers fertile loam soil

Sorbus aucuparia (mountain ash) in late summer, showing clusters of decorative red berries, which are edible as preserves.

Spiraea prunifolia (Bridal wreath) makes a beautiful flowering hedge as well as an eye-catching lawn highlight.

Staphylea trifolia (bladdernut) is an attractive flowering shade tree.

Stewartia pseudo-camellia (Chinese stewartia) produces exquisite, camellia-type flowers in early summer.

in full sun. Can be pruned back to the roots to rejuvenate. Grows from Zones 4 to 8.

Landscape Use — Old fashioned favorite for mixed-shrub borders and foundations. Good lawn highlight and flowering hedge.

STAPHYLEA TRIFOLIA
Bladdernut

Hardy deciduous flowering shade tree native to North America, from Canada to Georgia. Grows to 15 feet high, spreads 10 feet. White, bell-shaped flowers are produced in dense clusters in spring.

How to Grow—Plant balled-and-burlapped. Propagated mostly from softwood cuttings. Prefers moist loam or humus-rich soil in full sun. Grows from Zones 3 to 8.

Landscape Use—Good lawn specimen. Also effective in naturalized plantings.

STEWARTIA SINENSIS
Chinese Stewartia

Although many stewartias are native to North America, including the mountain stewartia *(S. ovata),* it is the Japanese stewartia *(S. pseudocamellia)* and the Chinese stewartia *(S. chinensis),* which are most often grown as small ornamental flowering trees. The Chinese stewartia has especially attractive, large, white, camellialike flowers appearing in early summer. The trunk is also a decorative feature, its flaking bark making a mottled effect with gray, green and brown coloring. Plants grow to 20 feet high, spread 15 feet wide.

How to Grow—Plant balled-and-burlapped or from containers. Propagated from seeds and cuttings. Prefers moist, acid, humus-rich soil in a sunny location. Grows from Zones 5 to 8. The Japanese stewartia is more widely adapted to the South.

Landscape Use—Good lawn highlight. Also used to line driveways. Popular in Oriental landscapes and rock gardens, especially with lower branches pruned to expose the beautiful, flaking trunk.

SYRINGA
Lilac

Native to Southern Europe, these hardy spring-flowering shrubs have showy, highly fragrant flower clusters in white, red, blue and purple. Grows to 15 feet high and spreads 12 feet, forming a thicket of long, slender trunks.

Double-flowered hybrid varieties are especially beautiful. Particularly good are the so-called *French hybrids*— 'Mme Lemoine' (white) 'Marechal Lannes' (violet), 'President Grevy' (blue), 'Victor Lemoine' (lilac) and 'Charles Joly' (magenta). Several fine species are also good for home gardens, including the tall, billowing, Persian lilac *(S. persica)* with fragrant, pale blue flowers and graceful, arching branches, and the Chinese lilac *(S.*

chinensis), which produces exceedingly large quantities of fragrant, purple-lilac flowers.

How to Grow—Best planted from containers. Propagated mostly from softwood cuttings taken in spring and early summer. Plants prefer acid loam or sandy soil in full sun. Takes heavy pruning, which should be done immediately after flowering. Older plants that look overgrown can be cut back to the ground and fertilized to rejuvenate. Lilacs are susceptible to powdery mildew disease, which covers the leaf surfaces with dirty white patches. Though ugly, the disease is generally not fatal. For control, see page 58. Grows from Zones 3 to 7.

Landscape Use—Popular foundation shrubs planted close to the house, where the fragrance can be appreciated. However, one of the best uses for lilacs is in a *lilac garden* whereby a semi-circle of different colors is planted to surround a gazebo or a garden seat.

TAMARIX RAMSISSIMA
Tamarix

Hardy deciduous flowering shrub native to southeast Europe and Asia. Grows to 15 feet, spreads 10 feet, with a cascading habit. Wispy, pink flowers form slender, arching plumes in spring.

How to Grow — Plant from containers. Propagated from seeds and cuttings. Prefers sandy, moist, acid soil in full sun. Tolerates salt spray. Grows from Zones 2 to 9.

Landscape Use — Mostly used in mixed-shrub borders and foundation plantings, particularly against a wall or fence where its arching stems can cascade over the top.

TAXODIUM DISTICHUM
Bald Cypress

Hardy deciduous conifer native to North America, from Delaware to Florida. Cypress swamps along the Atlantic coast are relics of a prehistoric past. Plants grow 50 to 70 feet high, spread 20 feet. It has an upright, spirelike habit. The tree has needles like other conifers, but they are one of a small number that are *deciduous*—needles turn bronze in fall before dropping. Mature trees have flared, *buttressed* trunks. They are able to live permanently in water by means of 'knees'—knobby protrusions that grow up from the roots and project above the water surface.

How to Grow—Though bare-root stock is available, bald cypress is best planted balled-and-burlapped or from containers. Propagated mostly from seeds. In the wild, plants grow mostly in swampy water, but as a landscape tree it grows well in relatively dry soils. Grows from Zones 4 to 10.

Landscape Use—Highly resistant to wind storms. Wood is extremely hard, and like redwood, is highly rot-resistant. As a landscape tree it is valued for lining avenues and driveways, also as a lawn accent. One of the very few trees that thrives in permanently wet soil.

Syringa vulgaris (common lilac) has fragrant purple flowers in spring.

Taxodium distichum (bald cypress) growing in water at Magnolia Gardens, South Carolina.

Taxus baccata (Irish yew) forms a beautiful evergreen avenue at Filoli Garden, near San Francisco, California.

Thuja occidentalis (American arborvitae) creates a perfect spire, can be trimmed to make a symmetrical column.

TAXUS
Yews

Among evergreen conifers, the yew family has a reputation for immense strength and longevity similar to that of oaks among deciduous trees. There are eight species known in cultivation, including the American yew. However, it is the English yew and the Japanese yew that are most popular as landscape plants. There is also an excellent hybrid form, *T. × media,* that is a cross between the English and Japanese yews, commonly called Anglojap yew. These yews are all similar in appearance, though the Japanese yew and Anglojap yew are hardier and therefore more widely planted in the Northern states and Canada. They have fine, short, dark green—almost black—needles and smooth, reddish-brown bark. The foliage cover is dense, and female plants produce poisonous red berries that persist through winter.

Caution: Yews are extremely toxic plants. The toxin, called *taxine,* is present in the foliage, bark and seeds. It is poisonous to both humans and livestock. The fleshy part of the fruit is not toxic, but the hard seed at its center will poison if crushed.

ENGLISH YEW *(Taxus baccata)*

Native to Europe, plants are slow growing to 60 feet, spread 30 feet. They can live for 1,000 years. Trunks of older trees usually become hollow. Mature plants have wide, upright, spreading branches and a rounded crown. However, one of the most popular garden varieties is 'Fastigiata', a narrow, upright form discovered growing wild in Ireland and popularly called Irish yew.

How to Grow — Although widely available as bare-root stock, large specimens are best planted balled-and-burlapped. Propagated mostly from cuttings. Prefers fertile, acid loam soil in full sun or partial shade. Must have good drainage because it hates "wet feet." Takes heavy pruning and shearing. Grows from Zones 6 to 7. Marginally hardy in Zone 5.

Landscape Use — Hedges and windbreaks. Good lawn highlight. Popular for topiary and mazes. 'Fastigiata' makes a particularly fine *avenue* for driveways and vistas.

JAPANESE YEW *(Taxus cuspidata)*

Native to Japan, plants are slow growing to 50 feet, spread 50 feet. Mature plants have a broad crown and spreading habit, often multi-stemmed. However, most garden plants are kept low and compact by severe shearing, often shaped into squares or mounds. The varieties 'Capitata' and 'Nana' are particularly fine for shaping. The hybrid form, *T. × media* is available in numerous varieties, the most popular being 'Hicks', which has an upright habit and is often pruned to create a rounded column.

How to Grow — Same requirements as English yew, but more widely adapted and hardier. Grows from Zones 4 to 7 and Zone 8 on the Pacific coast.

Landscape Use — Excellent for hedges, screens and windbreaks, also as foundation plantings and topiary when sheared.

THUJA OCCIDENTALIS
American Arborvitae

Hardy evergreen conifer native to North America from Canada to North Carolina. Though numerous dwarf and mutant forms have been introduced into cultivation, the species is fairly fast growing to 60 feet, spreading 15 feet, with a dense, upright spire-shaped habit. Scaly leaves resemble those of cedars—soft to touch and splayed out like a fan. Related species include the Western arborvitae *(T. plicata)*—widely planted in the Pacific Northwest— and the Oriental arborvitae *(T. orientalis),* which is mostly used in the southeastern and western states.

How to Grow—Plant balled-and-burlapped. Propagated mostly from cuttings taken in early spring. Tolerates a wide range of soils, including moist soil and alkaline soil, but needs good fertility to maintain an attractive, dense column. Susceptible to infestations of bagworms. For control, see page 55. Grows from Zones 2 to 8.

Landscape Use—Excellent tall hedge or screen. Also makes a good backdrop for flower beds and perennial borders. Good windbreak tree. Also popular for foundation plantings and as a matched pair at entryways.

Tilia americana (American linden) presents a towering outline over a spacious lawn.

TILIA CORDATA
Littleleaf Linden

Hardy deciduous shade tree native to Europe. Plants grow to 60 feet, spread 30 feet, have an attractive, rounded pyramidal habit. Leaves resemble those of poplars— heart-shaped, serrated and dark green in summer, changing to buttercup-yellow in fall. 'Greenspire' is a particularly fine form, developing a strong leader and distinctive pear shape. A native American species, the American linden *(T. americana)* does not have such good fall color.

How to Grow—Plant balled-and-burlapped. Propagated from seeds and budding onto seedling understocks. Prefers deep, moist, fertile loam soil in sun or partial shade. Grows from Zones 3 to 7.

Landscape Use—Good lawn highlight. Also widely planted as a street tree and to line driveways, though plants are susceptible to damage from de-icing salts.

TRACHELOSPERMUM JASMINOIDES
Confederate Jasmine

Tender evergreen flowering vine native to China. Also called star jasmine. Popular throughout the South and Southern California. Plants grow to 15 feet, spread 15 feet. Numerous fragrant, white flowers cover the vine in summer.

How to Grow—Plant from containers. Propagated from softwood cuttings taken in summer. Plants prefer moist, humus-rich, acid soil in full sun or partial shade. Takes heavy pruning to keep it within bounds. Grows from Zones 8 to 10.

Landscape Use—Mostly used to cover a trellis, wall or fence. Also planted where its pleasant fragrance can be enjoyed.

Trachelospermum jasminoides (star jasmine) is a fast-growing vine for covering arbors and trellises. Flowers are fragrant.

Tsuga canadensis 'Pendula' (Sargent's weeping hemlock) is considered among the finest of all weeping evergreen trees.

Ulmus parvifolia (Chinese elm) has leaves that grow directly from the trunk and main branches, giving the appearance of a tree covered with epiphytic ferns.

TSUGA
Hemlock

Hardy evergreen conifers native to North America and Asia. The most popular species is the Canadian hemlock *(T. canadensis),* which grows slowly to 75 feet, spreading 35 feet. Pyramidal habit, with sweeping branches that touch the ground. Needles are small, medium green.

Sargent's weeping hemlock is a particularly fine weeping variety. Habit is wide-spreading and billowing, resembling a green waterfall. Exquisite when planted beside a lake and as a lawn highlight.

How to Grow — Widely planted from bare-root stock for hedges and windbreaks; otherwise planted balled-and-burlapped. Propagated from seeds and by layering. Prefers moist, well-drained, acid soil in sun or partial shade. Grows from Zones 3 to 8.

Landscape Use — Good lawn highlight, but most often used as a windbreak and formal hedge. At the Ladew Topiary Gardens, near Monkton, Maryland, some particularly fine hemlock hedges can be seen, their tops artistically sheared to create waves with topiary swans swimming along.

ULMUS
Elms

Hardy deciduous shade trees native to North America, Europe and Asia. The American elm *(U. americana)* was at one time a widely planted street tree, but as a result of the accidental introduction of Dutch elm disease from Europe, it is considered too risky to establish any new American elms for decorative value. Plant breeders at the U.S. National Arboretum, in Washington, D.C., recently announced the introduction of three new elm varieties that are highly resistant to this disease, each from a different genetic background. One of them, 'Dynasty', is a variety of Chinese elm *(U. parvifolia)* with an upright, fast-growing, rounded habit. The second, 'Pioneer', has Scotch elm *(U. glabra)* in its parentage and makes a spreading, globe-shaped shade tree. The third of the group, 'Homestead', has Siberian elm *(U. pumila)* in its background and develops a pyramidal crown and strong, stout central trunk.

Of the many species available to home gardeners, perhaps the most desirable substitute for American elm is the Chinese elm. It is an upright, spreading tree that grows to 50 feet and spreads 50 feet. It is often confused with Siberian elm, which is not as desirable for landscape use. Scotch elm *(U. glabra)* includes a beautiful weeping form known as the 'Camperdown' elm, valued as a lawn highlight. All elms have oval, pointed, serrated leaves with prominent leaf veins.

How to Grow — Plant balled-and-burlapped or from bare-root stock. Propagated from seeds and cuttings. Elms are not fussy about soil but prefer deep, moist loam. Chinese and Scotch elms grow from Zones 4 to 9.

Landscape Use — Chinese elm and the new National Arboretum varieties make good street trees and wooded lots.

VIBURNUM
Viburnum

Native to North America, Europe and Asia, there are more than 200 species of viburnum worldwide. They are broadly divided into deciduous and evergreen kinds. Plants grow bushy, with beautiful white flowers followed in most cases by ornamental berries. Here is a sampling of the best kinds:

BLACKHAW VIBURNUM (V. prunifolium)
Deciduous North American species distributed from New England south to Florida and Texas. It has many small, flattened, creamy white flower clusters in early spring. The most vigorous, durable and earliest-flowering of viburnums. Grows to 12 feet, spreads 12 feet, but usually kept 5 to 6 feet by pruning. Grows from Zones 3 to 9.

CHINESE SNOWBALL (V. macrocephalum)
Deciduous Chinese species with dense, upright habit. Grows to 15 feet, spreads 10 feet. The most spectacular of all viburnums because the size and quality of the flowers. Individual flowers are completely round, up to 8 inches across, and can completely cover the plant in spring. Does not produce berries because flowers are sterile. Grows from Zones 6 to 10.

DOUBLEFILE VIBURNUM (V. plicatum 'Tomentosum')
Deciduous Chinese species. Flower clusters are white, up to 4 inches across, resembling those of lacecap hydrangeas, and crowd the long, sweeping branches that appear to be arranged in tiers. Flowering in spring, these are followed by decorative, bright red fruits that are eagerly devoured by birds. Grows to 10 feet, spreads 12 feet. 'Shasta'—a recent introduction from the U.S. National Arboretum—has flower clusters up to 6 inches across. Grows from Zones 5 to 8.

KOREAN SPICE VIBURNUM (V. carlesii)
Deciduous Korean species. Rounded flower clusters are up to 3 inches across, extremely fragrant, white tinged with pink, appearing in spring. Grows 6 to 8 feet, spreads to 8 feet. Dense habit and upright, spreading branches. Grows from Zones 5 to 8.

LEATHERLEAF VIBURNUM (V. rhytidophyllum)
Evergreen Chinese species. The shiny, dark green leaves are leathery and lance-shaped. They add a distinctive contrast and unusual texture to foundation plantings and mixed-shrub borders. Decorative, creamy white, flat flower clusters up to 4 inches across appear in spring, followed by blue-black ornamental berries. Upright, rounded, open habit. Grows to 15 feet, spreads 15 feet. Grows from Zones 5 to 8.

Viburnum macrocephalum (Chinese snowball bush) produces the largest flowers of any viburnum.

Viburnum tomentosum (doublefile viburnum) radiates long, sweeping branches crowded with lovely, flat flower clusters.

Viburnum dilatatum (linden viburnum) produces one of the finest berry displays for fall color.

LINDEN VIBURNUM *(V. dilatatum)*

In spring, this deciduous Asian species puts forth a profusion of white, flat flower clusters that resemble elderberry blossoms. But its main attraction is its astonishing scarlet berry display in fall. Grows to 10 feet, spreads 8 feet. Grows from Zones 4 to 8.

SNOWBALL BUSH *(V. opulus 'Sterile')*

This is an outstanding fully double white-flowering variety, though there is a rare pale pink form of *V. opulus*. Probably the most widely planted of all viburnums. Initially, the flower balls are an appealing lime-green, changing to snow white when fully open. Because the flowers are sterile, no berries are produced. Grows 8 to 10 feet, spreads 10 feet, forming a thicket of arching branches. Young plants are susceptible to aphids. For controls, see page 55. Grows from Zones 3 to 8.

TEA VIBURNUM *(V. setigerum)*

Deciduous Chinese species. One of the best for berry displays. Leggy, mounded plants are slow growing, usually kept to below 6 feet by pruning. Though the spring floral display is not as showy as other viburnums, the bright red berry clusters are reason enough to grow it. Its common name derives from the leaves that were once used to make tea.

How to Grow—Viburnums generally are fibrous rooted and are best planted from containers. Propagated from cuttings. Prefer moist, humus-rich soil, heavily mulched to keep the roots cool. Hardiness extends from Zones 2 to 10, depending on variety.

Landscape Use—Versatile plants that make excellent lawn highlights. Good to use in mixed-shrub borders. Dense forms a make good informal hedges.

VITEX AGNUS-CASTUS
Chaste Tree

Tender deciduous flowering shrub native to Asia. Popular in the South and on the West Coast. Fragrant deep blue flowers are borne in spires that cover the multistemmed bushy plants in late spring. Grows to 12 feet, spreads 10 feet. 'Alba' is a white-flowered form, 'Rosea', a pink.

How to Grow—Plant from containers. Propagated from cuttings. Prefers moist, sandy or loam soil with good humus content. Grows from Zones 6 to 10.

Landscape Use—Good lawn highlight, foundation plant or informal hedge.

Vitex agnus-castus 'Latifolia' (blue chaste tree) is popular in Southern gardens.

WEIGELA FLORIDA
Weigela

Hardy deciduous flowering shrub native to Japan. Covers itself in pink, red or white blossoms in spring. 'Bristol Ruby' is a good deep red hybrid, 'Pink Princess' a lovely pink. 'Variegata' has rose-pink flowers and beautiful green leaves edged creamy white.

How to Grow—Plant from containers. Propagated from seeds, cuttings and layering. Prefers sandy or loam soil in full sun. Grows from Zones 5 to 8.

Landscape Use—Good for mixed-shrub borders, lawn highlight and informal hedge.

WISTERIA FLORIBUNDA
Wisteria

Deciduous flowering vine native to Japan. Wisterias are vigorous plants capable of strangling even mature trees, unless controlled by heavy pruning after flowering. Grows 30 feet and more. In spring, the beautiful blue flowers hang like clusters of grapes, up to 20 inches in length and extremely fragrant. 'Alba' is a beautiful white; 'Rosea' an unusual pink. 'Violacea plena' is also a beautiful, double-flowered blue variety.

How to Grow—Plant from containers. Propagated from seeds and cuttings. Prefers a humus-rich, acid soil in sun or partial shade. Grows from Zones 4 to 10, though flowering may not occur every year above Zone 6 because flower buds may be damaged by late frosts.

Landscape Use—Wonderful as a wall cover or trained up a sturdy trellis. Also forms a good, dense canopy to cover arbors.

ZELKOVA SERRATA
Japanese Zelkova

Hardy deciduous shade tree native to Japan. Grows to 60 feet and more, spreads 50 feet. Rounded crown, elm-shaped appearance and fast growth are some of its desirable qualities. It has oval, pointed, serrated leaves that turn russet-red in fall.

How to Grow—Plant balled-and-burlapped. Propagated from seeds. Tolerates a wide range of soils, including alkaline soil. Needs full sun. Grows from Zones 5 to 8.

Landscape Use—Recommended as a substitute for the American elm, which has been largely destroyed by Dutch elm disease. Good lawn specimen and street tree.

Weigela florida is so full of flowers it is often mistaken for an azalea.

Wisteria floribunda planted as a lawn highlight.

Index